Data Mining with Python

Data is everywhere and it's growing at an unprecedented rate. But making sense of all that data is a challenge. Data Mining is the process of discovering patterns and knowledge from large data sets, and *Data Mining with Python* focuses on the hands-on approach to learning Data Mining. It showcases how to use Python Packages to fulfil the Data Mining pipeline, which is to collect, integrate, manipulate, clean, process, organize, and analyze data for knowledge.

The contents are organized based on the Data Mining pipeline, so readers can naturally progress step by step through the process. Topics, methods, and tools are explained in three aspects: "What it is" as a theoretical background, "why we need it" as an application orientation, and "how we do it" as a case study.

This book is designed to give students, data scientists, and business analysts an understanding of Data Mining concepts in an applicable way. Through interactive tutorials that can be run, modified, and used for a more comprehensive learning experience, this book will help its readers gain practical skills to implement Data Mining techniques in their work.

Dr. Di Wu is an Assistant Professor of Finance, Information Systems, and Economics department of Business School, Lehman College. He obtained a Ph.D. in Computer Science from the Graduate Center, CUNY. Dr. Wu's research interests includeTemporal extensions to RDF and semantic web, Applied Data Science, and Experiential Learning and Pedagogy in Business Education. Dr. Wu developed and taught courses including Strategic Management, Databases, Business Statistics, Management Decision Making, Programming Languages (C++, Java, and Python), Data Structures and Algorithms, Data Mining, Big Data, and Machine Learning.

Chapman & Hall/CRC

The Python Series

About the Series

Python has been ranked as the most popular programming language, and it is widely used in education and industry. This book series will offer a wide range of books on Python for students and professionals. Titles in the series will help users learn the language at an introductory and advanced level, and explore its many applications in data science, AI, and machine learning. Series titles can also be supplemented with Jupyter notebooks.

Image Processing and Acquisition using Python, Second Edition
Ravishankar Chityala, Sridevi Pudipeddi

Python Packages
Tomas Beuzen and Tiffany-Anne Timbers

Statistics and Data Visualisation with Python
Jesús Rogel-Salazar

Introduction to Python for Humanists
William J.B. Mattingly

Python for Scientific Computation and Artificial Intelligence
Stephen Lynch

Learning Professional Python Volume 1: The Basics
Usharani Bhimavarapu and Jude D. Hemanth

Learning Professional Python Volume 2: Advanced
Usharani Bhimavarapu and Jude D. Hemanth

Learning Advanced Python from Open Source Projects
Rongpeng Li

Foundations of Data Science with Python
John Mark Shea

Data Mining with Python: Theory, Application, and Case Studies
Di Wu

For more information about this series please visit: https://www.crcpress.com/Chapman--Hall-CRC/book-series/PYTH

Data Mining with Python
Theory, Application, and Case Studies

Di Wu

CRC Press
Taylor & Francis Group
Boca Raton London New York

CRC Press is an imprint of the
Taylor & Francis Group, an **informa** business

A CHAPMAN & HALL BOOK

First edition published 2024
by CRC Press
2385 Executive Center Drive, Suite 320, Boca Raton, FL 33431

and by CRC Press
4 Park Square, Milton Park, Abingdon, Oxon, OX14 4RN

CRC Press is an imprint of Taylor & Francis Group, LLC

© 2024 Di Wu

ISBN: 978-1-032-61264-5 (hbk)
ISBN: 978-1-032-59890-1 (pbk)
ISBN: 978-1-003-46278-1 (ebk)

DOI: 10.1201/9781003462781

Typeset in Latin Modern font
by KnowledgeWorks Global Ltd.

Publisher's note: This book has been prepared from camera-ready copy provided by the authors.

Access the Support Material]: https://www.routledge.com/9781032598901

Dedication
Students, Staff, and Colleagues
at University of Colorado Boulder and Lehman College

Contents

List of Figures

Foreword

WHY WE NEED THIS BOOK

Data is everywhere and it's growing at an unprecedented rate. But making sense of all that data is a challenge. Data Mining is the process of discovering patterns and knowledge from large data sets. This book focuses on the hands-on approach to learn Data Mining. This book is designed to give you an understanding of Data Mining concepts in an applicable way. The tutorials in this book will help you to gain practical skills to implement Data Mining techniques in your work. Whether you are a student, a data scientist, or a business analyst, this book is a must-read for you.

Preface

HOW TO USE THIS BOOK

This book is served as complementary to a theoretical Data Mining course. We intend to keep the introductions brief and simple and concentrate on detailed tutorials. The book is divided into two parts: Part 1 covers the preparation of data or Data Wrangling. Part 2 covers the analysis of data or Data Analysis. For readers' convenience, besides including all tutorials within pages, we also provide the .ipynb files with associated data sets through links. When you run the .ipynb files, please make sure the data path is updated in your local/cloud environment.

WHY THIS BOOK IS DIFFERENT

While there are many books, websites, online courses about the topic, we differentiate our book in multiple ways:

- We organized the contents based on the Data Mining pipeline, so readers can naturally gain the formal process from raw data to knowledge step by step. Readers can have a full stack of consistent learning, rather than learning from pieces from multiple sources.

- For the topics, methods, and tools we cover in the book, we explain them in three aspects: "What it is" as a theoretical background, "Why we need it" as an application orientation, and "How we do it" as a case study.

- Our book is "LIVE". All tutorials are runnable interactive Python notebooks in .ipynb format. Students can run them, modify them, and use them.

Author Bios

Dr. Di Wu is an Assistant Professor of Finance, Information Systems, and Economics department of Business School, Lehman College. He obtained a Ph.D. in Computer Science from the Graduate Center, CUNY. Dr. Wu's research interests are 1) Temporal extensions to RDF and semantic web, 2) Applied Data Science, and 3) Experiential Learning and Pedagogy in business education. Dr. Wu developed and taught courses including Strategic Management, Databases, Business Statistics, Management Decision Making, Programming Languages (C++, Java, and Python), Data Structures and Algorithms, Data Mining, Big Data, and Machine Learning.

I

Data Wrangling

## CHAPTER 1

Data Collection

D
ATA COLLECTION is a crucial step in the process of obtaining valuable insights and making informed decisions. In today's interconnected world, data can be found in a multitude of sources, ranging from traditional files such as .csv, .html, .txt, .xlsx, .html, and .json, to databases powered by SQL, websites hosting relevant information, and APIs (Application Programming Interfaces) offered by companies. To efficiently gather data from these diverse sources, various tools can be employed. These tools encompass an array of technologies, including web scraping frameworks, database connectors, data extraction libraries, and specialized APIs, all designed to facilitate the collection and extraction of data from different sources. By leveraging these tools, organizations can harness the power of data and gain valuable insights to drive their decision-making processes.

Python offers a rich ecosystem of packages for data collection. Some commonly used Python packages for data collection include: including:

- Pandas: Pandas is a powerful library for data manipulation and analysis. It provides data structures and functions to efficiently work with structured data, making it suitable for data collection from CSV files, Excel spreadsheets, and SQL databases.

- BeautifulSoup: Beautiful Soup is a Python library for web scraping. It helps parse HTML and XML documents, making it useful for extracting data from websites.

- Requests: Requests is a versatile library for making HTTP requests. It simplifies the process of interacting with web services and APIs, allowing data retrieval from various sources.

- mysql-connector-python, psycopg2, and sqlite3: These libraries are Python connectors for MySQL, PostgreSQL, and sqlite databases, respectively. They enable data collection by establishing connections to these databases, executing queries, and retrieving data.

DOI: 10.1201/9781003462781-1

- Yahoo Finance: The Yahoo Finance library provides an interface to access financial data from Yahoo Finance. It allows you to fetch historical stock prices, company information, and other financial data.

These are just a few examples of Python packages commonly used for data collection. We will cover them in detail with tutorials and case studies. Depending on the specific data sources and requirements, there are many more packages available to facilitate data collection in Python.

1.1 COLLECT DATA FROM FILES

Storing data in different file formats allows for versatility and compatibility with various applications and tools.

- CSV (Comma-Separated Values): CSV files store tabular data in plain text format, where each line represents a row, and values are separated by commas (or other delimiters). CSV files are simple, human-readable, and widely supported. They can be easily opened and edited using spreadsheet software or text editors. However, CSV files may not support complex data structures, and there is no standardized format for metadata or data types. Pandas provides the read_csv() function, allowing you to read CSV files into a DataFrame object effortlessly. It automatically detects the delimiter, handles missing values, and provides convenient methods for data manipulation and analysis.

- TXT (Plain Text): TXT files contain unformatted text with no specific structure or metadata. TXT files are lightweight, widely supported, and can be easily opened with any text editor. However, TXT files lack a standardized structure or format, making it challenging to handle data that requires specific organization or metadata. Pandas offers the read_csv() function with customizable delimiters to read text files with structured data. By specifying the appropriate delimiter, you can read text files into a DataFrame for further analysis.

- XLSX (Microsoft Excel): XLSX is a file format used by Microsoft Excel to store spreadsheet data with multiple sheets, formatting, formulas, and metadata. XLSX files support complex spreadsheets with multiple tabs, cell formatting, and formulas. They are widely used in business and data analysis scenarios. However, XLSX files can be large, and manipulating them directly can be memory-intensive. Additionally, XLSX files require software like Microsoft Excel to view and edit. Pandas provides the read_excel() function, enabling the reading of XLSX files into DataFrames. It allows you to specify the sheet name, range of cells, and other parameters to extract data easily.

- JSON (JavaScript Object Notation): JSON is a lightweight, human-readable data interchange format that represents structured data as key-value pairs, lists, and nested objects. JSON is easy to read and write, supports complex nested structures, and is widely used for data interchange between systems. However, JSON files can be larger than their equivalent CSV representations, and handling complex nested structures may require additional processing. Pandas provides the read_json() function to read JSON data directly into a DataFrame. It handles both simple and nested JSON structures, allowing for convenient data exploration and analysis.

- XML (eXtensible Markup Language): XML files store structured data using tags that define elements and their relationships. XML is designed to be self-descriptive and human-readable. XML files provide a flexible and extensible format for storing structured data. They are widely used for data interchange and can represent complex hierarchical structures. However, XML files can be verbose and have larger file sizes compared to other formats. Parsing XML files can be more complex due to the nested structure and the need for specialized parsing libraries. Pandas provides the read_xml() function to directly read XML files into a DataFrame. It provides several options for handling different XML structures, such as extracting data from specific tags, handling attributes, and parsing nested elements.

- HTML (Hypertext Markup Language): HTML files are primarily used for structuring and presenting content on the web. They consist of tags that define the structure and formatting of the data. HTML files provide a rich structure for representing web content and can include images, links, and other multimedia elements. However, HTML files are designed for web display, so extracting structured data from them can be more complex due to the presence of non-tabular content and formatting tags. Pandas provides the read_html() function, which can extract tabular data from HTML tables into a DataFrame.

1.1.1 Tutorial – Collect Data from Files

We may have stored data in multiple types of files, such as text, csv, excel, xml, html, etc. We can load them into dataframes.

```
import pandas as pd
```

1.1.1.1 CSV

We have done this when we learned pandas. You can get the path of your csv file, and feed the path to the function read_csv.

Default setting   A lot cases, default setting will do the job.

```
df = pd.read_csv('/content/ds_salaries.csv')
```

```
df.head()
```

```
   Unnamed: 0  work_year  experience_level  employment_type  \
0           0       2020                MI               FT
1           1       2020                SE               FT
```

```
2            2        2020            SE            FT
3            3        2020            MI            FT
4            4        2020            SE            FT

                       job_title   salary salary_currency  salary_in_usd  \
0             Data Scientist        70000             EUR          79833
1   Machine Learning Scientist    260000             USD         260000
2            Big Data Engineer      85000             GBP         109024
3          Product Data Analyst     20000             USD          20000
4   Machine Learning Engineer     150000             USD         150000

   employee_residence  remote_ratio company_location company_size
0                  DE             0               DE            L
1                  JP             0               JP            S
2                  GB            50               GB            M
3                  HN             0               HN            S
4                  US            50               US            L
```

```
df.info()
```

```
<class 'pandas.core.frame.DataFrame'>
RangeIndex: 607 entries, 0 to 606
Data columns (total 12 columns):
 #   Column              Non-Null Count  Dtype
---  ------              --------------  -----
 0   Unnamed: 0          607 non-null    int64
 1   work_year           607 non-null    int64
 2   experience_level    607 non-null    object
 3   employment_type     607 non-null    object
 4   job_title           607 non-null    object
 5   salary              607 non-null    int64
 6   salary_currency     607 non-null    object
 7   salary_in_usd       607 non-null    int64
 8   employee_residence  607 non-null    object
 9   remote_ratio        607 non-null    int64
 10  company_location    607 non-null    object
 11  company_size        607 non-null    object
dtypes: int64(5), object(7)
memory usage: 57.0+ KB
```

Customize setting You can manipulate arguments for your specific csv file

```
df = pd.read_csv('/content/ds_salaries.csv', header = None)
df.head()
```

```
     0            1                 2                 3  \
0  NaN    work_year  experience_level  employment_type
1  0.0         2020                MI               FT
2  1.0         2020                SE               FT
3  2.0         2020                SE               FT
4  3.0         2020                MI               FT

              4            5                 6                 7  \
```

```
0                     job_title   salary  salary_currency  salary_in_usd
1                Data Scientist    70000              EUR          79833
2     Machine Learning Scientist   260000             USD         260000
3              Big Data Engineer    85000              GBP         109024
4            Product Data Analyst   20000              USD          20000

                        8               9               10            11
0     employee_residence  remote_ratio  company_location  company_size
1                     DE             0                DE             L
2                     JP             0                JP             S
3                     GB            50                GB             M
4                     HN             0                HN             S
```

```
df.info()
```

```
<class 'pandas.core.frame.DataFrame'>
RangeIndex: 608 entries, 0 to 607
Data columns (total 12 columns):
 #   Column  Non-Null Count  Dtype
---  ------  --------------  -----
 0   0       607 non-null    float64
 1   1       608 non-null    object
 2   2       608 non-null    object
 3   3       608 non-null    object
 4   4       608 non-null    object
 5   5       608 non-null    object
 6   6       608 non-null    object
 7   7       608 non-null    object
 8   8       608 non-null    object
 9   9       608 non-null    object
 10  10      608 non-null    object
 11  11      608 non-null    object
dtypes: float64(1), object(11)
memory usage: 57.1+ KB
```

```
df = pd.read_csv('/content/ds_salaries.csv', header = None, skiprows=1)
df.head()
```

```
   0   1    2   3                          4       5    6       7    8   9  \
0  0  2020  MI  FT             Data Scientist   70000  EUR   79833  DE   0
1  1  2020  SE  FT  Machine Learning Scientist  260000  USD  260000  JP   0
2  2  2020  SE  FT           Big Data Engineer   85000  GBP  109024  GB  50
3  3  2020  MI  FT        Product Data Analyst   20000  USD   20000  HN   0
4  4  2020  SE  FT  Machine Learning Engineer  150000  USD  150000  US  50

   10 11
0  DE  L
1  JP  S
2  GB  M
3  HN  S
4  US  L
```

```
df.info()
```

```
<class 'pandas.core.frame.DataFrame'>
RangeIndex: 607 entries, 0 to 606
Data columns (total 12 columns):
 #   Column  Non-Null Count  Dtype
---  ------  --------------  -----
 0   0       607 non-null    int64
 1   1       607 non-null    int64
 2   2       607 non-null    object
 3   3       607 non-null    object
 4   4       607 non-null    object
 5   5       607 non-null    int64
 6   6       607 non-null    object
 7   7       607 non-null    int64
 8   8       607 non-null    object
 9   9       607 non-null    int64
 10  10      607 non-null    object
 11  11      607 non-null    object
dtypes: int64(5), object(7)
memory usage: 57.0+ KB
```

```
df = pd.read_csv('/content/ds_salaries.csv', header = None,
        skiprows=1, skipfooter=300)
df.head()
```

```
   0  1     2   3                            4       5    6       7   8   9  \
0  0  2020  MI  FT              Data Scientist   70000  EUR   79833  DE   0
1  1  2020  SE  FT   Machine Learning Scientist  260000  USD  260000  JP   0
2  2  2020  SE  FT            Big Data Engineer   85000  GBP  109024  GB  50
3  3  2020  MI  FT          Product Data Analyst   20000  USD   20000  HN   0
4  4  2020  SE  FT   Machine Learning Engineer  150000  USD  150000  US  50

   10 11
0  DE  L
1  JP  S
2  GB  M
3  HN  S
4  US  L
```

```
df.info()
```

```
<class 'pandas.core.frame.DataFrame'>
RangeIndex: 307 entries, 0 to 306
Data columns (total 12 columns):
 #   Column  Non-Null Count  Dtype
---  ------  --------------  -----
 0   0       307 non-null    int64
 1   1       307 non-null    int64
 2   2       307 non-null    object
 3   3       307 non-null    object
 4   4       307 non-null    object
 5   5       307 non-null    int64
 6   6       307 non-null    object
```

```
7    7         307 non-null     int64
8    8         307 non-null     object
9    9         307 non-null     int64
10   10        307 non-null     object
11   11        307 non-null     object
dtypes: int64(5), object(7)
memory usage: 28.9+ KB
```

1.1.1.2 TXT

If the txt follows csv format, then it can be read as a csv file

```
df = pd.read_csv('/content/ds_salaries.txt')
df
```

```
     Unnamed: 0  work_year experience_level employment_type  \
0             0       2020              MI              FT
1             1       2020              SE              FT
2             2       2020              SE              FT
3             3       2020              MI              FT
4             4       2020              SE              FT
..          ...        ...             ...             ...
602         602       2022              SE              FT
603         603       2022              SE              FT
604         604       2022              SE              FT
605         605       2022              SE              FT
606         606       2022              MI              FT

                         job_title   salary salary_currency  salary_in_usd  \
0                   Data Scientist    70000             EUR          79833
1        Machine Learning Scientist   260000             USD         260000
2                 Big Data Engineer    85000             GBP         109024
3              Product Data Analyst    20000             USD          20000
4        Machine Learning Engineer   150000             USD         150000
..                             ...      ...             ...             ...
602                  Data Engineer   154000             USD         154000
603                  Data Engineer   126000             USD         126000
604                   Data Analyst   129000             USD         129000
605                   Data Analyst   150000             USD         150000
606                    AI Scientist  200000             USD         200000

     employee_residence  remote_ratio company_location company_size
0                    DE             0               DE            L
1                    JP             0               JP            S
2                    GB            50               GB            M
3                    HN             0               HN            S
4                    US            50               US            L
..                  ...           ...              ...          ...
602                  US           100               US            M
603                  US           100               US            M
604                  US             0               US            M
605                  US           100               US            M
606                  IN           100               US            L

[607 rows x 12 columns]
```

1.1.1.3 Excel

```
df = pd.read_excel('/content/ds_salaries.xlsx')
```

```
df.head()
```

```
   Unnamed: 0  work_year experience_level employment_type  \
0           0       2020               MI              FT
1           1       2020               SE              FT
2           2       2020               SE              FT
3           3       2020               MI              FT
4           4       2020               SE              FT

                      job_title  salary salary_currency  salary_in_usd  \
0                Data Scientist   70000             EUR          79833
1      Machine Learning Scientist  260000             USD         260000
2             Big Data Engineer   85000             GBP         109024
3           Product Data Analyst   20000             USD          20000
4      Machine Learning Engineer  150000             USD         150000

   employee_residence  remote_ratio company_location company_size
0                  DE             0               DE            L
1                  JP             0               JP            S
2                  GB            50               GB            M
3                  HN             0               HN            S
4                  US            50               US            L
```

```
df.info()
```

```
<class 'pandas.core.frame.DataFrame'>
RangeIndex: 607 entries, 0 to 606
Data columns (total 12 columns):
 #   Column            Non-Null Count  Dtype
---  ------            --------------  -----
 0   Unnamed: 0        607 non-null    int64
 1   work_year         607 non-null    int64
 2   experience_level  607 non-null    object
 3   employment_type   607 non-null    object
 4   job_title         607 non-null    object
 5   salary            607 non-null    int64
 6   salary_currency   607 non-null    object
 7   salary_in_usd     607 non-null    int64
 8   employee_residence 607 non-null   object
 9   remote_ratio      607 non-null    int64
 10  company_location  607 non-null    object
 11  company_size      607 non-null    object
dtypes: int64(5), object(7)
memory usage: 57.0+ KB
```

1.1.1.4 json

```
df = pd.read_json('/content/ds_salaries.json')
df.head()
```

```
   FIELD1  work_year experience_level employment_type  \
0       0       2020               MI              FT
1       1       2020               SE              FT
2       2       2020               SE              FT
3       3       2020               MI              FT
4       4       2020               SE              FT

                     job_title  salary salary_currency  salary_in_usd  \
0               Data Scientist   70000             EUR          79833
1    Machine Learning Scientist  260000             USD         260000
2             Big Data Engineer   85000             GBP         109024
3           Product Data Analyst   20000             USD          20000
4    Machine Learning Engineer  150000             USD         150000

   employee_residence  remote_ratio company_location company_size
0                 DE             0               DE            L
1                 JP             0               JP            S
2                 GB            50               GB            M
3                 HN             0               HN            S
4                 US            50               US            L
```

```
df.info()
```

```
<class 'pandas.core.frame.DataFrame'>
RangeIndex: 607 entries, 0 to 606
Data columns (total 12 columns):
 #   Column            Non-Null Count  Dtype
---  ------            --------------  -----
 0   FIELD1            607 non-null    int64
 1   work_year         607 non-null    int64
 2   experience_level  607 non-null    object
 3   employment_type   607 non-null    object
 4   job_title         607 non-null    object
 5   salary            607 non-null    int64
 6   salary_currency   607 non-null    object
 7   salary_in_usd     607 non-null    int64
 8   employee_residence 607 non-null   object
 9   remote_ratio      607 non-null    int64
 10  company_location  607 non-null    object
 11  company_size      607 non-null    object
dtypes: int64(5), object(7)
memory usage: 57.0+ KB
```

1.1.1.5 *XML*

```
df = pd.read_xml('/content/ds_salaries.xml')
df.head()
```

```
   FIELD1  work_year experience_level employment_type  \
0       0       2020               MI              FT
1       1       2020               SE              FT
2       2       2020               SE              FT
3       3       2020               MI              FT
4       4       2020               SE              FT

                   job_title  salary salary_currency  salary_in_usd  \
0             Data Scientist   70000             EUR          79833
1   Machine Learning Scientist  260000           USD         260000
2           Big Data Engineer   85000             GBP         109024
3         Product Data Analyst   20000            USD          20000
4   Machine Learning Engineer  150000            USD         150000

  employee_residence  remote_ratio company_location company_size
0                 DE             0               DE            L
1                 JP             0               JP            S
2                 GB            50               GB            M
3                 HN             0               HN            S
4                 US            50               US            L
```

```
df.info()
```

```
<class 'pandas.core.frame.DataFrame'>
RangeIndex: 607 entries, 0 to 606
Data columns (total 12 columns):
 #   Column             Non-Null Count  Dtype
---  ------             --------------  -----
 0   FIELD1             607 non-null    int64
 1   work_year          607 non-null    int64
 2   experience_level   607 non-null    object
 3   employment_type    607 non-null    object
 4   job_title          607 non-null    object
 5   salary             607 non-null    int64
 6   salary_currency    607 non-null    object
 7   salary_in_usd      607 non-null    int64
 8   employee_residence 607 non-null    object
 9   remote_ratio       607 non-null    int64
 10  company_location   607 non-null    object
 11  company_size       607 non-null    object
dtypes: int64(5), object(7)
memory usage: 57.0+ KB
```

1.1.1.6 HTM

```
df = pd.read_html('/content/ds_salaries.htm')[0]
df.head()
```

```
   FIELD1  work_year experience_level employment_type  \
0       0       2020               MI              FT
1       1       2020               SE              FT
2       2       2020               SE              FT
3       3       2020               MI              FT
4       4       2020               SE              FT

                      job_title  salary salary_currency  salary_in_usd  \
0                Data Scientist   70000             EUR          79833
1      Machine Learning Scientist 260000             USD         260000
2              Big Data Engineer   85000             GBP         109024
3           Product Data Analyst   20000             USD          20000
4      Machine Learning Engineer  150000             USD         150000

   employee_residence  remote_ratio company_location company_size
0                 DE              0               DE            L
1                 JP              0               JP            S
2                 GB             50               GB            M
3                 HN              0               HN            S
4                 US             50               US            L
```

```
df.info()
```

```
<class 'pandas.core.frame.DataFrame'>
RangeIndex: 607 entries, 0 to 606
Data columns (total 12 columns):
 #   Column              Non-Null Count  Dtype
---  ------              --------------  -----
 0   FIELD1              607 non-null    int64
 1   work_year           607 non-null    int64
 2   experience_level    607 non-null    object
 3   employment_type     607 non-null    object
 4   job_title           607 non-null    object
 5   salary              607 non-null    int64
 6   salary_currency     607 non-null    object
 7   salary_in_usd       607 non-null    int64
 8   employee_residence  607 non-null    object
 9   remote_ratio        607 non-null    int64
 10  company_location    607 non-null    object
 11  company_size        607 non-null    object
dtypes: int64(5), object(7)
memory usage: 57.0+ KB
```

1.1.2 Documentation

It is always good to have a reference of the read files functions in pandas. You can find it via https://pandas.pydata.org/docs/reference/io.html

1.2 COLLECT DATA FROM THE WEB

Collecting data from the web is essential for various reasons:

- Access to vast amounts of information: The web contains an immense amount of data on diverse topics. By collecting data from the web, you can tap into this vast information pool and gain insights that can inform decision-making, research, analysis, and more.

- Real-time and up-to-date data: The web provides a platform for the dissemination of real-time and up-to-date information. By collecting data from the web, you can stay informed about the latest news, trends, market updates, social media activity, and other dynamic sources of information.

- Competitive intelligence: Collecting data from the web allows you to monitor your competitors, track their activities, analyze their strategies, and gain insights into the market landscape. This can help you make informed decisions and stay ahead in a competitive environment.

- Research and analysis: Web data collection is crucial for research, analysis, and data-driven insights. By collecting data from diverse sources, you can validate hypotheses, perform statistical analysis, conduct sentiment analysis, and uncover patterns or trends that can enhance understanding and drive informed decision-making.

The web has many websites, including structured websites, semi-structured websites, and unstructured websites, that differ in terms of their organization and consistency.

- Structured Websites: Structured websites have a well-defined and organized format, making it easy to locate specific information. They often follow a consistent layout and have clearly defined sections. Structured websites generally pose fewer challenges for data collection as the information is neatly organized. However, occasional variations in page layouts or changes in website structure can introduce some level of complexity. To collect data from structured websites, you can utilize libraries like Beautiful Soup or lxml in Python. These libraries enable you to parse the HTML structure of the web pages and extract desired data using specific tags or CSS selectors.

- Semi-Structured Websites: Semi-structured websites contain a mixture of structured and unstructured data. While certain sections might be organized, others may have varying formats or lack consistent organization. The main challenge with semi-structured websites is the inconsistency in data presentation. The lack of uniformity in structure and formatting requires additional effort to identify and extract the relevant data. Similar to structured websites, libraries like Beautiful Soup or lxml can help parse and extract data from semi-structured websites. However, you may need to employ additional techniques such as regular expressions or data cleaning procedures to handle variations in data presentation.

- Unstructured Websites: Unstructured websites lack a clear organization or predefined structure. They may have free-form text, multimedia content, and unorganized data scattered across multiple pages. Unstructured websites pose the most significant challenges for data collection due to the absence of consistent structure. The data may be embedded within paragraphs, images, or other non-tabular formats, requiring sophisticated techniques for extraction. For unstructured websites, natural language processing (NLP) techniques and machine learning algorithms can be employed to extract relevant information. These methods involve parsing the web content, identifying patterns, and applying text processing algorithms to extract structured data.

In summary, structured websites provide a clear structure, making data collection relatively straightforward. Semi-structured websites introduce some variability, requiring careful handling of inconsistencies. Unstructured websites present the most significant challenges, necessitating advanced techniques such as NLP and machine learning to extract structured information. Python libraries like Beautiful Soup, lxml, and NLP frameworks can assist in parsing and extracting data from these different types of websites, adapting to their specific characteristics and complexities.

1.2.1 Tutorial – Collect Data from Web

```
import pandas as pd
```

1.2.1.1 Wiki

Some websites maintains structured data, which is easy to read

```
table = pd.read_html('https://en.wikipedia.org/wiki/
                      List_of_countries_by_GDP_(nominal)#Table')
```

```
for i in table:
  print(type(i))
```

```
<class 'pandas.core.frame.DataFrame'>
<class 'pandas.core.frame.DataFrame'>
<class 'pandas.core.frame.DataFrame'>
<class 'pandas.core.frame.DataFrame'>
<class 'pandas.core.frame.DataFrame'>
<class 'pandas.core.frame.DataFrame'>
<class 'pandas.core.frame.DataFrame'>
```

```
for i in table:
  print(i.columns)
```

```
Int64Index([0], dtype='int64')
Int64Index([0, 1, 2], dtype='int64')
MultiIndex([( 'Country/Territory', 'Country/Territory'),
           (         'UN Region',          'UN Region'),
```

```
          (        'IMF[1][13]',              'Estimate'),
          (        'IMF[1][13]',                  'Year'),
          (   'World Bank[14]',              'Estimate'),
          (   'World Bank[14]',                  'Year'),
          ('United Nations[15]',             'Estimate'),
          ('United Nations[15]',                 'Year')],
          )
...
Int64Index([0, 1], dtype='int64')
```

```
df = table[2]
df.head()
```

```
   Country/Territory UN Region IMF[1][13]           World Bank[14]           \
   Country/Territory UN Region   Estimate      Year      Estimate      Year
0             World         -  101560901      2022      96513077      2021
1     United States  Americas   25035164      2022      22996100      2021
2             China      Asia   18321197  [n 1]2022      17734063  [n 3]2021
3             Japan      Asia    4300621      2022       4937422      2021
4           Germany    Europe    4031149      2022       4223116      2021

   United Nations[15]
             Estimate      Year
0            85328323      2020
1            20893746      2020
2            14722801  [n 1]2020
3             5057759      2020
4             3846414      2020
```

```
df.info()
```

```
<class 'pandas.core.frame.DataFrame'>
RangeIndex: 217 entries, 0 to 216
Data columns (total 8 columns):
 #   Column                                Non-Null Count  Dtype
---  ------                                --------------  -----
 0   (Country/Territory, Country/Territory) 217 non-null   object
 1   (UN Region, UN Region)                217 non-null    object
 2   (IMF[1][13], Estimate)                217 non-null    object
 3   (IMF[1][13], Year)                    217 non-null    object
 4   (World Bank[14], Estimate)            217 non-null    object
 5   (World Bank[14], Year)                217 non-null    object
 6   (United Nations[15], Estimate)        217 non-null    object
 7   (United Nations[15], Year)            217 non-null    object
dtypes: object(8)
memory usage: 13.7+ KB
```

1.2.1.2 Web Scraping

Some websites are semi-structured, which has metadata, such as labels, classes, etc., so we can look into their source code, and do web scraping.

> Note: You need to have a basic understanding of html, xml, in order to understand the source code and collect data from these websites.

Note: Some websites prevent users from scraping or scraping rapidly.

The first thing we'll need to do to scrape a web page is to download the page. We can download pages using the Python `requests` library.

The requests library will make a `GET` request to a web server, which will download the HTML contents of a given web page for us. There are several different types of requests we can make using requests, of which `GET` is just one. If you want to learn more, check out our API tutorial.

Let's try downloading a simple sample website, https://dataquestio.github.io/web-scraping-pages/simple.html.

Download by requests   We'll need to first import the requests library, and then download the page using the requests.get method:

```python
import requests

page = requests.get("https://dataquestio.github.io/
                        web-scraping-pages/simple.html")
page
```

`<Response [200]>`

After running our request, we get a Response object. This object has a status_code property, which indicates if the page was downloaded successfully:

```python
page.status_code
```

`200`

A status_code of 200 means that the page downloaded successfully. We won't fully dive into status codes here, but a status code starting with a 2 generally indicates success, and a code starting with a 4 or a 5 indicates an error.

We can print out the HTML content of the page using the content property:

```python
page.content
```

```
b'<!DOCTYPE html>\n<html>\n    <head>\n        <title>A simple example
    page</title>\n    </head>\n    <body>\n        <p>Here is some
    simple content for this page.</p>\n    </body>\n</html>'
```

Parsing by BeautifulSoup   As you can see above, we now have downloaded an HTML document.

We can use the `BeautifulSoup` library to parse this document, and extract the text from the p tag.

```
from bs4 import BeautifulSoup
soup = BeautifulSoup(page.content, 'html.parser')
```

We can now print out the HTML content of the page, formatted nicely, using the prettify method on the BeautifulSoup object.

```
print(soup.prettify())
```

```
<!DOCTYPE html>
<html>
 <head>
  <title>
   A simple example page
  </title>
 </head>
 <body>
  <p>
   Here is some simple content for this page.
  </p>
 </body>
</html>
```

This step isn't strictly necessary, and we won't always bother with it, but it can be helpful to look at prettified HTML to make the structure of the and where tags are nested easier to see.

Finding Tags   Finding all instances of a tag at once What we did above was useful for figuring out how to navigate a page, but it took a lot of commands to do something fairly simple. If we want to extract a single tag, we can instead use the find_all method, which will find all the instances of a tag on a page.

if we are looking for the title, we can look for <title> tag

```
soup.find_all('title')
```

```
[<title>A simple example page</title>]
```

```
for t in soup.find_all('title'):
  print(t.get_text())
```

```
A simple example page
```

If we are looking for text, we can look for <p> tag

```
for t in soup.find_all('p'):
  print(t.get_text())
```

```
Here is some simple content for this page.
```

If you instead only want to find the first instance of a tag, you can use the find method, which will return a single BeautifulSoup object:

```
soup.find('p').get_text()
```

```
{"type":"string"}
```

Searching for tags by class and id:

Classes and ids are used by CSS to determine which HTML elements to apply certain styles to. But when we're scraping, we can also use them to specify the elements we want to scrape.

Let's try another page.

```
page = requests.get("https://dataquestio.github.io/
        web-scraping-pages/ids_and_classes.html")
soup = BeautifulSoup(page.content, 'html.parser')
soup
```

```
<html>
<head>
<title>A simple example page</title>
</head>
<body>
<div>
<p class="inner-text first-item" id="first">
            First paragraph.
        </p>
<p class="inner-text">
            Second paragraph.
        </p>
</div>
<p class="outer-text first-item" id="second">
<b>
            First outer paragraph.
        </b>
</p>
<p class="outer-text">
<b>
            Second outer paragraph.
        </b>
</p>
</body>
</html>
```

Now, we can use the find_all method to search for items by class or by id. In the below example, we'll search for any p tag that has the class outer-text:

```
soup.find_all('p', class_='outer-text')
```

```
[<p class="outer-text first-item" id="second">
 <b>
```

```
                    First outer paragraph.
            </b>
</p>, <p class="outer-text">
<b>
                Second outer paragraph.
            </b>
</p>]
```

In the below example, we'll look for any tag that has the class outer-text:

```
soup.find_all(class_="outer-text")
```

```
[<p class="outer-text first-item" id="second">
 <b>
                First outer paragraph.
            </b>
</p>, <p class="outer-text">
<b>
                Second outer paragraph.
            </b>
</p>]
```

We can also search for elements by id:

```
soup.find_all(id="first")
```

```
[<p class="inner-text first-item" id="first">
                First paragraph.
            </p>]
```

1.2.2   Case Study – Collect Weather Data from Web

1.2.2.1   Downloading Weather Data

We now know enough to proceed with extracting information about the local weather from the National Weather Service website!

The local weather of Boulder, CO is: https://forecast.weather.gov/MapClick.php?lat=40.0466&lon=-105.2523#.YwpRBy2B1f0

Time to Start Scraping!

We now know enough to download the page and start parsing it. In the below code, we will:

- Download the web page containing the forecast.
- Create a BeautifulSoup class to parse the page.
- Find the div with id seven-day-forecast, and assign to seven_day
- Inside seven_day, find each individual forecast item. Extract and print the first forecast item.

```
import requests
from bs4 import BeautifulSoup

page = requests.get("https://forecast.weather.gov/
        MapClick.php?lat=40.0466&lon=-105.2523#.YwpRBy2B1f0")
soup = BeautifulSoup(page.content, 'html.parser')
seven_day = soup.find(id="seven-day-forecast")
forecast_items = seven_day.find_all(class_="tombstone-container")
print(forecast_items)
```

```
[<div class="tombstone-container">
<p class="period-name">Today<br/><br/></p>
<p><img alt="Today: Sunny...>
<p class="period-name">Tonight<br/><br/></p>
<p><img alt="Tonight: Mostly clear...>
...
```

```
tonight = forecast_items[0]
print(tonight.prettify())
```

```
<div class="tombstone-container">
 <p class="period-name">
  Today
  <br/>
  <br/>
 </p>
 <p>
  <img alt="Today: Sunny, with a high near 88.
    Northwest wind 9 to 13 mph,
    with gusts as high as 21 mph. "
    class="forecast-icon" src="newimages/medium/few.png"
    title="Today: Sunny, with a high near 88.
    Northwest wind 9 to 13 mph,
    with gusts as high as 21 mph. "/>
 </p>
 <p class="short-desc">
  Sunny
 </p>
 <p class="temp temp-high">
  High: 88 °F
 </p>
</div>
```

1.2.2.2 Extracting Information of Tonight

As we can see, inside the forecast item tonight is all the information we want. There are four pieces of information we can extract:

- The name of the forecast item – in this case, Tonight.
- The description of the conditions – this is stored in the title property of img.
- A short description of the conditions – in this case, Sunny and hot.
- The temperature hight – in this case, 98 degrees.

We'll extract the name of the forecast item, the short description, and the temperature first, since they're all similar:

```
period = tonight.find(class_="period-name").get_text()
short_desc = tonight.find(class_="short-desc").get_text()
temp = tonight.find(class_="temp").get_text()
print(period)
print(short_desc)
print(temp)
```

```
Today
Sunny
High: 88 °F
```

Now, we can extract the title attribute from the img tag. To do this, we just treat the BeautifulSoup object like a dictionary, and pass in the attribute we want as a key:

```
img = tonight.find("img")
desc = img['title']
print(desc)
```

```
Today: Sunny,
    with a high near 88.
    Northwest wind 9 to 13 mph,
    with gusts as high as 21 mph.
```

1.2.2.3 Extract all Nights!

Now that we know how to extract each individual piece of information, we can combine our knowledge with CSS selectors and list comprehensions to extract everything at once.

In the below code, we will:

Select all items with the class period-name inside an item with the class tombstone-container in seven_day. Use a list comprehension to call the get_text method on each BeautifulSoup object.

```
period_tags = seven_day.select(".tombstone-container .period-name")
periods = [pt.get_text() for pt in period_tags]
periods
```

```
['Today',
 'Tonight',
 'Sunday',
 'SundayNight',
 'Monday',
 'MondayNight',
 'Tuesday',
 'TuesdayNight',
 'Wednesday']
```

As we can see above, our technique gets us each of the period names, in order.

We can apply the same technique to get the other three fields:

```
short_descs = [sd.get_text() for sd in seven_day.select(
    ".tombstone-container .short-desc")]
temps = [t.get_text() for t in seven_day.select(
    ".tombstone-container .temp")]
descs = [d["title"] for d in seven_day.select(
    ".tombstone-container img")]

print(short_descs)
print(temps)
print(descs)
```

```
['Sunny', 'Mostly Clear', 'Sunny thenSlight ChanceT-storms',...]
['High: 88 °F', 'Low: 59 °F', 'High: 88 °F', 'Low: 57 °F', ...]
['Today: Sunny, with a high near 88. Northwest wind 9 to 13 mph...]
```

1.2.2.4   Deal with Data

We can now combine the data into a Pandas DataFrame and analyze it. A DataFrame is an object that can store tabular data, making data analysis easy.

In order to do this, we'll call the DataFrame class, and pass in each list of items that we have. We pass them in as part of a dictionary.

Each dictionary key will become a column in the DataFrame, and each list will become the values in the column:

```
import pandas as pd
weather = pd.DataFrame({
    "period": periods,
    "short_desc": short_descs,
    "temp": temps,
    "desc":descs
})
weather
```

Now let's save it to CSV.

```
weather.to_csv('data/Boulder_Weather_7_Days.csv')
```

1.3   COLLECT DATA FROM SQL DATABASES

Storing data in SQL databases offers several advantages and considerations. The advantages are:

- Advantages of Storing Data in SQL Databases: Structured Storage: SQL databases provide a structured storage model with tables, rows, and columns, allowing for efficient organization and retrieval of data.

- Data Integrity and Consistency: SQL databases enforce data integrity through constraints, such as primary keys, unique keys, and referential integrity, ensuring the accuracy and consistency of the stored data.

- Querying and Analysis: SQL databases offer powerful query languages (e.g., SQL) that enable complex data retrieval, filtering, aggregations, and analysis operations.

- ACID Compliance: SQL databases adhere to ACID (Atomicity, Consistency, Isolation, Durability) properties, ensuring reliable and transactional data operations.

To collect data from a SQL database, you need to establish a connection to the database server. This typically involves providing connection details such as server address, port, username, and password. Once connected, you can use SQL queries to extract data from the database. Queries can range from simple retrieval of specific records to complex joins, aggregations, and filtering operations. Python provides several libraries for interacting with SQL databases, such as sqlite3, psycopg2, pymysql, and pyodbc. These libraries allow you to establish connections, execute SQL queries, and retrieve the query results into Python data structures for further processing.

1.3.1 Tutorial – Collect Data from SQLite

1.3.1.1 What is SQLite

A file with the .sqlite extension is a lightweight SQL database file created with the SQLite software. It is a database in a file itself and implements a self-contained, full-featured, highly-reliable SQL database engine.

We use SQLite to demonstrate the approach to access SQL databases. They follow similar steps. You just need to setup your account credentials in the `connect` so you can connect the server.

1.3.1.2 Read an SQLite Database in Python

We use a Python package, sqlite3, to deal with SQLite databases. Once the sqlite3 package is imported, the general steps are:

1. Create a connection object that connects the SQLite database.
2. Create a cursor object
3. Create a query statement
4. Execute the query statement
5. Fetch the query result to result
6. If all work is done, close the connection.

We use the built-in SQLite database Chinook as the example here. We connect with the database, and show all the tables it contains.

```
import sqlite3

connection = sqlite3.connect('/content/ds_salaries.sqlite')
cursor = connection.cursor()

query = '''
SELECT name FROM sqlite_master
WHERE type='table';
'''

cursor.execute(query)
results = cursor.fetchall()
results
```

`[('ds_salaries',)]`

1.3.1.3   Play with the SQLite Databases

Using SQL statements, you can play with the SQLite Databases and get the data you need.

```
query = '''SELECT *
FROM ds_salaries'''

cursor.execute(query)
results = cursor.fetchall()
results
```

```
[(None,
  'work_year',
  'experience_level',
  'employment_type',
  'job_title',
  'salary',
  'salary_currency',
  'salary_in_usd',
  'employee_residence',
  'remote_ratio',
  'company_location',
  'company_size'),
 (0,
  '2020',
  'MI',
  'FT',
  'Data Scientist',
  '70000',
  'EUR',
  '79833',
  'DE',
  '0',
  'DE',
  'L'),
```

```
...,
(606,
 '2022',
 'MI',
 'FT',
 'AI Scientist',
 '200000',
 'USD',
 '200000',
 'IN',
 '100',
 'US',
 'L')]
```

1.3.1.4 Save Data to CSV Files

Since CSV file is much more convenient to process, we still use pandas to convert and to write to CSV files.

```python
import pandas as pd

df = pd.DataFrame(results)
df.info()
```

```
<class 'pandas.core.frame.DataFrame'>
RangeIndex: 608 entries, 0 to 607
Data columns (total 12 columns):
 #   Column  Non-Null Count  Dtype
---  ------  --------------  -----
 0   0       607 non-null    float64
 1   1       608 non-null    object
 2   2       608 non-null    object
 3   3       608 non-null    object
 4   4       608 non-null    object
 5   5       608 non-null    object
 6   6       608 non-null    object
 7   7       608 non-null    object
 8   8       608 non-null    object
 9   9       608 non-null    object
 10  10      608 non-null    object
 11  11      608 non-null    object
dtypes: float64(1), object(11)
memory usage: 57.1+ KB
```

```python
df.iloc[0]
```

```
0                  NaN
1            work_year
2     experience_level
3      employment_type
4            job_title
5               salary
6       salary_currency
```

```
7           salary_in_usd
8      employee_residence
9           remote_ratio
10       company_location
11          company_size
Name: 0, dtype: object
```

```
cols = list(df.iloc[0])
cols
```

```
[nan,
 'work_year',
 'experience_level',
 'employment_type',
 'job_title',
 'salary',
 'salary_currency',
 'salary_in_usd',
 'employee_residence',
 'remote_ratio',
 'company_location',
 'company_size']
```

```
df.columns = cols
df.info()
```

```
<class 'pandas.core.frame.DataFrame'>
RangeIndex: 608 entries, 0 to 607
Data columns (total 12 columns):
 #   Column              Non-Null Count  Dtype
---  ------              --------------  -----
 0   nan                 607 non-null    float64
 1   work_year           608 non-null    object
 2   experience_level    608 non-null    object
 3   employment_type     608 non-null    object
 4   job_title           608 non-null    object
 5   salary              608 non-null    object
 6   salary_currency     608 non-null    object
 7   salary_in_usd       608 non-null    object
 8   employee_residence  608 non-null    object
 9   remote_ratio        608 non-null    object
 10  company_location    608 non-null    object
 11  company_size        608 non-null    object
dtypes: float64(1), object(11)
memory usage: 57.1+ KB
```

```
df.drop(0, inplace = True)
df
```

```
    NaN  work_year experience_level employment_type  \
1   0.0       2020               MI              FT
2   1.0       2020               SE              FT
3   2.0       2020               SE              FT
```

```
4       3.0      2020            MI            FT
5       4.0      2020            SE            FT
..      ...      ...             ...           ...
603     602.0    2022            SE            FT
604     603.0    2022            SE            FT
605     604.0    2022            SE            FT
606     605.0    2022            SE            FT
607     606.0    2022            MI            FT

                         job_title  salary salary_currency salary_in_usd  \
1                   Data Scientist   70000             EUR         79833
2       Machine Learning Scientist  260000             USD        260000
3                Big Data Engineer   85000             GBP        109024
4               Product Data Analyst  20000            USD         20000
5       Machine Learning Engineer  150000             USD        150000
..                             ...     ...             ...           ...
603                  Data Engineer  154000             USD        154000
604                  Data Engineer  126000             USD        126000
605                   Data Analyst  129000             USD        129000
606                   Data Analyst  150000             USD        150000
607                   AI Scientist  200000             USD        200000

     employee_residence remote_ratio company_location company_size
1                    DE            0               DE            L
2                    JP            0               JP            S
3                    GB           50               GB            M
4                    HN            0               HN            S
5                    US           50               US            L
..                  ...          ...              ...          ...
603                  US          100               US            M
604                  US          100               US            M
605                  US            0               US            M
606                  US          100               US            M
607                  IN          100               US            L

[607 rows x 12 columns]
```

```
cursor.close()
connection.close()
```

1.3.2 Case Study – Collect Shopping Data from SQLite

Now you have learned how to collect data from a SQLite databse. Let's practice!

The attached **shopping.sqlite** file contains a dummy shopping dataset. Try to use your knowledge of collecting data from a SQL database, and retrieve information from it.

1.3.2.1 Establish the connection

```
import sqlite3

connection = sqlite3.connect('/content/shopping.sqlite')
cursor = connection.cursor()

query = '''
SELECT name FROM sqlite_master
WHERE type='table';
'''

cursor.execute(query)
results = cursor.fetchall()
results
```

```
[('customer_shopping_data',)]
```

1.3.2.2 Retrieve Information from the Database

```
query = '''SELECT *
FROM customer_shopping_data
Limit 3'''

cursor.execute(query)
results = cursor.fetchall()
results
```

```
[('I138884',
  'C241288',
  'Female',
  28,
  'Clothing',
  5,
  1500.4,
  'Credit Card',
  '5/8/2022',
  'Kanyon'),
 ('I317333',
  'C111565',
  'Male',
  21,
  'Shoes',
  3,
  1800.51,
  'Debit Card',
  '12/12/2021',
  'Forum Istanbul'),
 ('I127801',
  'C266599',
  'Male',
  20,
```

```
'Clothing',
1,
300.08,
'Cash',
'9/11/2021',
'Metrocity')]
```

1.3.2.3 Fetch all Records

```
query = '''SELECT *
FROM customer_shopping_data
'''

cursor.execute(query)
results = cursor.fetchall()
```

1.3.2.4 Columns' Names

We learned that the missing columns' names are: ['invoice_no', 'customer_id', 'gender', 'age', 'category', 'quantity', 'price', 'payment_method', 'invoice_date', 'shopping_mall'].

Combine this information and create a DataFrame of the shopping data, then save it to a CSV file for later use.

```
cols = ['invoice_no',
        'customer_id',
        'gender',
        'age',
        'category',
        'quantity',
        'price',
        'payment_method',
        'invoice_date',
        'shopping_mall']
```

```
import pandas as pd
```

```
df = pd.DataFrame(results, columns= cols)
df.info()
```

```
<class 'pandas.core.frame.DataFrame'>
RangeIndex: 16029 entries, 0 to 16028
Data columns (total 10 columns):
 #   Column          Non-Null Count  Dtype
---  ------          --------------  -----
 0   invoice_no      16029 non-null  object
 1   customer_id     16029 non-null  object
 2   gender          16029 non-null  object
 3   age             16029 non-null  int64
 4   category        16029 non-null  object
 5   quantity        16029 non-null  int64
```

```
6   price           16029 non-null  float64
7   payment_method  16029 non-null  object
8   invoice_date    16029 non-null  object
9   shopping_mall   16029 non-null  object
dtypes: float64(1), int64(2), object(7)
memory usage: 1.2+ MB
```

```
df.head()
```

```
   invoice_no customer_id  gender  age  category  quantity     price  \
0    I138884     C241288  Female   28  Clothing         5   1500.40
1    I317333     C111565    Male   21     Shoes         3   1800.51
2    I127801     C266599    Male   20  Clothing         1    300.08
3    I173702     C988172  Female   66     Shoes         5   3000.85
4    I337046     C189076  Female   53     Books         4     60.60

  payment_method invoice_date    shopping_mall
0    Credit Card      5/8/2022          Kanyon
1     Debit Card    12/12/2021  Forum Istanbul
2           Cash     9/11/2021       Metrocity
3    Credit Card    16/05/2021    Metropol AVM
4           Cash    24/10/2021          Kanyon
```

1.3.2.5 Save your retrieve information as a CSV file

```
df.to_csv('/content/shopping.csv')
```

1.4 COLLECT DATA THROUGH APIS

Collecting data through APIs (Application Programming Interfaces) offers several advantages:

- Structured Data: APIs provide structured and standardized data formats, making it easier to consume and integrate into applications or analysis pipelines.

- Real-time and Updated Data: APIs often provide real-time or near-real-time data, allowing you to access the latest information dynamically.

- Controlled Access: APIs allow data providers to control access to their data by implementing authentication mechanisms, usage limits, and access permissions.

- Targeted Data: APIs enable you to request specific data elements or subsets of data, minimizing unnecessary data transfer and processing.

- Automation and Integration: APIs facilitate automated data collection and integration into your workflows or systems.

There are some limitations and considerations too:

- Rate Limits and Usage Restrictions: Some APIs impose rate limits, usage quotas, or require subscription plans for accessing data beyond certain thresholds.

- Data Quality and Reliability: API data quality and reliability depend on the data provider. It's important to verify the accuracy, completeness, and consistency of the data obtained through APIs.

- API Changes and Deprecation: APIs may evolve over time, and changes to endpoints, parameters, or authentication mechanisms can require updates in your data collection code.

Examples of APIs are:

- Yahoo Finance API: The Yahoo Finance API provides access to financial market data, including stock quotes, historical prices, company information, and more. By interacting with the Yahoo Finance API, you can programmatically retrieve financial data for analysis, investment strategies, or market monitoring.

- OpenWeatherMap API: The OpenWeatherMap API offers weather data for various locations worldwide. You can fetch weather conditions, forecasts, historical weather data, and other meteorological information through their API.

- Twitter API: The Twitter API enables access to Twitter's vast collection of tweets and user data. You can use the API to retrieve tweets, monitor hashtags or keywords, analyze sentiment, and gain insights from Twitter's social media data.

- Google Maps API: The Google Maps API provides access to location-based services, including geocoding, distance calculations, routing, and map visualization. It allows you to integrate maps and location data into your applications or retrieve information related to places, addresses, or geographic features.

To collect data through APIs, you need to understand the API's documentation, authentication mechanisms, request formats (often in JSON or XML), and available endpoints. Python provides libraries such as requests and urllib that facilitate making HTTP requests to interact with APIs. You typically send HTTP requests with the required parameters, handle the API responses, and process the returned data according to your needs.

1.4.1   Tutorial – Collect Data from Yahoo

This tutorial will demonstrate how to use Python to retrieve financial data from Yahoo Finance. Using this, we may access historical market data as well as financial information about the company (for example, financial ratios).

1.4.1.1   Installation

```
!pip install yfinance
!pip install yahoofinancials
```

1.4.1.2 Analysis

The yfinance package can be imported into Python programs once it has been installed. We must use the company's ticker as an example in our argument.

A security is given a specific set of letters called a ticker or a stock symbol for trading purposes. For instance:

For Amazon, it is "AMZN" For Facebook, it is "FB" For Google, it is "GOOGL" For Microsoft, it is "MSFT"

```python
import yfinance as yahooFinance

# Here We are getting Google's financial information
GoogleInfo = yahooFinance.Ticker("GOOGL")
```

1.4.1.3 Whole Python Dictionary is Printed Here

```python
print(GoogleInfo.info)
```

```
{'zip': '94043', 'sector': 'Communication Services', ...
'logo_url': 'https://logo.clearbit.com/abc.xyz', 'trailingPegRatio': 1.3474}
```

The print statement produces a Python dictionary, which we can analyze and use to get the specific financial data we're looking for from Yahoo Finance. Let's take a few financial critical metrics as an example.

The info dictionary contains all firm information. As a result, we may extract the desired elements from the dictionary by parsing it:

We can retrieve financial key metrics like Company Sector, Price Earnings Ratio, and Company Beta from the above dictionary of items easily. Let us see the below code.

```python
# display Company Sector
print("Company Sector : ", GoogleInfo.info['sector'])

# display Price Earnings Ratio
print("Price Earnings Ratio : ", GoogleInfo.info['trailingPE'])

# display Company Beta
print(" Company Beta : ", GoogleInfo.info['beta'])
```

```
Company Sector :  Communication Services
Price Earnings Ratio :  1.6200992
 Company Beta :  1.078487
```

There are a ton of more stuff in the information. By printing the informational keys, we can view all of them:

```
# get all key value pairs that are available
for key, value in GoogleInfo.info.items():
    print(key, ":", value)
```

```
zip : 94043
sector : Communication Services
fullTimeEmployees : 174014
longBusinessSummary : Alphabet Inc. ... in Mountain View, California.
city : Mountain View
...
logo_url : https://logo.clearbit.com/abc.xyz
trailingPegRatio : 1.3474
```

We can retrieve historical market prices too and display them. Additionally, we can utilize it to get earlier market data.

We will use historical Google stock values over the past few years as our example. It is a relatively easy assignment to complete, as demonstrated below:

```
# covering the past few years.
# max->maximum number of daily prices available
# for Google.
# Valid options are 1d, 5d, 1mo, 3mo, 6mo, 1y, 2y,
# 5y, 10y and ytd.
print(GoogleInfo.history(period="max"))
```

Date	Open	High	Low	Close	Volume \
2004-08-19	2.502503	2.604104	2.401401	2.511011	893181924
2004-08-20	2.527778	2.729730	2.515015	2.710460	456686856
2004-08-23	2.771522	2.839840	2.728979	2.737738	365122512
2004-08-24	2.783784	2.792793	2.591842	2.624374	304946748
2004-08-25	2.626627	2.702703	2.599600	2.652653	183772044
...	...	...	...	...	...
2022-08-29	109.989998	110.949997	108.800003	109.419998	21191200
2022-08-30	110.169998	110.500000	107.800003	108.940002	27513300
2022-08-31	110.650002	110.849998	108.129997	108.220001	28627000
2022-09-01	108.279999	110.449997	107.360001	109.739998	28360900
2022-09-02	110.589996	110.739998	107.261597	107.849998	23528231

Date	Dividends	Stock Splits
2004-08-19	0	0.0
2004-08-20	0	0.0
2004-08-23	0	0.0
2004-08-24	0	0.0
2004-08-25	0	0.0
...	...	...
2022-08-29	0	0.0
2022-08-30	0	0.0
2022-08-31	0	0.0
2022-09-01	0	0.0
2022-09-02	0	0.0

```
[4543 rows x 7 columns]
```

We can pass our own start and end dates.

```
import datetime

start = datetime.datetime(2012,5,31)
end = datetime.datetime(2013,1,30)
print(GoogleInfo.history(start=start, end=end))
```

```
             Open       High        Low      Close    Volume  Dividends  \
Date
2012-05-31  14.732733  14.764765  14.489489  14.536036  118613268         0
2012-06-01  14.309059  14.330581  14.222973  14.288789  122193684         0
2012-06-04  14.269770  14.526777  14.264515  14.479229   97210692         0
2012-06-05  14.400651  14.467718  14.175926  14.274525   93502404         0
2012-06-06  14.426426  14.563814  14.354605  14.528779   83748168         0
...               ...        ...        ...        ...        ...       ...
2013-01-23  18.418167  18.743744  18.413162  18.556055  236127636         0
2013-01-24  18.549549  18.939690  18.531281  18.874125  135172692         0
2013-01-25  18.788038  18.980982  18.775024  18.860611   88946964         0
2013-01-28  18.812813  18.908909  18.715965  18.787037   65018916         0
2013-01-29  18.687437  18.942694  18.682182  18.860861   69814116         0

             Stock Splits
Date
2012-05-31            0
2012-06-01            0
2012-06-04            0
2012-06-05            0
2012-06-06            0
...                 ...
2013-01-23            0
2013-01-24            0
2013-01-25            0
2013-01-28            0
2013-01-29            0

[166 rows x 7 columns]
```

We can simultaneously download historical prices for many stocks:

The code below Pandas DataFrame including the different price data for the requested stocks. We now select the individual stock by printing df.GOOGL to have the historical market data for Google:

```
df = yahooFinance.download("AMZN GOOGL",
    start="2019-01-01", end="2020-01-01",group_by="ticker")
print(df)
print(df.GOOGL)
```

```
[*********************100%***********************]  2 of 2 completed
                    AMZN                                                  \
                    Open       High        Low      Close  Adj Close      Volume
```

```
Date
2019-01-02   73.260002   77.667999   73.046501   76.956497   76.956497   159662000
2019-01-03   76.000504   76.900002   74.855499   75.014000   75.014000   139512000
2019-01-04   76.500000   79.699997   75.915497   78.769501   78.769501   183652000
2019-01-07   80.115501   81.727997   79.459503   81.475502   81.475502   159864000
2019-01-08   83.234497   83.830498   80.830498   82.829002   82.829002   177628000
...               ...          ...          ...          ...          ...          ...
2019-12-24   89.690498   89.778503   89.378998   89.460503   89.460503    17626000
2019-12-26   90.050499   93.523003   89.974998   93.438499   93.438499   120108000
2019-12-27   94.146004   95.070000   93.300499   93.489998   93.489998   123732000
2019-12-30   93.699997   94.199997   92.030998   92.344498   92.344498    73494000
2019-12-31   92.099998   92.663002   91.611504   92.391998   92.391998    50130000

                 GOOGL
                 Open        High         Low        Close    Adj Close      Volume
Date
2019-01-02   51.360001   53.039501   51.264000   52.734001   52.734001    31868000
2019-01-03   52.533501   53.313000   51.118500   51.273499   51.273499    41960000
2019-01-04   52.127998   54.000000   51.842999   53.903500   53.903500    46022000
2019-01-07   54.048500   54.134998   53.132000   53.796001   53.796001    47446000
2019-01-08   54.299999   54.667500   53.417500   54.268501   54.268501    35414000
...               ...          ...          ...          ...          ...          ...
2019-12-24   67.510498   67.600502   67.208504   67.221497   67.221497    13468000
2019-12-26   67.327499   68.160004   67.275497   68.123497   68.123497    23662000
2019-12-27   68.199997   68.352501   67.650002   67.732002   67.732002    23212000
2019-12-30   67.840500   67.849998   66.891998   66.985497   66.985497    19994000
2019-12-31   66.789497   67.032997   66.606499   66.969498   66.969498    19514000

[252 rows x 12 columns]
                 Open        High         Low        Close    Adj Close      Volume
Date
2019-01-02   51.360001   53.039501   51.264000   52.734001   52.734001    31868000
2019-01-03   52.533501   53.313000   51.118500   51.273499   51.273499    41960000
2019-01-04   52.127998   54.000000   51.842999   53.903500   53.903500    46022000
2019-01-07   54.048500   54.134998   53.132000   53.796001   53.796001    47446000
2019-01-08   54.299999   54.667500   53.417500   54.268501   54.268501    35414000
...               ...          ...          ...          ...          ...          ...
2019-12-24   67.510498   67.600502   67.208504   67.221497   67.221497    13468000
2019-12-26   67.327499   68.160004   67.275497   68.123497   68.123497    23662000
2019-12-27   68.199997   68.352501   67.650002   67.732002   67.732002    23212000
2019-12-30   67.840500   67.849998   66.891998   66.985497   66.985497    19994000
2019-12-31   66.789497   67.032997   66.606499   66.969498   66.969498    19514000

[252 rows x 6 columns]
```

1.4.1.4 *Save the Data to CSV*

```
df.to_csv('data/FinanceData.csv')
```

## CHAPTER 2

Data Integration

D ATA INTEGRATION is the process of combining data from different sources into a single, unified view. It involves the combination of data from different data types, structures, and formats to form a single dataset that can be used for analysis and reporting. This step is important because it allows for the analysis of data from multiple sources, which can provide a more complete and accurate picture of the data being analyzed.

There are several Python packages that are commonly used for data integration, including:

- Pandas: A powerful library for data manipulation and analysis that provides data structures such as DataFrame and Series, that allow you to combine, filter, transform, and shape your data.

- NumPy: A powerful library for array computation that provides a high-performance multidimensional array object and tools to work with these arrays.

2.1 DATA INTEGRATION

Objective: Collect data from various files, an SQLite database, and webpages for a client.

Steps to fulfill the request:

- Understand the requirements: Schedule a meeting with the client to gather detailed requirements. Determine the specific files, SQLite database, and webpages from which the client wants to collect data. Clarify the desired data format, extraction criteria, and any specific data processing requirements.

- Data collection from files: Identify the file formats (e.g., CSV, HTML, TXT, XLSX, JSON) and their locations. Utilize the appropriate Python libraries (e.g., Pandas) to read and extract data from each file format. Iterate through the

DOI: 10.1201/9781003462781-2

files, apply the relevant parsing techniques, and store the extracted data in a unified format (e.g., DataFrame).

- Data collection from SQLite database: Obtain the SQLite database file and connection details. Use a Python library (e.g., sqlite3) to establish a connection to the SQLite database. Execute SQL queries to retrieve the desired data from specific tables or views. Fetch the query results into a Python data structure (e.g., DataFrame) for further processing or integration with other data.

- Data collection from webpages: Identify the target webpages and determine the appropriate approach for data extraction. If the webpages are structured or semi-structured, leverage Python libraries (e.g., BeautifulSoup) to parse the HTML/XML content and extract the required data using tags or CSS selectors. If the webpages are unstructured or require interaction, consider tools like Selenium to automate browser interactions and extract data through web scraping or API calls. Apply relevant data cleaning and transformation steps as needed.

Remember to maintain clear communication with the client throughout the process, seeking clarification when needed and delivering the final dataset according to their specifications. Regularly document your progress and keep track of any challenges faced or solutions implemented.

2.1.1 Tutorial – Data Integration

2.1.1.1 Setup

```
import numpy as np
import pandas as pd
```

```
df = pd.read_csv('/content/sample_data/california_housing_test.csv').
df.head()
```

```
   longitude  latitude  housing_median_age  total_rooms  total_bedrooms  \
0   -122.05     37.37                 27.0       3885.0           661.0
1   -118.30     34.26                 43.0       1510.0           310.0
2   -117.81     33.78                 27.0       3589.0           507.0
3   -118.36     33.82                 28.0         67.0            15.0
4   -119.67     36.33                 19.0       1241.0           244.0

   population  households  median_income  median_house_value
0      1537.0       606.0         6.6085            344700.0
1       809.0       277.0         3.5990            176500.0
2      1484.0       495.0         5.7934            270500.0
3        49.0        11.0         6.1359            330000.0
4       850.0       237.0         2.9375             81700.0
```

```
df.info()
```

```
<class 'pandas.core.frame.DataFrame'>
```

```
RangeIndex: 3000 entries, 0 to 2999
Data columns (total 9 columns):
 #   Column              Non-Null Count  Dtype
---  ------              --------------  -----
 0   longitude           3000 non-null   float64
 1   latitude            3000 non-null   float64
 2   housing_median_age  3000 non-null   float64
 3   total_rooms         3000 non-null   float64
 4   total_bedrooms      3000 non-null   float64
 5   population          3000 non-null   float64
 6   households          3000 non-null   float64
 7   median_income       3000 non-null   float64
 8   median_house_value  3000 non-null   float64
dtypes: float64(9)
memory usage: 211.1 KB
```

2.1.1.2 Concatenation

Documentation: https://pandas.pydata.org/pandas-docs/stable/reference/api/pandas.concat.html

```python
df_1 = df[['longitude','latitude','median_income']].sample(n=5)
df_2 = df[['longitude','latitude','median_income']].sample(n=5)
df_3 = df[['longitude','latitude','median_income']].sample(n=5)
```

df_1

```
      longitude  latitude  median_income
362   -117.19    32.77     3.8571
2425  -121.32    38.62     3.0864
1863  -118.36    33.82     3.3565
1059  -119.75    36.78     2.3333
1751  -121.96    37.34     5.7910
```

df_2

```
      longitude  latitude  median_income
2286  -122.20    37.47     4.2083
1933  -118.27    33.93     2.6458
1214  -121.00    37.60     2.6899
2372  -122.04    37.97     2.3152
483   -115.90    32.69     1.5417
```

df_3

```
      longitude  latitude  median_income
2731  -117.69    34.04     4.0096
1902  -117.90    36.95     1.7292
2683  -118.05    34.14     8.9728
937   -121.27    38.14     2.2883
1671  -117.98    33.76     4.4545
```

```
df_cat1 = pd.concat([df_1,df_2,df_3], axis=0)
df_cat1
```

```
      longitude  latitude  median_income
362    -117.19     32.77         3.8571
2425   -121.32     38.62         3.0864
1863   -118.36     33.82         3.3565
1059   -119.75     36.78         2.3333
1751   -121.96     37.34         5.7910
2286   -122.20     37.47         4.2083
1933   -118.27     33.93         2.6458
1214   -121.00     37.60         2.6899
2372   -122.04     37.97         2.3152
483    -115.90     32.69         1.5417
2731   -117.69     34.04         4.0096
1902   -117.90     36.95         1.7292
2683   -118.05     34.14         8.9728
937    -121.27     38.14         2.2883
1671   -117.98     33.76         4.4545
```

```
df_cat1.info()
```

```
<class 'pandas.core.frame.DataFrame'>
Int64Index: 15 entries, 362 to 1671
Data columns (total 3 columns):
 #   Column         Non-Null Count  Dtype
---  ------         --------------  -----
 0   longitude      15 non-null     float64
 1   latitude       15 non-null     float64
 2   median_income  15 non-null     float64
dtypes: float64(3)
memory usage: 480.0 bytes
```

```
df_cat2 = pd.concat([df_1,df_2,df_3], axis=1)
df_cat2
```

```
      longitude  latitude  median_income  longitude  latitude  median_income  \
362    -117.19     32.77         3.8571        NaN       NaN           NaN
2425   -121.32     38.62         3.0864        NaN       NaN           NaN
1863   -118.36     33.82         3.3565        NaN       NaN           NaN
1059   -119.75     36.78         2.3333        NaN       NaN           NaN
1751   -121.96     37.34         5.7910        NaN       NaN           NaN
2286      NaN       NaN           NaN      -122.20     37.47         4.2083
1933      NaN       NaN           NaN      -118.27     33.93         2.6458
1214      NaN       NaN           NaN      -121.00     37.60         2.6899
2372      NaN       NaN           NaN      -122.04     37.97         2.3152
483       NaN       NaN           NaN      -115.90     32.69         1.5417
2731      NaN       NaN           NaN         NaN       NaN           NaN
1902      NaN       NaN           NaN         NaN       NaN           NaN
2683      NaN       NaN           NaN         NaN       NaN           NaN
937       NaN       NaN           NaN         NaN       NaN           NaN
1671      NaN       NaN           NaN         NaN       NaN           NaN
```

```
        longitude   latitude   median_income
362          NaN        NaN             NaN
2425         NaN        NaN             NaN
1863         NaN        NaN             NaN
1059         NaN        NaN             NaN
1751         NaN        NaN             NaN
2286         NaN        NaN             NaN
1933         NaN        NaN             NaN
1214         NaN        NaN             NaN
2372         NaN        NaN             NaN
483          NaN        NaN             NaN
2731      -117.69      34.04          4.0096
1902      -117.90      36.95          1.7292
2683      -118.05      34.14          8.9728
937       -121.27      38.14          2.2883
1671      -117.98      33.76          4.4545
```

```
df_cat2.info()
```

```
<class 'pandas.core.frame.DataFrame'>
Int64Index: 15 entries, 362 to 1671
Data columns (total 9 columns):
 #   Column          Non-Null Count   Dtype
---  ------          --------------   -----
 0   longitude       5 non-null       float64
 1   latitude        5 non-null       float64
 2   median_income   5 non-null       float64
 3   longitude       5 non-null       float64
 4   latitude        5 non-null       float64
 5   median_income   5 non-null       float64
 6   longitude       5 non-null       float64
 7   latitude        5 non-null       float64
 8   median_income   5 non-null       float64
dtypes: float64(9)
memory usage: 1.2 KB
```

```
df_1 = df[['longitude']][:5]
df_2 = df[['latitude']][:5]
df_3 = df[['median_income']][:5]
df_1, df_2, df_3
```

```
(   longitude
0    -122.05
1    -118.30
2    -117.81
3    -118.36
4    -119.67,
     latitude
0      37.37
1      34.26
2      33.78
3      33.82
4      36.33,
```

```
   median_income
0         6.6085
1         3.5990
2         5.7934
3         6.1359
4         2.9375)
```

```
df_cat2 = pd.concat([df_1,df_2,df_3], axis=1)
df_cat2
```

```
   longitude  latitude  median_income
0    -122.05     37.37         6.6085
1    -118.30     34.26         3.5990
2    -117.81     33.78         5.7934
3    -118.36     33.82         6.1359
4    -119.67     36.33         2.9375
```

2.1.1.3 Merging

Documentation: https://pandas.pydata.org/docs/reference/api/pandas.DataFrame.merge.html

```
df_1=df[['longitude','median_income']][0:5]
df_1
```

```
   longitude  median_income
0    -122.05         6.6085
1    -118.30         3.5990
2    -117.81         5.7934
3    -118.36         6.1359
4    -119.67         2.9375
```

```
df_2=df[['longitude','median_house_value']][0:5]
df_2
```

```
   longitude  median_house_value
0    -122.05            344700.0
1    -118.30            176500.0
2    -117.81            270500.0
3    -118.36            330000.0
4    -119.67             81700.0
```

```
pd.merge(df_1,df_2,on=['longitude'],how='inner')
```

```
   longitude  median_income  median_house_value
0    -122.05         6.6085            344700.0
1    -118.30         3.5990            176500.0
2    -117.81         5.7934            270500.0
3    -118.36         6.1359            330000.0
4    -119.67         2.9375             81700.0
```

```
df_3=df[['longitude','population',]][2:7]
df_3
```

```
   longitude  population
2   -117.81      1484.0
3   -118.36        49.0
4   -119.67       850.0
5   -119.56       663.0
6   -121.43       604.0
```

```
pd.merge(df_1,df_3,on='longitude',how='inner')
```

```
   longitude  median_income  population
0   -117.81         5.7934      1484.0
1   -118.36         6.1359        49.0
2   -119.67         2.9375       850.0
```

```
pd.merge(df_1,df_3,on='longitude',how='outer').drop_duplicates()
```

```
   longitude  median_income  population
0   -122.05         6.6085         NaN
1   -118.30         3.5990         NaN
2   -117.81         5.7934      1484.0
3   -118.36         6.1359        49.0
4   -119.67         2.9375       850.0
5   -119.56            NaN       663.0
6   -121.43            NaN       604.0
```

Joining

Documentation: https://pandas.pydata.org/docs/reference/api/pandas.DataFrame.join.html

```
df_1=df[['longitude']][0:5]
df_1
```

```
   longitude
0   -122.05
1   -118.30
2   -117.81
3   -118.36
4   -119.67
```

```
df_2=df[['latitude']][2:7]
df_2
```

```
   latitude
2     33.78
3     33.82
4     36.33
```

```
5      36.51
6      38.63
```

```
df_1.join(df_2,how='left')
```

```
     longitude  latitude
0     -122.05       NaN
1     -118.30       NaN
2     -117.81     33.78
3     -118.36     33.82
4     -119.67     36.33
```

```
df_1.join(df_2,how='right')
```

```
     longitude  latitude
2     -117.81     33.78
3     -118.36     33.82
4     -119.67     36.33
5         NaN     36.51
6         NaN     38.63
```

```
df_1.join(df_2,how='inner')
```

```
     longitude  latitude
2     -117.81     33.78
3     -118.36     33.82
4     -119.67     36.33
```

```
df_1.join(df_2,how='outer')
```

```
     longitude  latitude
0     -122.05       NaN
1     -118.30       NaN
2     -117.81     33.78
3     -118.36     33.82
4     -119.67     36.33
5         NaN     36.51
6         NaN     38.63
```

2.1.2 Case Study – Data Science Salary

2.1.2.1 Setup

```
import numpy as np
import pandas as pd
import matplotlib.pyplot as plt
```

```
df = pd.read_csv('/content/Data Science Jobs Salaries.csv', skiprows=2)
df.head()
```

```
   work_year experience_level employment_type              job_title  \
0     2021e               EN              FT   Data Science Consultant
1      2020               SE              FT            Data Scientist
2     2021e               EX              FT       Head of Data Science
3     2021e               EX              FT              Head of Data
4     2021e               EN              FT  Machine Learning Engineer

   salary salary_currency  salary_in_usd employee_residence  remote_ratio  \
0   54000             EUR          64369                 DE            50
1   60000             EUR          68428                 GR           100
2   85000             USD          85000                 RU             0
3  230000             USD         230000                 RU            50
4  125000             USD         125000                 US           100

  company_location company_size
0               DE            L
1               US            L
2               RU            M
3               RU            L
4               US            S
```

```
df.info()
```

```
<class 'pandas.core.frame.DataFrame'>
RangeIndex: 245 entries, 0 to 244
Data columns (total 11 columns):
 #   Column             Non-Null Count  Dtype
---  ------             --------------  -----
 0   work_year          245 non-null    object
 1   experience_level   245 non-null    object
 2   employment_type    245 non-null    object
 3   job_title          245 non-null    object
 4   salary             245 non-null    int64
 5   salary_currency    245 non-null    object
 6   salary_in_usd      245 non-null    int64
 7   employee_residence 245 non-null    object
 8   remote_ratio       245 non-null    int64
 9   company_location   245 non-null    object
 10  company_size       245 non-null    object
dtypes: int64(3), object(8)
memory usage: 21.2+ KB
```

2.1.2.2 Concatenation

Documentation: https://pandas.pydata.org/pandas-docs/stable/reference/api/pandas.concat.html

```
df_1 = df[['company_location','job_title',
    'experience_level','salary_in_usd']].sample(n=5)
df_2 = df[['company_location','job_title',
    'experience_level','salary_in_usd']].sample(n=5)
df_3 = df[['company_location','job_title',
    'experience_level','salary_in_usd']].sample(n=5)
```

```
df_1
```

	company_location	job_title	experience_level	salary_in_usd
16	US	Data Engineer	MI	90000
125	IN	Data Scientist	MI	16949
25	PL	Director of Data Science	EX	154963
22	US	ML Engineer	MI	270000
41	US	Head of Data	EX	235000

```
df_2
```

	company_location	job_title	experience_level	salary_in_usd
216	ES	Data Scientist	MI	38776
73	US	Data Analyst	MI	93000
137	US	Data Scientist	MI	147000
28	GB	Research Scientist	EN	83000
45	DE	Data Science Consultant	EN	77481

```
df_3
```

	company_location	job_title	experience_level	salary_in_usd
92	AE	Lead Data Scientist	MI	115000
70	US	Data Scientist	MI	105000
242	US	Data Scientist	EN	105000
130	CA	Data Analyst	SE	71968
84	GB	Data Engineer	MI	72625

```
df_cat1 = pd.concat([df_1,df_2,df_3], axis=0)
df_cat1
```

	company_location	job_title	experience_level	salary_in_usd
16	US	Data Engineer	MI	90000
125	IN	Data Scientist	MI	16949
25	PL	Director of Data Science	EX	154963
22	US	ML Engineer	MI	270000
41	US	Head of Data	EX	235000
216	ES	Data Scientist	MI	38776
73	US	Data Analyst	MI	93000
137	US	Data Scientist	MI	147000
28	GB	Research Scientist	EN	83000
45	DE	Data Science Consultant	EN	77481
92	AE	Lead Data Scientist	MI	115000
70	US	Data Scientist	MI	105000
242	US	Data Scientist	EN	105000
130	CA	Data Analyst	SE	71968
84	GB	Data Engineer	MI	72625

```
df_cat1.info()
```

```
<class 'pandas.core.frame.DataFrame'>
Int64Index: 15 entries, 16 to 84
Data columns (total 4 columns):
 #   Column            Non-Null Count  Dtype
---  ------            --------------  -----
 0   company_location  15 non-null     object
 1   job_title         15 non-null     object
 2   experience_level  15 non-null     object
 3   salary_in_usd     15 non-null     int64
dtypes: int64(1), object(3)
memory usage: 600.0+ bytes
```

```
df_cat2 = pd.concat([df_1,df_2,df_3], axis=1)
df_cat2
```

	company_location	job_title	experience_level \
16	US	Data Engineer	MI
125	IN	Data Scientist	MI
25	PL	Director of Data Science	EX
22	US	ML Engineer	MI
41	US	Head of Data	EX
216	NaN	NaN	NaN
73	NaN	NaN	NaN
137	NaN	NaN	NaN
28	NaN	NaN	NaN
45	NaN	NaN	NaN
92	NaN	NaN	NaN
70	NaN	NaN	NaN
242	NaN	NaN	NaN
130	NaN	NaN	NaN
84	NaN	NaN	NaN

	salary_in_usd	company_location	job_title	experience_level \
16	90000.0	NaN	NaN	NaN
125	16949.0	NaN	NaN	NaN
25	154963.0	NaN	NaN	NaN
22	270000.0	NaN	NaN	NaN
41	235000.0	NaN	NaN	NaN
216	NaN	ES	Data Scientist	MI
73	NaN	US	Data Analyst	MI
137	NaN	US	Data Scientist	MI
28	NaN	GB	Research Scientist	EN
45	NaN	DE	Data Science Consultant	EN
92	NaN	NaN	NaN	NaN
70	NaN	NaN	NaN	NaN
242	NaN	NaN	NaN	NaN
130	NaN	NaN	NaN	NaN
84	NaN	NaN	NaN	NaN

	salary_in_usd	company_location	job_title	experience_level \
16	NaN	NaN	NaN	NaN

125	NaN	NaN	NaN	NaN
25	NaN	NaN	NaN	NaN
22	NaN	NaN	NaN	NaN
41	NaN	NaN	NaN	NaN
216	38776.0	NaN	NaN	NaN
73	93000.0	NaN	NaN	NaN
137	147000.0	NaN	NaN	NaN
28	83000.0	NaN	NaN	NaN
45	77481.0	NaN	NaN	NaN
92	NaN	AE	Lead Data Scientist	MI
70	NaN	US	Data Scientist	MI
242	NaN	US	Data Scientist	EN
130	NaN	CA	Data Analyst	SE
84	NaN	GB	Data Engineer	MI

	salary_in_usd
16	NaN
125	NaN
25	NaN
22	NaN
41	NaN
216	NaN
73	NaN
137	NaN
28	NaN
45	NaN
92	115000.0
70	105000.0
242	105000.0
130	71968.0
84	72625.0

```
df_cat2.info()
```

```
<class 'pandas.core.frame.DataFrame'>
Int64Index: 15 entries, 16 to 84
Data columns (total 12 columns):
 #   Column            Non-Null Count  Dtype
---  ------            --------------  -----
 0   company_location  5 non-null      object
 1   job_title         5 non-null      object
 2   experience_level  5 non-null      object
 3   salary_in_usd     5 non-null      float64
 4   company_location  5 non-null      object
 5   job_title         5 non-null      object
 6   experience_level  5 non-null      object
 7   salary_in_usd     5 non-null      float64
 8   company_location  5 non-null      object
 9   job_title         5 non-null      object
 10  experience_level  5 non-null      object
 11  salary_in_usd     5 non-null      float64
dtypes: float64(3), object(9)
memory usage: 1.5+ KB
```

2.1.2.3 Merging

Documentation: https://pandas.pydata.org/docs/reference/api/pandas.DataFrame.merge.html

```
df_1=df[['company_location','experience_level','salary_in_usd']][0:5]
df_1
```

	company_location	experience_level	salary_in_usd
0	DE	EN	64369
1	US	SE	68428
2	RU	EX	85000
3	RU	EX	230000
4	US	EN	125000

```
df_2=df[['company_location','job_title','salary_in_usd']][0:5]
df_2
```

	company_location	job_title	salary_in_usd
0	DE	Data Science Consultant	64369
1	US	Data Scientist	68428
2	RU	Head of Data Science	85000
3	RU	Head of Data	230000
4	US	Machine Learning Engineer	125000

```
pd.merge(df_1,df_2,on='company_location',how='inner')
```

	company_location	experience_level	salary_in_usd_x \
0	DE	EN	64369
1	US	SE	68428
2	US	SE	68428
3	US	EN	125000
4	US	EN	125000
5	RU	EX	85000
6	RU	EX	85000
7	RU	EX	230000
8	RU	EX	230000

	job_title	salary_in_usd_y
0	Data Science Consultant	64369
1	Data Scientist	68428
2	Machine Learning Engineer	125000
3	Data Scientist	68428
4	Machine Learning Engineer	125000
5	Head of Data Science	85000
6	Head of Data	230000
7	Head of Data Science	85000
8	Head of Data	230000

```
pd.merge(df_1,df_2,on='company_location',how='inner').drop_duplicates()
```

```
  company_location experience_level  salary_in_usd_x  \
0               DE               EN            64369
1               US               SE            68428
2               US               SE            68428
3               US               EN           125000
4               US               EN           125000
5               RU               EX            85000
6               RU               EX            85000
7               RU               EX           230000
8               RU               EX           230000

                   job_title  salary_in_usd_y
0    Data Science Consultant            64369
1             Data Scientist            68428
2  Machine Learning Engineer           125000
3             Data Scientist            68428
4  Machine Learning Engineer           125000
5        Head of Data Science           85000
6               Head of Data          230000
7        Head of Data Science           85000
8               Head of Data          230000
```

```
df_3=df[['company_location','job_title','experience_level',]][2:6]
df_3
```

```
  company_location                  job_title experience_level
2               RU       Head of Data Science               EX
3               RU               Head of Data               EX
4               US  Machine Learning Engineer               EN
5               US     Data Analytics Manager               SE
```

```
pd.merge(df_1,df_3,on='company_location',how='inner').drop_duplicates()
```

```
  company_location experience_level_x  salary_in_usd  \
0               US                 SE          68428
1               US                 SE          68428
2               US                 EN         125000
3               US                 EN         125000
4               RU                 EX          85000
5               RU                 EX          85000
6               RU                 EX         230000
7               RU                 EX         230000

                   job_title experience_level_y
0  Machine Learning Engineer                 EN
1     Data Analytics Manager                 SE
2  Machine Learning Engineer                 EN
3     Data Analytics Manager                 SE
4        Head of Data Science                 EX
5               Head of Data                 EX
```

```
6        Head of Data Science              EX
7             Head of Data                 EX
```

```
pd.merge(df_1,df_3,on='company_location',how='outer').drop_duplicates()
```

```
   company_location experience_level_x  salary_in_usd  \
0                DE                 EN          64369
1                US                 SE          68428
2                US                 SE          68428
3                US                 EN         125000
4                US                 EN         125000
5                RU                 EX          85000
6                RU                 EX          85000
7                RU                 EX         230000
8                RU                 EX         230000

                   job_title experience_level_y
0                        NaN                NaN
1  Machine Learning Engineer                 EN
2     Data Analytics Manager                 SE
3  Machine Learning Engineer                 EN
4     Data Analytics Manager                 SE
5        Head of Data Science                EX
6             Head of Data                   EX
7        Head of Data Science                EX
8             Head of Data                   EX
```

Joining

Documentation: https://pandas.pydata.org/docs/reference/api/pandas.DataFrame.join.html

```
df_1=df[['experience_level']][0:5]
df_1
```

```
   experience_level
0                EN
1                SE
2                EX
3                EX
4                EN
```

```
df_2=df[['job_title']][2:7]
df_2
```

```
                   job_title
2        Head of Data Science
3             Head of Data
4  Machine Learning Engineer
5     Data Analytics Manager
6        Research Scientist
```

```
df_1.join(df_2,how='left').drop_duplicates()
```

```
  experience_level                   job_title
0               EN                         NaN
1               SE                         NaN
2               EX         Head of Data Science
3               EX                 Head of Data
4               EN    Machine Learning Engineer
```

```
df_1.join(df_2,how='right').drop_duplicates()
```

```
  experience_level                   job_title
2               EX         Head of Data Science
3               EX                 Head of Data
4               EN    Machine Learning Engineer
5              NaN        Data Analytics Manager
6              NaN            Research Scientist
```

```
df_1.join(df_2,how='inner').drop_duplicates()
```

```
  experience_level                   job_title
2               EX         Head of Data Science
3               EX                 Head of Data
4               EN    Machine Learning Engineer
```

```
df_1.join(df_2,how='outer').drop_duplicates()
```

```
  experience_level                   job_title
0               EN                         NaN
1               SE                         NaN
2               EX         Head of Data Science
3               EX                 Head of Data
4               EN    Machine Learning Engineer
5              NaN        Data Analytics Manager
6              NaN            Research Scientist
```

## CHAPTER 3

Data Statistics

D ATA STATISTICAL UNDERSTANDING is the process of gaining insights and knowledge about the data through statistical analysis. This step involves tasks such as descriptive statistics, probability distributions, hypothesis testing, and inferential statistics. The goal is to understand the characteristics of the data, identify patterns, and make predictions about future data.

There are several Python packages that are commonly used for data statistical understanding, including:

- Pandas: It provides a wide range of built-in functions for calculating summary statistics of the data, such as mean, median, standard deviation, and more.

- NumPy: It provides tools for working with arrays and matrices, and also provides a wide range of mathematical and statistical functions.

- SciPy: It builds on NumPy and provides a wide range of scientific and technical computing tools, including optimization, signal processing, and statistics.

- statsmodels: It provides a wide range of statistical models, estimation procedures, and tests for use in data analysis.

3.1 DESCRIPTIVE DATA ANALYSIS

We begin with a thorough examination of data types. We categorize data into two distinct groups: non-numerical and numerical. Nonnumerical data encompasses qualitative information, such as categories or labels, while numerical data consists of quantitative values. Understanding the characteristics and significance of these data types is crucial for effective data analysis.

Central tendency measures are fundamental to statistical analysis. In this section, we delve into the heart of data summarization by introducing key measures, including the mean, median, and mode. These measures provide insights into the central or typical value within a dataset and are invaluable tools for data interpretation.

DOI: 10.1201/9781003462781-3

Our exploration continues with a focus on dispersion and location metrics. Dispersion measures, such as standard deviation and variance, quantify the spread or variability of data points. Location metrics, on the other hand, help pinpoint central positions within a dataset. We explore how these metrics contribute to a deeper understanding of data patterns and variability.

The Interquartile Range (IQR) is a powerful tool for understanding data variability. We not only explain how to calculate the IQR but also provide practical guidance on its interpretation. This measure is particularly useful for identifying outliers and assessing data distribution.

By the end of this chapter, you will have a solid foundation in these key concepts, making you better equipped to navigate the complexities of data analysis. These concepts serve as the building blocks for more advanced topics in the field and will empower you to extract meaningful insights from your datasets. As we progress through this chapter, remember that our aim is to provide you with both theoretical understanding and practical applications of these concepts, ensuring that you can confidently apply them to real-world data scenarios.

3.1.1 Tutorial – Statistical Understanding

3.1.1.1 Setup

```
import pandas as pd
import numpy as np
```

3.1.1.2 Load the Data

```
df = pd.read_csv("/content/Spotify_Youtube_Sample.csv")
df.head()
```

```
     Artist                                    Track  \
0  Gorillaz                           Feel Good Inc.
1  Gorillaz                          Rhinestone Eyes
2  Gorillaz  New Gold (feat. Tame Impala and Bootie Brown)
3  Gorillaz                         On Melancholy Hill
4  Gorillaz                            Clint Eastwood

                                          Album Album_type       Views  \
0                                    Demon Days      album  693555221.0
1                                 Plastic Beach      album   72011645.0
2  New Gold (feat. Tame Impala and Bootie Brown)     single    8435055.0
3                                 Plastic Beach      album  211754952.0
4                                      Gorillaz      album  618480958.0

       Likes   Comments Licensed official_video       Stream
0  6220896.0  169907.0     True           True  1.040235e+09
1  1079128.0   31003.0     True           True  3.100837e+08
2   282142.0    7399.0     True           True  6.306347e+07
3  1788577.0   55229.0     True           True  4.346636e+08
4  6197318.0  155930.0     True           True  6.172597e+08
```

3.1.1.3 General Idea

```
df.info()
```

```
<class 'pandas.core.frame.DataFrame'>
RangeIndex: 20718 entries, 0 to 20717
Data columns (total 10 columns):
 #   Column          Non-Null Count  Dtype
---  ------          --------------  -----
 0   Artist          20718 non-null  object
 1   Track           20718 non-null  object
 2   Album           20718 non-null  object
 3   Album_type      20718 non-null  object
 4   Views           20248 non-null  float64
 5   Likes           20177 non-null  float64
 6   Comments        20149 non-null  float64
 7   Licensed        20248 non-null  object
 8   official_video  20248 non-null  object
 9   Stream          20142 non-null  float64
dtypes: float64(4), object(6)
memory usage: 1.6+ MB
```

```
df.describe()
```

	Views	Likes	Comments	Stream
count	2.024800e+04	2.017700e+04	2.014900e+04	2.014200e+04
mean	9.393782e+07	6.633411e+05	2.751899e+04	1.359422e+08
std	2.746443e+08	1.789324e+06	1.932347e+05	2.441321e+08
min	0.000000e+00	0.000000e+00	0.000000e+00	6.574000e+03
25%	1.826002e+06	2.158100e+04	5.090000e+02	1.767486e+07
50%	1.450110e+07	1.244810e+05	3.277000e+03	4.968298e+07
75%	7.039975e+07	5.221480e+05	1.436000e+04	1.383581e+08
max	8.079649e+09	5.078865e+07	1.608314e+07	3.386520e+09

3.1.1.4 Non-Numerical Attributes

```
df['Artist'].value_counts()
```

```
Gorillaz                10
Die drei !!!            10
Hollywood Undead        10
Empire of the Sun       10
White Noise for Babies  10
                        ..
NewJeans                 6
Alfonso Herrera          6
Jimin                    3
Stars Music Chile        1
Bootie Brown             1
Name: Artist, Length: 2079, dtype: int64
```

```
df['Artist'].unique()
```

```
array(['Gorillaz', 'Red Hot Chili Peppers', '50 Cent', ..., 'LE SSERAFIM',
       'ThxSoMch', 'SICK LEGEND'], dtype=object)
```

```
df['Artist'].nunique()
```

2079

```
nonnumericalcols = ['Artist', 'Track', 'Album',
    'Album_type', 'Licensed', 'official_video']
df[nonnumericalcols].nunique()
```

```
Artist              2079
Track              17841
Album              11937
Album_type             3
Licensed               2
official_video         2
dtype: int64
```

3.1.1.5 Categorical Attributes

```
album_type = pd.DataFrame({'Album_type' : df[
    'Album_type'].value_counts()})
album_type
```

```
             Album_type
album             14926
single             5004
compilation         788
```

```
licensed = pd.DataFrame({'Licensed' : df['Licensed'].value_counts()})
licensed
```

```
        Licensed
True       14140
False       6108
```

```
official_video = pd.DataFrame({'official_video' : df['official_video'].
        value_counts()})
official_video
```

```
        official_video
True             15723
False             4525
```

3.1.1.6 Numerical Attributes

Central Tendency

min, max, median, mode, midrange

```
col = 'Views'
min = df[col].min()
max = df[col].max()
median = df[col].median()
mode = df[col].mode()[0]
midrange = (max - min)/2
print('col:',col,
      '\n\tmin:', min,
      'max:',max,
      'median:', median,
      'mode:', mode,
      'midrange:', midrange)
```

```
col: Views
min: 0.0 max: 8079649362.0 median: 14501095.0 mode: 6639.0
      midrange: 4039824681.0
```

```
def getCentralTendency(col):
    min = df[col].min()
    max = df[col].max()
    median = df[col].median()
    mode = df[col].mode()[0]
    midrange = (max - min)/2
    print('col:',col,
       '\n\tmin:', min,
       'max:',max,
       'median:', median,
       'mode:', mode,
       'midrange:', midrange)

numericalcols = ['Views', 'Likes', 'Comments', 'Stream']

for col in numericalcols:
    getCentralTendency(col)
```

```
col: Views
min: 0.0 max: 8079649362.0
        median: 14501095.0 mode: 6639.0 midrange: 4039824681.0
col: Likes
min: 0.0 max: 50788652.0
        median: 124481.0 mode: 0.0 midrange: 25394326.0
col: Comments
min: 0.0 max: 16083138.0
        median: 3277.0 mode: 0.0 midrange: 8041569.0
col: Stream
min: 6574.0 max: 3386520288.0
        median: 49682981.5 mode: 169769959.0 midrange: 1693256857.0
```

Dispersion

range, quantiles, var, std

```python
col = 'Views'
range = df[col].max() - df[col].min()
quantiles = df[col].quantile([0.25, 0.5, 0.75])
IQR = quantiles[0.75] - quantiles[0.25]
var = df[col].var()
std = df[col].std()

print('col:',col,
      '\n\trange:', range,
      'Q1:',quantiles[0.25],
      'Q2:', quantiles[0.5],
      'Q3:', quantiles[0.75],
      'IQR:', IQR,
      'var:', var,
      'std:', std)
```

```
col: Views
range: 8079649362.0 Q1: 1826001.5 Q2: 14501095.0 Q3: 70399749.0
        IQR: 68573747.5 var: 7.542950360937822e+16 std: 274644322.0046215
```

```python
def getDispersion(col):
    range = df[col].max() - df[col].min()
    quantiles = df[col].quantile([0.25, 0.5, 0.75])
    IQR = quantiles[0.75] - quantiles[0.25]
    var = df[col].var()
    std = df[col].std()
    print('col:',col,
        '\n\trange:', range,
        'Q1:',quantiles[0.25],
        'Q2:', quantiles[0.5],
        'Q3:', quantiles[0.75],
        'IQR:', IQR,
        'var:', var,
        'std:', std)
numericalcols = ['Views', 'Likes', 'Comments', 'Stream']

for col in numericalcols:
    getDispersion(col)
```

```
col: Views
range: 8079649362.0 Q1: 1826001.5 Q2: 14501095.0 Q3: 70399749.0
        IQR: 68573747.5 var: 7.542950360937822e+16 std: 274644322.0046215
col: Likes
range: 50788652.0 Q1: 21581.0 Q2: 124481.0 Q3: 522148.0
        IQR: 500567.0 var: 3201681265274.244 std: 1789324.2482217257
col: Comments
range: 16083138.0 Q1: 509.0 Q2: 3277.0 Q3: 14360.0
```

```
      IQR: 13851.0 var: 37339645168.43132 std: 193234.68935062183
col: Stream
range: 3386513714.0 Q1: 17674864.25 Q2: 49682981.5 Q3: 138358065.25
      IQR: 120683201.0 var: 5.960047142258919e+16 std: 244132077.82384762
```

Correlation

```
df[numericalcols].corr()
```

	Views	Likes	Comments	Stream
Views	1.000000	0.891101	0.431185	0.601905
Likes	0.891101	1.000000	0.631670	0.654247
Comments	0.431185	0.631670	1.000000	0.267737
Stream	0.601905	0.654247	0.267737	1.000000

3.1.2 Case Study – Statistical Understanding of YouTube and Spotify

You have learned how to use Pandas to get a statistical understanding of your data. It is time to apply and to practice!

3.1.2.1 Setup

```
import pandas as pd
import numpy as np
```

3.1.2.2 Load the Data

We will use the dataset "ds-salaries.csv" for the case study.

```
df = pd.read_csv("/content/ds-salaries.csv")
df.head()
```

	work_year	experience_level	employment_type	job_title
0	2021e	EN	FT	Data Science Consultant
1	2020	SE	FT	Data Scientist
2	2021e	EX	FT	Head of Data Science
3	2021e	EX	FT	Head of Data
4	2021e	EN	FT	Machine Learning Engineer

	salary	salary_currency	salary_in_usd	employee_residence	remote_ratio
0	54000	EUR	64369	DE	50
1	60000	EUR	68428	GR	100
2	85000	USD	85000	RU	0
3	230000	USD	230000	RU	50
4	125000	USD	125000	US	100

	company_location	company_size
0	DE	L
1	US	L
2	RU	M
3	RU	L
4	US	S

3.1.2.3 General Idea

```
df.info()
```

```
<class 'pandas.core.frame.DataFrame'>
RangeIndex: 245 entries, 0 to 244
Data columns (total 11 columns):
 #   Column             Non-Null Count  Dtype
---  ------             --------------  -----
 0   work_year          245 non-null    object
 1   experience_level   245 non-null    object
 2   employment_type    245 non-null    object
 3   job_title          245 non-null    object
 4   salary             245 non-null    int64
 5   salary_currency    245 non-null    object
 6   salary_in_usd      245 non-null    int64
 7   employee_residence 245 non-null    object
 8   remote_ratio       245 non-null    int64
 9   company_location   245 non-null    object
 10  company_size       245 non-null    object
dtypes: int64(3), object(8)
memory usage: 21.2+ KB
```

```
df.describe()
```

	salary	salary_in_usd	remote_ratio
count	2.450000e+02	245.000000	245.000000
mean	5.025418e+05	99868.012245	69.183673
std	2.276230e+06	83983.326949	37.593421
min	4.000000e+03	2876.000000	0.000000
25%	6.000000e+04	45896.000000	50.000000
50%	1.030000e+05	81000.000000	100.000000
75%	1.740000e+05	130000.000000	100.000000
max	3.040000e+07	600000.000000	100.000000

3.1.2.4 Non-Numerical Attributes

```
df['work_year'].value_counts()
```

```
2021e    179
2020      66
Name: work_year, dtype: int64
```

```
df['experience_level'].value_counts()
```

```
MI    103
SE    77
EN    54
EX    11
Name: experience_level, dtype: int64
```

```
FT     231
PT       7
CT       4
FL       3
Name: employment_type, dtype: int64
```

```
df['company_location'].value_counts()
```

```
US     108
DE      19
IN      17
GB      16
FR      11
CA      11
...
CO       1
KE       1
HU       1
SG       1
MT       1
Name: company_location, dtype: int64
```

```
df['company_location'].unique()
```

```
array(['DE', 'US', 'RU', 'FR', 'AT', 'CA', 'UA', 'NG', 'IN', 'ES', 'PL',
       'GB', 'PT', 'DK', 'SG', 'MX', 'TR', 'NL', 'AE', 'JP', 'CN', 'HU',
       'KE', 'CO', 'NZ', 'IR', 'CL', 'PK', 'BE', 'GR', 'SI', 'BR', 'CH',
       'IT', 'MD', 'LU', 'VN', 'AS', 'HR', 'IL', 'MT'], dtype=object)
```

```
df['company_location'].nunique()
```

```
41
```

```
nonnumericalcols = ['work_year',
                    'experience_level',
                    'employment_type',
                    'job_title',
                    'salary_currency',
                    'employee_residence',
                    'company_location',
                    'company_size']
df[nonnumericalcols].nunique()
```

```
work_year            2
experience_level     4
employment_type      4
job_title           43
salary_currency     15
employee_residence  45
company_location    41
```

```
company_size              3
dtype: int64
```

3.1.2.5 Categorical Attributes

```
employment_type = pd.DataFrame({'employment_type' : df[
    'employment_type'].value_counts()})
employment_type
```

```
      employment_type
FT              231
PT                7
CT                4
FL                3
```

```
salary_currency  = pd.DataFrame({'salary_currency' : df[
    'salary_currency'].value_counts()})
salary_currency
```

```
      salary_currency
USD              126
EUR               57
INR               21
GBP               13
CAD               10
TRY                3
PLN                2
HUF                2
SGD                2
MXN                2
DKK                2
BRL                2
CLP                1
JPY                1
CNY                1
```

```
company_size = pd.DataFrame({'company_size' : df[
    'company_size'].value_counts()})
company_size
```

```
      company_size
L              132
S               58
M               55
```

3.1.2.6 Numerical Attributes

Central Tendency

   min, max, median, mode, midrange

```
col = 'salary_in_usd'
min = df[col].min()
max = df[col].max()
median = df[col].median()
mode = df[col].mode()[0]
midrange = (max - min)/2
print('col:',col,
      '\n\tmin:', min,
      'max:',max,
      'median:', median,
      'mode:', mode,
      'midrange:', midrange)
```

```
col: salary_in_usd
min: 2876 max: 600000 median: 81000.0 mode: 150000 midrange: 298562.0
```

```
def getCentralTendency(col):
    min = df[col].min()
    max = df[col].max()
    median = df[col].median()
    mode = df[col].mode()[0]
    midrange = (max - min)/2
    print('col:',col,
      '\n\tmin:', min,
      'max:',max,
      'median:', median,
      'mode:', mode,
      'midrange:', midrange)

numericalcols = ['salary', 'salary_in_usd', 'remote_ratio']

for col in numericalcols:
    getCentralTendency(col)
```

```
col: salary
min: 4000 max: 30400000 median: 103000.0 mode: 80000 midrange: 15198000.0
col: salary_in_usd
min: 2876 max: 600000 median: 81000.0 mode: 150000 midrange: 298562.0
col: remote_ratio
min: 0 max: 100 median: 100.0 mode: 100 midrange: 50.0
```

Dispersion

range, quantiles, var, std

```
col = 'salary'
range = df[col].max() - df[col].min()
quantiles = df[col].quantile([0.25, 0.5, 0.75])
IQR = quantiles[0.75] - quantiles[0.25]
```

```
var = df[col].var()
std = df[col].std()

print('col:',col,
      '\n\trange:', range,
      'Q1:',quantiles[0.25],
      'Q2:', quantiles[0.5],
      'Q3:', quantiles[0.75],
      'IQR:', IQR,
      'var:', var,
      'std:', std)
```

:

```
\index{IQR}
col: salary
range: 30396000 Q1 60000.0 Q2: 103000.0 Q3: 174000.0
        IQR: 114000.0 var: 5181223548855.596 std: 2276230.117728784
```

```
def getDispersion(col):
    range = df[col].max() - df[col].min()
    quantiles = df[col].quantile([0.25, 0.5, 0.75])
    IQR = quantiles[0.75] - quantiles[0.25]
    var = df[col].var()
    std = df[col].std()
    print('col:',col,
          '\n\trange:', range,
          'Q1:',quantiles[0.25],
          'Q2:', quantiles[0.5],
          'Q3:', quantiles[0.75],
          'IQR:', IQR,
          'var:', var,
          'std:', std)
nnumericalcols = ['salary', 'salary_in_usd', 'remote_ratio']

for col in numericalcols:
    getDispersion(col)
```

```
col: salary
range: 30396000 Q1: 60000.0 Q2: 103000.0 Q3: 174000.0
        IQR: 114000.0 var: 5181223548855.596 std: 2276230.117728784
col: salary_in_usd
range: 597124 Q1: 45896.0 Q2: 81000.0 Q3: 130000.0
        IQR: 84104.0 var: 7053199205.446571 std: 83983.32694914255
col: remote_ratio
range: 100 Q1: 50.0 Q2: 100.0 Q3: 100.0
        IQR: 50.0 var: 1413.265306122449 std: 37.59342104840219
```

Correlation

```
df[numericalcols].corr()
```

```
                    salary  salary_in_usd  remote_ratio
salary            1.000000      -0.087365     -0.004775
salary_in_usd    -0.087365       1.000000      0.171240
remote_ratio     -0.004775       0.171240      1.000000
```

## CHAPTER 4

Data Visualization

D ATA VISUALIZATION is the process of creating graphical representations of data in order to communicate information and insights effectively. The goal is to use visual elements such as charts, plots, and maps to make the data more accessible, understandable, and actionable for different audiences.

There are several Python packages that are commonly used for data visualization, including:

- Pandas: It integrates with other libraries such as Matplotlib and Seaborn that allow to generate various types of plots and visualizations, that can help understand the data and, identify patterns and trends.

- Matplotlib: It is a 2D plotting library that provides a wide range of tools for creating static, animated, and interactive visualizations. It is widely used as the foundation for other libraries.

- Seaborn: It is a library built on top of Matplotlib that provides a higher-level interface for creating more attractive and informative statistical graphics. It is particularly useful for data visualization in statistics and data science.

- Plotly: It is a library for creating interactive and web-based visualizations and provides a wide range of tools for creating plots, maps, and dashboards. It is particularly useful for creating interactive visualizations that can be embedded in web pages or apps.

- PyViz: It is a library that is composed of a set of libraries such as Holoviews, Geoviews, Datashader and more, for creating visualizations for complex data and large datasets.

DOI: 10.1201/9781003462781-4

4.1 DATA VISUALIZATION WITH PANDAS

Data visualization is a critical aspect of data analysis, and the Pandas library embraces this need by providing built-in functionalities for it. In this section, we focus on harnessing these built-in functionalities for data visualization. Whether you are new to data visualization or looking for a quick and convenient way to explore your data, Pandas provides a powerful toolset.

4.1.1 Tutorial – Data Visualization with Pandas

It is hard to digest many data at the same time. Data visualizaiton is a way to make the process simple and straightforward.

Because data visualization is so important and essential in today's business, Pandas as a data-driven package provides built-in plotting functions. We will learn some of their basic usage today.

4.1.1.1 Setup

```
import numpy as np
import pandas as pd
```

```
df = pd.read_csv('/content/Economy_of_US.csv')
df
```

	Year	GDP_PPP	GDP_PerCapita_PPP	GDP_Nominal	GDP_PerCapita_Nominal \
0	1980	2857.3	12552.9	2857.3	12552.9
1	1981	3207.0	13948.7	3207.0	13948.7
2	1982	3343.8	14405.0	3343.8	14405.0
3	1983	3634.0	15513.7	3634.0	15513.7
4	1984	4037.7	17086.4	4037.7	17086.4
...					
42	2022	25035.2	75179.6	25035.2	75179.6
43	2023	26185.2	78421.9	26185.2	78421.9
44	2024	27057.2	80779.3	27057.2	80779.3
45	2025	28045.3	83463.2	28045.3	83463.2
46	2026	29165.5	86521.2	29165.5	86521.2
47	2027	30281.5	89546.4	30281.5	89546.4

	GDP_Growth	Inflation	Unemployment	Inflation_Change
0	-0.003	0.135	0.072	NaN
1	0.025	0.104	0.076	Decrease
2	-0.018	0.062	0.097	Decrease
3	0.046	0.032	0.096	Decrease
4	0.072	0.044	0.075	Increase
...				
42	0.016	0.081	0.037	Increase
43	0.010	0.035	0.046	Decrease
44	0.012	0.022	0.054	Decrease
45	0.018	0.020	0.054	Decrease
46	0.021	0.020	0.049	No change
47	0.019	0.020	0.047	No change

```
df.info()
```

```
<class 'pandas.core.frame.DataFrame'>
RangeIndex: 48 entries, 0 to 47
Data columns (total 9 columns):
 #   Column                 Non-Null Count  Dtype
---  ------                 --------------  -----
 0   Year                   48 non-null     int64
 1   GDP_PPP                48 non-null     float64
 2   GDP_PerCapita_PPP      48 non-null     float64
 3   GDP_Nominal            48 non-null     float64
 4   GDP_PerCapita_Nominal  48 non-null     float64
 5   GDP_Growth             48 non-null     float64
 6   Inflation              48 non-null     float64
 7   Unemployment           48 non-null     float64
 8   Inflation_Change       47 non-null     object
dtypes: float64(7), int64(1), object(1)
memory usage: 3.5+ KB
```

```
df.describe()
```

```
            Year      GDP_PPP  GDP_PerCapita_PPP   GDP_Nominal  \
count      48.00    48.000000          48.000000     48.000000
mean     2003.50  13182.360417       43192.318750  13182.360417
std        14.00   7817.386178       21396.888688   7817.386178
min      1980.00   2857.300000       12552.900000   2857.300000
25%      1991.75   6429.750000       25120.375000   6429.750000
50%      2003.50  11836.850000       40523.500000  11836.850000
75%      2015.25  18328.275000       57007.275000  18328.275000
max      2027.00  30281.500000       89546.400000  30281.500000

       GDP_PerCapita_Nominal  GDP_Growth  Inflation  Unemployment
count              48.000000   48.000000  48.000000     48.000000
mean            43192.318750    0.024458   0.032208      0.060500
std             21396.888688    0.019611   0.023672      0.016391
min             12552.900000   -0.034000  -0.003000      0.037000
25%             25120.375000    0.017000   0.020000      0.048500
50%             40523.500000    0.026000   0.028000      0.055500
75%             57007.275000    0.037250   0.035250      0.072000
max             89546.400000    0.072000   0.135000      0.097000
```

4.1.1.2 Scatter Plots

```
df.plot(x = 'Year', y = 'Inflation', kind = 'scatter')
```

```
<Axes: xlabel='Year', ylabel='Inflation'>
```

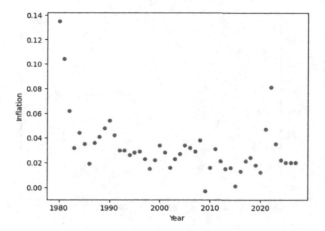

Figure 4.1 · A Scatter Plot

4.1.1.3 Line Plots

```
df.plot(y = 'Inflation', kind = 'line')
```

```
<Axes: >
```

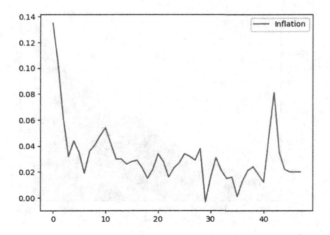

Figure 4.2 A Line Plot

```
df.plot(x = 'Year', y = 'Inflation', kind = 'line')
```

```
<Axes: xlabel='Year'>
```

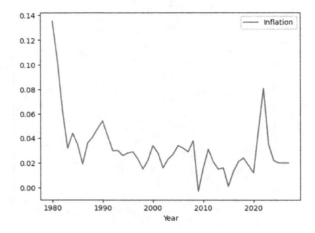

Figure 4.3 Another Line Plot

4.1.1.4 Area Plots

```
df.plot(x = 'Year', y = 'GDP_PPP', kind = 'area')
```

```
<Axes: xlabel='Year'>
```

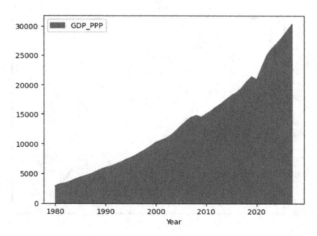

Figure 4.4 An Area Plot

```
df.plot(x = 'Year', y = 'GDP_Nominal', kind = 'area')
```

```
<Axes: xlabel='Year'>
```

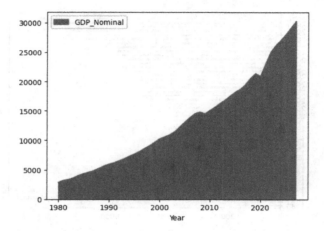

Figure 4.5   Another Area Plot

4.1.1.5   Bar Charts

```
df.plot(x = 'Year', y = 'GDP_PerCapita_PPP', kind = 'bar')
```

```
<Axes: xlabel='Year'>
```

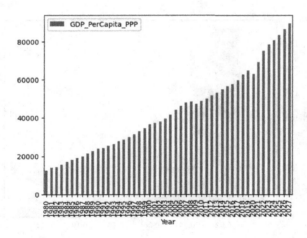

Figure 4.6   A Bar Plot

```
df.plot(x = 'Year', y = 'GDP_PerCapita_Nominal', kind = 'barh')
```

```
<Axes: ylabel='Year'>
```

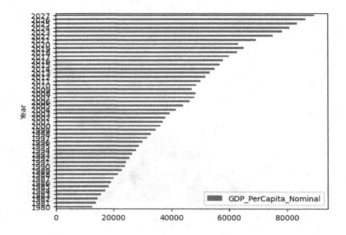

Figure 4.7 A Horizontal Bar Plot

4.1.1.6 *Histograms*

```
df['Inflation'].plot(kind = 'hist')
```

```
<Axes: ylabel='Frequency'>
```

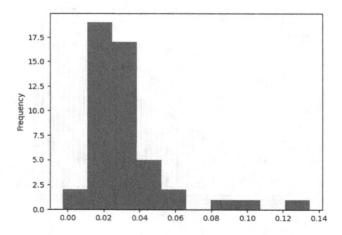

Figure 4.8 A Histogram

```
df['Inflation'].plot(kind = 'hist', bins = 100)
```

```
<Axes: ylabel='Frequency'>
```

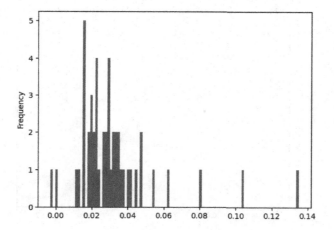

Figure 4.9   Another Histogram Plot

```
df['Unemployment'].plot(kind = 'hist')
```

```
<Axes: ylabel='Frequency'>
```

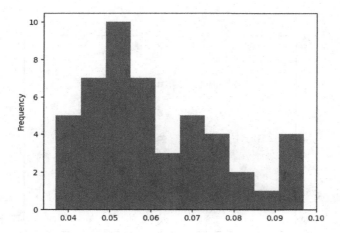

Figure 4.10   Another Histogram Plot

```
df['Unemployment'].plot(kind = 'kde')
```

```
<Axes: ylabel='Density'>
```

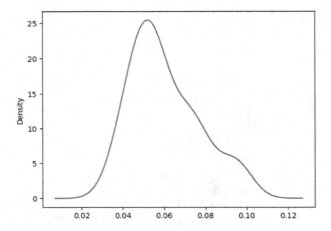

Figure 4.11 Another Histogram Plot with Density

4.1.1.7 Box Plot

```
df['Inflation'].plot(kind = 'box')
```

`<Axes: >`

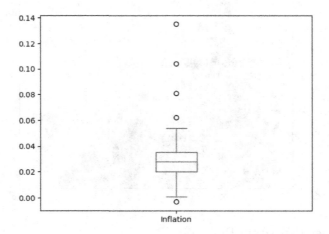

Figure 4.12 A Box Plot

```
df['Unemployment'].plot(kind = 'box')
```

`<Axes: >`

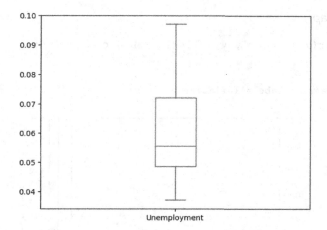

Figure 4.13   Another Box Plot

4.1.1.8   Pie Charts

```
df['Inflation_Change'].value_counts()
```

```
Decrease     23
Increase     21
No change     3
Name: Inflation_Change, dtype: int64
```

```
df['Inflation_Change'].value_counts().plot(kind = 'pie')
```

```
<Axes: ylabel='Inflation_Change'>
```

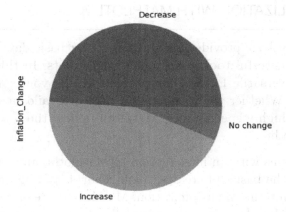

Figure 4.14   A Pie Plot

4.1.1.9 Color Map

```
df.plot.scatter(x = 'Year', y = 'Inflation', c = 'Unemployment')
```

```
<Axes: xlabel='Year', ylabel='Inflation'>
```

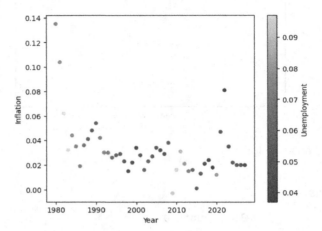

Figure 4.15 A Color Map

4.1.1.10 Documentation

- You can find more details in the documentation here: https://pandas.pydata.or
  g/pandas-docs/stable/reference/api/pandas.DataFrame.plot.html
- Here is another useful reference: https://pandas.pydata.org/docs/user_guide/
  visualization.html

4.2 DATA VISUALIZATION WITH MATPLOTLIB

While the Pandas package provides certain support for basic data visualization, users may need a more powerful tool to customize their plots. In this section, we delve into Matplotlib, a versatile Python library that grants you complete control over your visualizations. Whether you're aiming for intricate, tailor-made plots or need to visualize data in a highly specific way, Matplotlib offers the tools and flexibility to bring your vision to life.

Our exploration begins with an introduction to Matplotlib and its capabilities. We'll guide you through the basics of creating plots, charts, and figures, emphasizing the library's flexibility in terms of customization. Matplotlib is renowned for its customization options. We delve deep into the art of fine-tuning your visualizations. From adjusting colors, markers, and line styles to controlling axis scales and annotations, you'll have the tools to craft visualizations that precisely convey your insights. Multipanel figures and subplots are essential when visualizing complex data. We explore how Matplotlib allows you to create grids of subplots, enabling you to present multiple views of your data in a single, coherent figure.

4.2.1 Tutorial – Data Visualization with Matplotlib

Document: https://matplotlib.org

4.2.1.1 Setup

```
import matplotlib.pyplot as plt
import pandas as pd
import numpy as np
```

```
df = pd.read_csv('/content/Economy_of_US.csv')
df
```

	Year	GDP_PPP	GDP_PerCapita_PPP	GDP_Nominal	GDP_PerCapita_Nominal	\
0	1980	2857.3	12552.9	2857.3	12552.9	
1	1981	3207.0	13948.7	3207.0	13948.7	
2	1982	3343.8	14405.0	3343.8	14405.0	
3	1983	3634.0	15513.7	3634.0	15513.7	
4	1984	4037.7	17086.4	4037.7	17086.4	
5	1985	4339.0	18199.3	4339.0	18199.3	
...						
42	2022	25035.2	75179.6	25035.2	75179.6	
43	2023	26185.2	78421.9	26185.2	78421.9	
44	2024	27057.2	80779.3	27057.2	80779.3	
45	2025	28045.3	83463.2	28045.3	83463.2	
46	2026	29165.5	86521.2	29165.5	86521.2	
47	2027	30281.5	89546.4	30281.5	89546.4	

	GDP_Growth	Inflation	Unemployment	Inflation_Change
0	-0.003	0.135	0.072	NaN
1	0.025	0.104	0.076	Decrease
2	-0.018	0.062	0.097	Decrease
3	0.046	0.032	0.096	Decrease
4	0.072	0.044	0.075	Increase
5	0.042	0.035	0.072	Decrease
...				
43	0.010	0.035	0.046	Decrease
44	0.012	0.022	0.054	Decrease
45	0.018	0.020	0.054	Decrease
46	0.021	0.020	0.049	No change
47	0.019	0.020	0.047	No change

4.2.1.2 A Simple Plot

```
plt.plot(df['Year'], df['GDP_Growth'])
plt.xlabel('Year')
plt.ylabel('GDP GRowth')
plt.title('Economy of US')
```

Text(0.5, 1.0, 'Economy of US')

Figure 4.16   A Simple Plot

Change markers

```
plt.plot(df['Year'], df['GDP_Growth'], 'o')
plt.xlabel('Year')
plt.ylabel('GDP GRowth')
plt.title('Economy of US')
```

Text(0.5, 1.0, 'Economy of US')

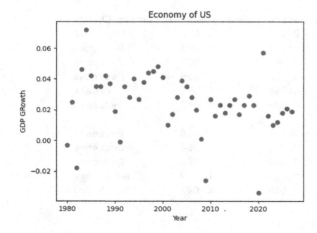

Figure 4.17   A Scatter Plot with Marker o

```
markers = ['o', '*', '.', ',', 'x', 'X', '+', 'P', 's', 'D', 'd', 'p',
    'H', 'h', 'v', '^', '<', '>', '1', '2', '3', '4', '|', '_']

for m in markers:
  print(m)
  plt.plot(df['Year'], df['GDP_Growth'], m)
  plt.xlabel('Year')
  plt.ylabel('GDP GRowth')
  plt.title('Economy of US')
  plt.show()
```

*

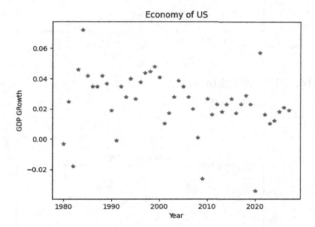

Figure 4.18 A Scatter Plot with Marker *

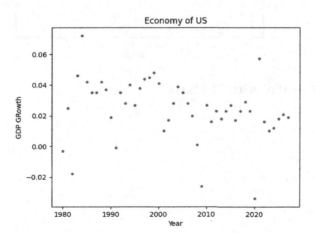

Figure 4.19 A Scatter Plot with Marker.

,

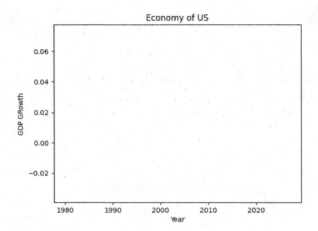

Figure 4.20 A Scatter Plot with Marker ,

x

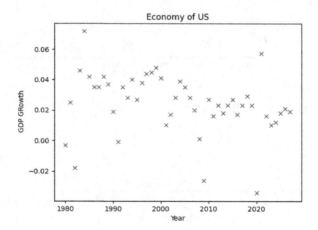

Figure 4.21 A Scatter Plot with Marker x

X

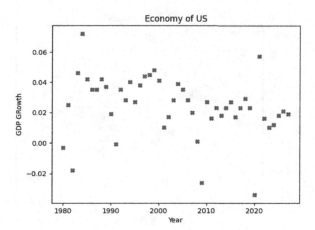

Figure 4.22 A Scatter Plot with Marker X

+

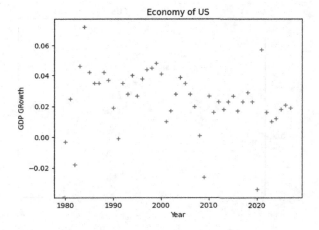

Figure 4.23 A Scatter Plot with Marker +

P

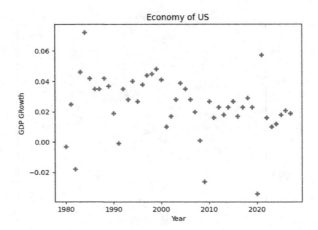

Figure 4.24 A Scatter Plot with Marker P

s

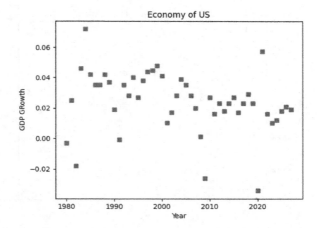

Figure 4.25 A Scatter Plot with Marker s

D

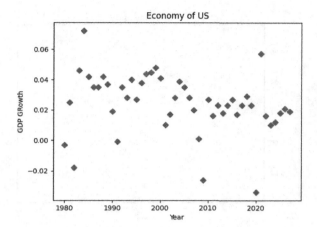

Figure 4.26 A Scatter Plot with Marker D

d

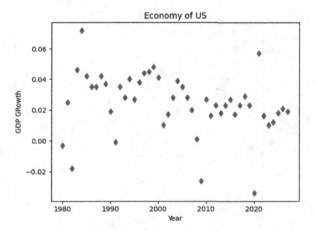

Figure 4.27 A Scatter Plot with Marker d

p

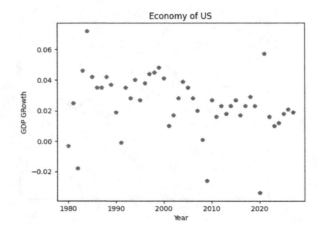

Figure 4.28 A Scatter Plot with Marker p

H

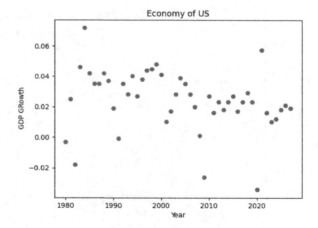

Figure 4.29 A Scatter Plot with Marker H

h

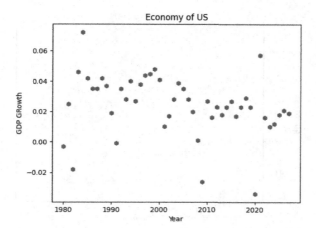

Figure 4.30   A Scatter Plot with Marker h

v

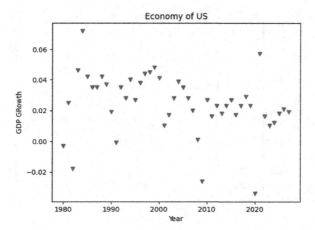

Figure 4.31   A Scatter Plot with Marker o

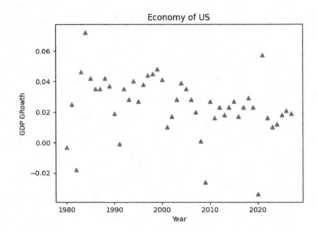

Figure 4.32 A Scatter Plot with Marker ˆ

<

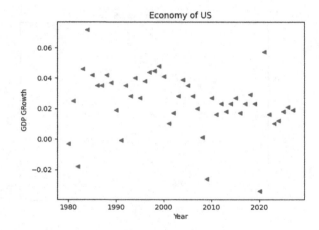

Figure 4.33 A Scatter Plot with Marker <

>

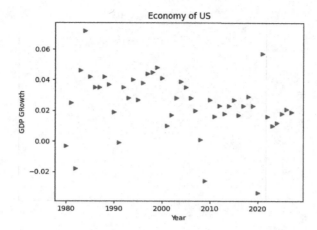

Figure 4.34 A Scatter Plot with Marker >

1

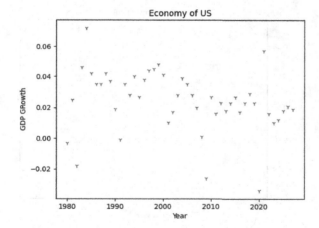

Figure 4.35 A Scatter Plot with Marker 1

2

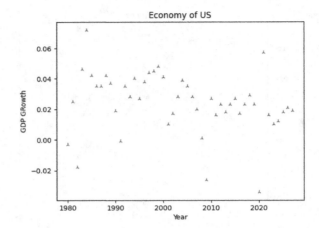

Figure 4.36 A Scatter Plot with Marker 2

3

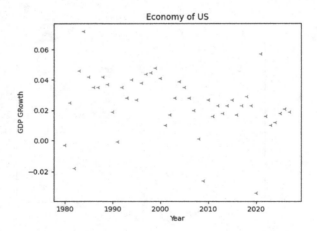

Figure 4.37 A Scatter Plot with Marker 3

4

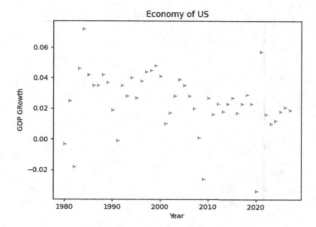

Figure 4.38 A Scatter Plot with Marker 4

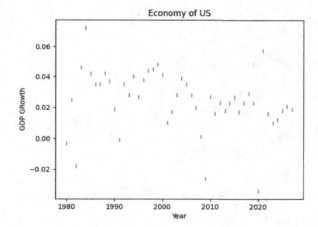

Figure 4.39 A Scatter Plot with Marker |

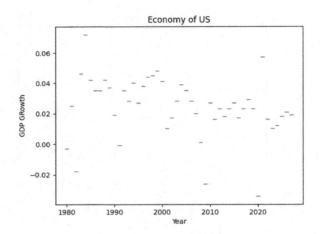

Figure 4.40 A Scatter Plot with Marker -

Change line style

```
line = ['-',':','--','-.']
for l in line:
  print(l)
  l = 'o' + l + 'r'
  plt.plot(df['Year'], df['GDP_Growth'], l)
  plt.xlabel('Year')
  plt.ylabel('GDP GRowth')
  plt.title('Economy of US')
  plt.show()
```

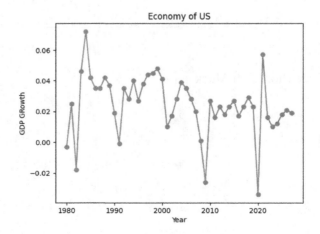

Figure 4.41 A Line Plot

:

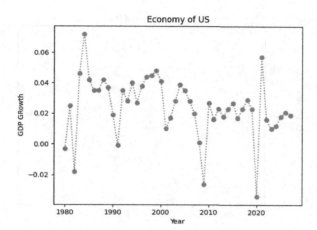

Figure 4.42   A Line Plot

--

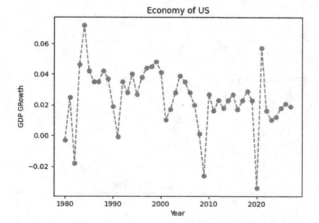

Figure 4.43   A Line Plot

_.

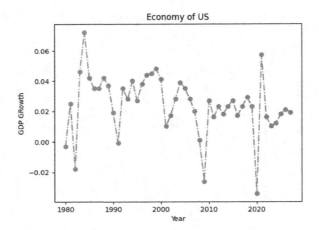

Figure 4.44   A Line Plot

Change color

```
color = ['r','g','b','c','m','y','k','w']
for c in color:
  print(c)
  c = 'o:' + c
  plt.plot(df['Year'], df['GDP_Growth'], c)
  plt.xlabel('Year')
  plt.ylabel('GDP GRowth')
  plt.title('Economy of US')
  plt.show()
```

r

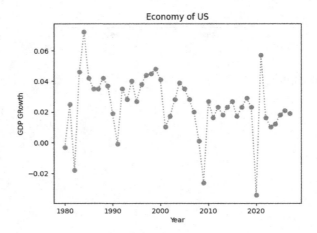

Figure 4.45   A Line Plot

g

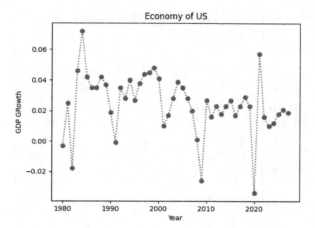

Figure 4.46   A Line Plot

b

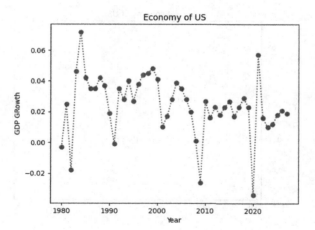

Figure 4.47   A Line Plot

c

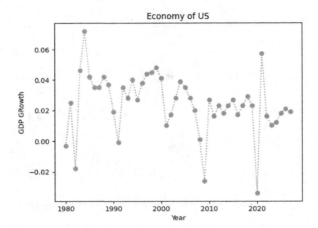

Figure 4.48 A Line Plot

m

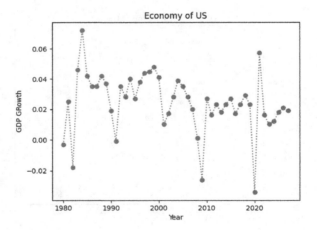

Figure 4.49 A Line Plot

y

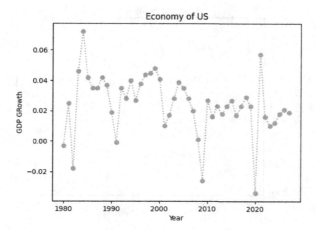

Figure 4.50 A Line Plot

k

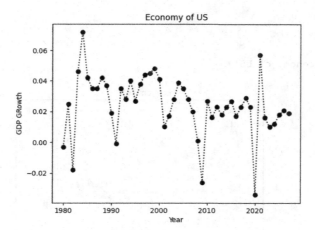

Figure 4.51 A Line Plot

w

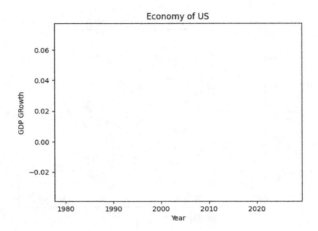

Figure 4.52 A Line Plot

Change marker size

```
plt.plot(df['Year'], df['GDP_Growth'], marker = '^', ms = 15)
plt.xlabel('Year')
plt.ylabel('GDP GRowth')
plt.title('Economy of US')
```

Text(0.5, 1.0, 'Economy of US')

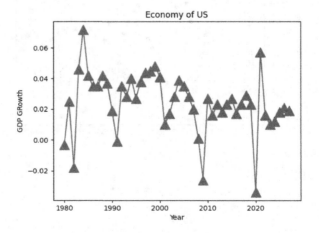

Figure 4.53 A Line Plot

4.2.1.3 Scatter Plot

```
plt.plot(df['Year'], df['GDP_Growth'], 'o')
plt.xlabel('Year')
plt.ylabel('GDP GRowth')
plt.title('Economy of US')
```

Text(0.5, 1.0, 'Economy of US')

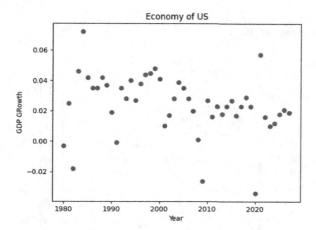

Figure 4.54 A Line Plot

```
plt.scatter(df['Year'], df['GDP_Growth'])
plt.xlabel('Year')
plt.ylabel('GDP GRowth')
plt.title('Economy of US')
```

Text(0.5, 1.0, 'Economy of US')

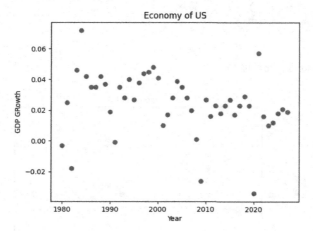

Figure 4.55 A Scatter Plot

Colorbar

```
plt.scatter(df['Year'], df['GDP_Growth'], c=df['Inflation'], cmap='hot')
plt.colorbar()
plt.xlabel('Year')
```

```
plt.ylabel('GDP GRowth')
plt.title('Economy of US')
```

Text(0.5, 1.0, 'Economy of US')

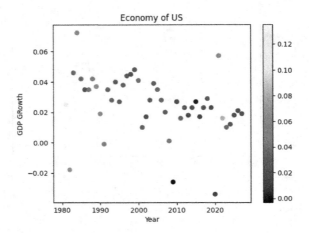

Figure 4.56 A Colorbar Plot

Size

```
plt.scatter(df['Year'], df['GDP_Growth'], s= df['Unemployment']*1000)
plt.xlabel('Year')
plt.ylabel('GDP GRowth')
plt.title('Economy of US')
```

Text(0.5, 1.0, 'Economy of US')

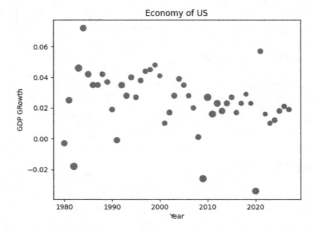

Figure 4.57 A Scatter Plot with Different Dot-Sizes

Colorbar and size

```
plt.scatter(df['Year'], df['GDP_Growth'], c=df['Inflation'], cmap='hot'
    , alpha = 0.5, s= df['Unemployment']*1000)
plt.colorbar()
plt.xlabel('Year')
plt.ylabel('GDP GRowth')
plt.title('Economy of US')
```

Text(0.5, 1.0, 'Economy of US')

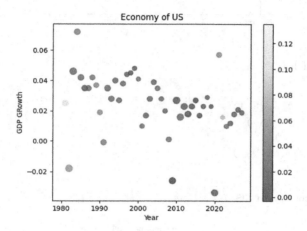

Figure 4.58 A Scatter Plot with Colorbar and Different Dot-Sizes

```
plt.bar(df['Year'], df['GDP_Growth'])
plt.xlabel('Year')
plt.ylabel('GDP GRowth')
plt.title('Economy of US')
```

Text(0.5, 1.0, 'Economy of US')

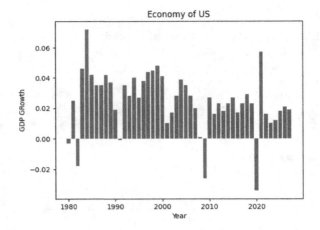

Figure 4.59 A Bar Plot

```
plt.hist(df['GDP_Growth'])
plt.xlabel('GDP Growth')
plt.ylabel('Counts')
plt.title('Economy of US')
```

Text(0.5, 1.0, 'Economy of US')

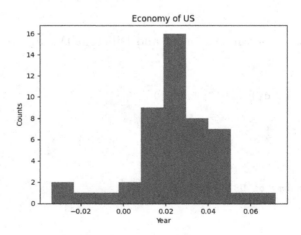

Figure 4.60 A Histogram Plot

```
plt.hist(df['GDP_Growth'], bins = 50)
plt.xlabel('GDP Growth')
plt.ylabel('Counts')
plt.title('Economy of US')
```

Text(0.5, 1.0, 'Economy of US')

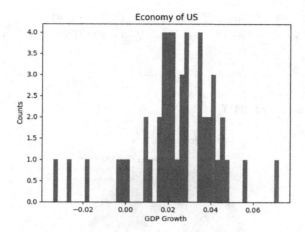

Figure 4.61 Another Histogram Plot

4.2.1.4 Pie Plot

```
df['Inflation_Change'].value_counts()
```

```
Decrease    23
Increase    21
No change    3
Name: Inflation_Change, dtype: int64
```

```
plt.pie(df['Inflation_Change'].value_counts(), labels
    = ['Decrease', 'Increase', 'No change'])
plt.legend()
plt.title('Economy of US')
```

```
Text(0.5, 1.0, 'Economy of US')
```

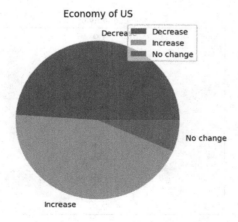

Figure 4.62 A Pie Plot

```
plt.pie(df['Inflation_Change'].value_counts(), labels =
    ['Decrease', 'Increase', 'No change'], explode = [0.0, 0.2, 0])
plt.legend()
plt.title('Economy of US')
```

Text(0.5, 1.0, 'Economy of US')

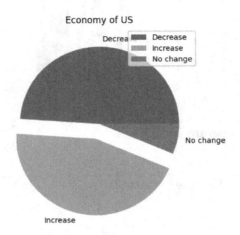

Figure 4.63 An Explode Pie Plot

4.2.1.5 Box Plot

```
plt.boxplot(df['Inflation'])
plt.ylabel('Inflation')
plt.title('Economy of US')
```

Text(0.5, 1.0, 'Economy of US')

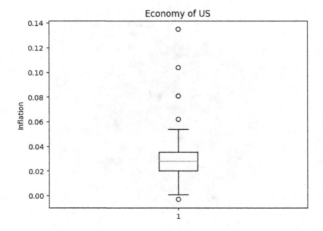

Figure 4.64 A Box Plot

4.2.1.6   Violin Plot

```
plt.violinplot(df['Inflation'])
plt.ylabel('Inflation')
plt.title('Economy of US')
```

Text(0.5, 1.0, 'Economy of US')

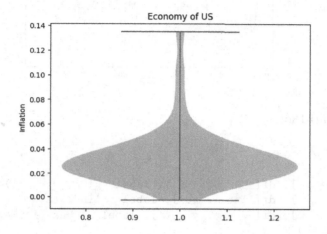

Figure 4.65   A Violin Plot

4.2.1.7   Multi-Plots

```
plt.plot(df['Year'], df['GDP_Growth'])
plt.plot(df['Year'], df['Inflation'])
plt.plot(df['Year'], df['Unemployment'])
plt.xlabel('Year')
plt.title('Economy of US')
```

Text(0.5, 1.0, 'Economy of US')

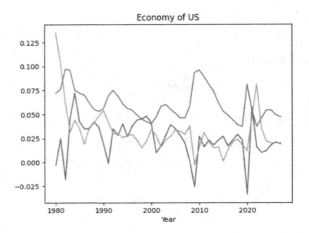

Figure 4.66   A Multi-Plot

Add legend

```
plt.plot(df['Year'], df['GDP_Growth'], label = 'GDP_Growth')
plt.plot(df['Year'], df['Inflation'], label = 'Inflation' )
plt.plot(df['Year'], df['Unemployment'], label = 'Unemployment')
plt.xlabel('Year')
plt.ylabel('Economy')
plt.grid()
plt.legend()
```

```
<matplotlib.legend.Legend at 0x7f27844e3e20>
```

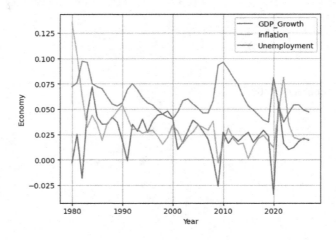

Figure 4.67   A Multi-Plot with Legend and Grid

Change arrangement

```
plt.subplot(3, 1, 1)
plt.plot(df['Year'], df['GDP_Growth'], label = 'GDP_Growth')
plt.legend()
plt.xlabel('Year')
plt.ylabel('Economy')
plt.subplot(3, 1, 2)
plt.plot(df['Year'], df['Inflation'], label = 'Inflation' )
plt.legend()
plt.xlabel('Year')
plt.ylabel('Economy')
plt.subplot(3, 1, 3)
plt.plot(df['Year'], df['Unemployment'], label = 'Unemployment')
plt.legend()
plt.xlabel('Year')
plt.ylabel('Economy')
plt.grid()
```

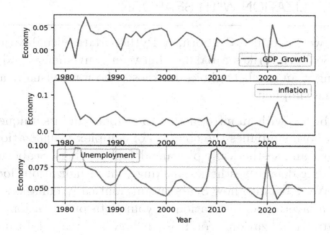

Figure 4.68   A Multi-Plot as Stacks

```
plt.subplot(1, 3, 1)
plt.plot(df['Year'], df['GDP_Growth'], label = 'GDP_Growth')
plt.legend()
plt.xlabel('Year')
plt.ylabel('Economy')
plt.subplot(1, 3, 2)
plt.plot(df['Year'], df['Inflation'], label = 'Inflation' )
plt.legend()
plt.xlabel('Year')
plt.subplot(1, 3, 3)
plt.plot(df['Year'], df['Unemployment'], label = 'Unemployment')
plt.legend()
plt.xlabel('Year')
plt.grid()
```

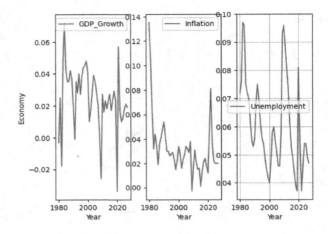

Figure 4.69 A Multi-Plot as Columns

4.3 DATA VISUALIZATION WITH SEABORN

In this section, we introduce Seaborn, a Python data visualization library built on Matplotlib. Seaborn strikes a balance between convenience and elegant default aesthetics, making it an excellent choice for those who want visually appealing results without sacrificing simplicity.

Our exploration begins with an introduction to Seaborn and its unique features. You'll discover how Seaborn simplifies the creation of complex visualizations by providing high-level functions and aesthetically pleasing default settings. Seaborn is renowned for its visually appealing default aesthetics, making your visualizations look polished with minimal effort. We delve into how Seaborn automatically enhances the appearance of plots, adding a layer of sophistication to your data presentations. Seaborn excels in statistical data visualization. You'll learn how to create informative statistical plots like violin plots, box plots, and regression plots, allowing you to explore and communicate data distributions and relationships effortlessly. Customizing the look of your visualizations is made easy with Seaborn's color palettes and themes. We'll guide you through the process of selecting color schemes and themes that align with your data and presentation style.

4.3.1 Tutorial – Data Visualization with Seaborn

Document: https://seaborn.pydata.org

4.3.1.1 *Setup*

```
import numpy as np
import pandas as pd
import matplotlib.pyplot as plt
import seaborn as sns

tips = sns.load_dataset('tips')
```

4.3.1.2 Relational Plots

```
sns.relplot(data = tips, x = 'total_bill', y = 'tip')
```

```
<seaborn.axisgrid.FacetGrid at 0x7f0e5b9e6280>
```

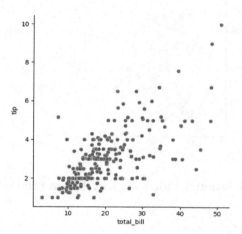

Figure 4.70 A Default Relational Plot

```
sns.relplot(data = tips, x = 'total_bill', y = 'tip', hue = 'sex')
```

```
<seaborn.axisgrid.FacetGrid at 0x7f0e4d8e1fd0>
```

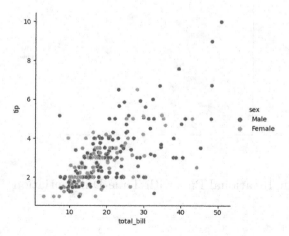

Figure 4.71 A Default Relational Plot with Gender Differentiation

```
sns.relplot(data = tips, x = 'total_bill', y = 'tip', hue = 'day')
```

```
<seaborn.axisgrid.FacetGrid at 0x7f0e4b62f370>
```

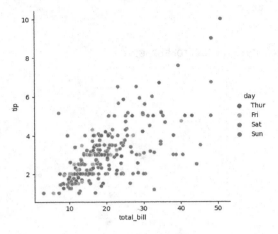

Figure 4.72 A Default Relational Plot with Day Differentiation

```
sns.relplot(data = tips, x = 'total_bill', y = 'tip', hue = 'time')
```

```
<seaborn.axisgrid.FacetGrid at 0x7f0e4b54d310>
```

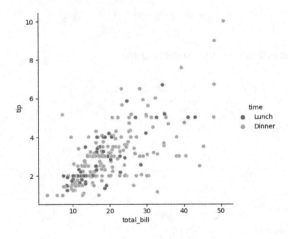

Figure 4.73 A Default Relational Plot with Time Differentiation

```
sns.relplot(data = tips, x = 'total_bill', y = 'tip'
    , hue = 'smoker', col = 'time')
```

```
<seaborn.axisgrid.FacetGrid at 0x7f0e5b9e6df0>
```

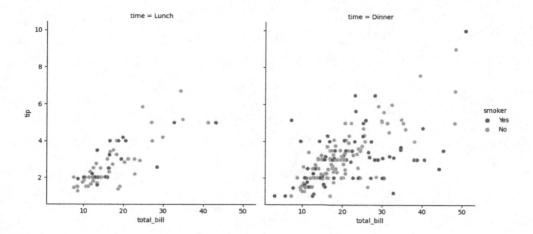

Figure 4.74   A Default Relational Plot with Time Differentiation in Multicolumns

```
sns.relplot(data = tips, x = 'total_bill', y = 'tip'
    , hue = 'size')
```

<seaborn.axisgrid.FacetGrid at 0x7f0e5b970970>

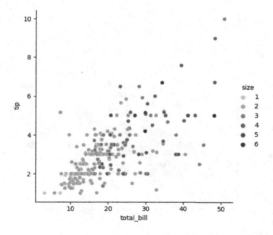

Figure 4.75   A Default Relational Plot with Size Differentiation

```
sns.relplot(data = tips, x = 'total_bill', y = 'tip'
    , size = 'size', hue = 'size')
```

<seaborn.axisgrid.FacetGrid at 0x7f0e4b192c40>

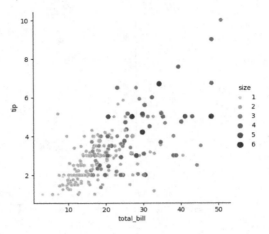

Figure 4.76   A Default Relational Plot with Size Differentiation and Different Dot-Sizes

```
sns.relplot(data = tips, x = 'total_bill', y = 'tip'
    , size = 'size', sizes = (15, 200), hue = 'size')
```

`<seaborn.axisgrid.FacetGrid at 0x7f0e4aff1f10>`

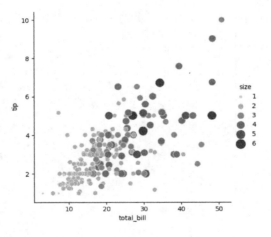

Figure 4.77   A Default Relational Plot with Large Size Differentiation

```
sns.relplot(data = tips, x = 'total_bill', y = 'tip'
    , size = 'size', sizes = (15, 200), alpha= 0.5, hue = 'size')
```

`<seaborn.axisgrid.FacetGrid at 0x7f0e4ad0d370>`

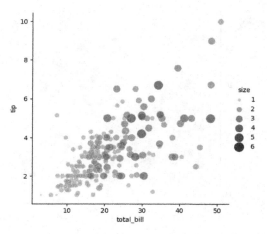

Figure 4.78   A Default Relational Plot with Large Size Differentiation and Transparency

```
sns.relplot(data = tips, x = 'day', y = 'total_bill')
```

<seaborn.axisgrid.FacetGrid at 0x7f0e4ad26310>

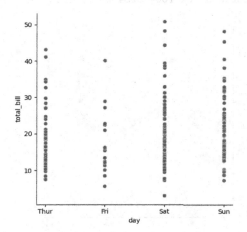

Figure 4.79   A Default Relational Plot with Categorical Xs

```
sns.relplot(data = tips, x = 'day', y = 'total_bill', kind = 'line')
```

<seaborn.axisgrid.FacetGrid at 0x7f0e4aff1ee0>

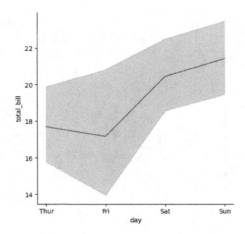

Figure 4.80 A Line Relational Plot

```
sns.relplot(data = tips, x = 'day', y = 'total_bill'
    , hue = 'sex', kind = 'line')
```

<seaborn.axisgrid.FacetGrid at 0x7f0e48eb3400>

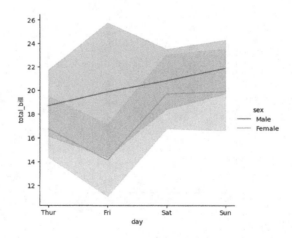

Figure 4.81 A Line Relational Plot with Gender Differentiation

```
sns.relplot(data = tips, x = 'day', y = 'total_bill'
    , hue = 'sex', kind = 'line', col = 'time')
```

<seaborn.axisgrid.FacetGrid at 0x7f0e48d7e100>

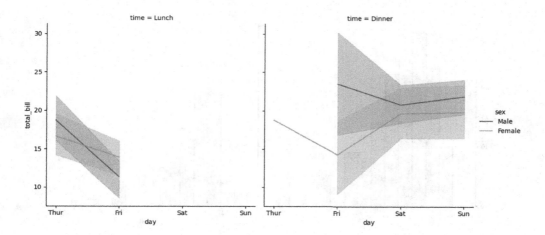

Figure 4.82 A Line Relational Plot with Gender Differentiation in Multicolumns

4.3.1.3 Distribution Plots

```
sns.displot(data = tips, x = 'total_bill')
```

```
<seaborn.axisgrid.FacetGrid at 0x7f0e48ccdc40>
```

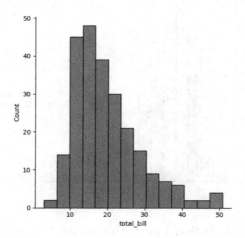

Figure 4.83 A Default Distribution Plot

```
sns.displot(data = tips, x = 'total_bill', col = 'sex')
```

```
<seaborn.axisgrid.FacetGrid at 0x7f0e48b70a30>
```

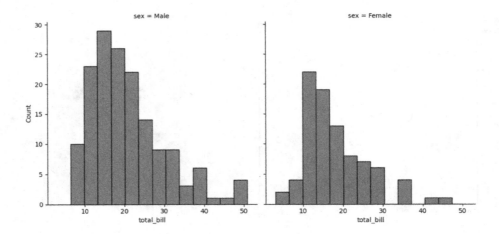

Figure 4.84 A Default Distribution Plot in Multicolumns

```
sns.displot(data = tips, x = 'total_bill', hue = 'sex')
```

<seaborn.axisgrid.FacetGrid at 0x7f0e48a0c760>

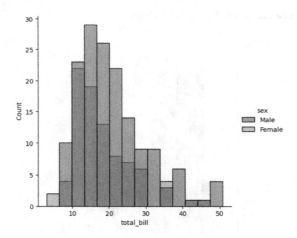

Figure 4.85 A Default Distribution Plot with Gender Differentiation

```
sns.displot(data = tips, x = 'total_bill', hue = 'sex', col = 'day')
```

<seaborn.axisgrid.FacetGrid at 0x7f0e489e8cd0>

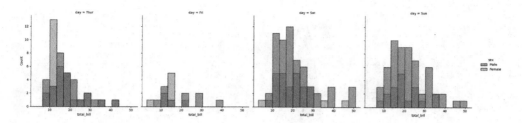

Figure 4.86 A Default Distribution Plot with Gender Differentiation in Multicolumns

```
sns.displot(data = tips, x = 'total_bill', hue = 'sex', kind = 'kde')
```

<seaborn.axisgrid.FacetGrid at 0x7f0e4b3ecfd0>

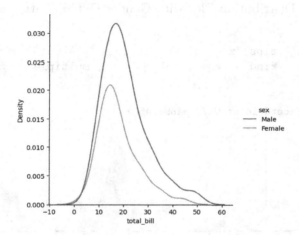

Figure 4.87 A KDE Distribution Plot with Gender Differentiation

```
sns.displot(data = tips, x = 'total_bill'
    , hue = 'sex', kind = 'kde', multiple = 'stack')
```

<seaborn.axisgrid.FacetGrid at 0x7f0e482d6550>

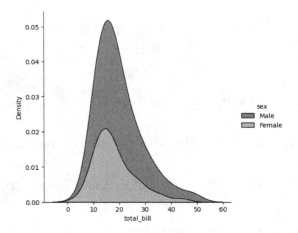

Figure 4.88 A KDE Distribution Plot with Gender Differentiation and Stacking

```
sns.displot(data = tips, x = 'total_bill'
    , hue = 'sex', kind = 'kde', col = 'day', multiple = 'stack')
```

<seaborn.axisgrid.FacetGrid at 0x7f0e489dee50>

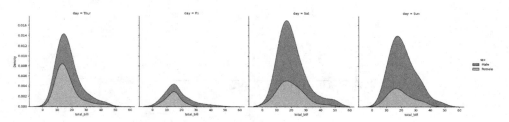

Figure 4.89 A KDE Distribution Plot with Gender Differentiation, Stacking in Multi-columns

```
sns.displot(data = tips, x = 'total_bill', y = 'tip', kind = 'kde')
```

<seaborn.axisgrid.FacetGrid at 0x7f0e480b4fd0>

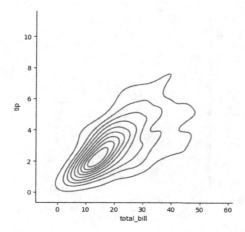

Figure 4.90   A KDE Distribution Plot with Two Attributes

```
sns.displot(data = tips, x = 'total_bill', y = 'tip'
    , kind = 'kde', hue = 'sex')
```

<seaborn.axisgrid.FacetGrid at 0x7f0e480ac9d0>

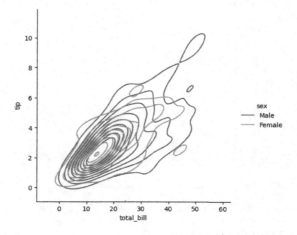

Figure 4.91   A KDE Distribution Plot with Two Attributes and Gender Differentiation

```
sns.displot(data = tips, x = 'total_bill', y = 'tip'
    , kind = 'kde', rug = True)
```

<seaborn.axisgrid.FacetGrid at 0x7f0e43d65640>

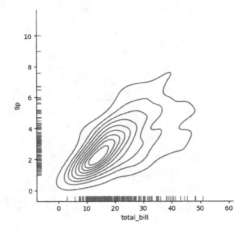

Figure 4.92   A KDE Distribution Plot with Two Attributes and Rug

```
sns.displot(data = tips, x = 'total_bill', kind = 'ecdf')
```

```
<seaborn.axisgrid.FacetGrid at 0x7f0e43c4c610>
```

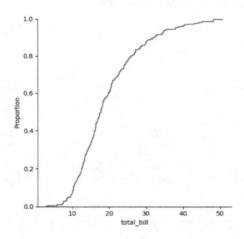

Figure 4.93   An ECDF Distribution Plot

```
sns.displot(data = tips, x = 'total_bill'
    , kind = 'ecdf', hue = 'sex')
```

```
<seaborn.axisgrid.FacetGrid at 0x7f0e417a4b50>
```

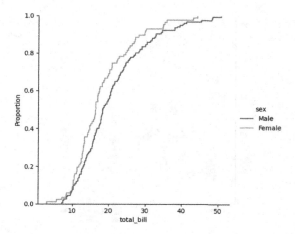

Figure 4.94 An ECDF Distribution Plot with Gender Differentiation

```
sns.displot(data = tips, x = 'total_bill', kind = 'ecdf'
    , hue = 'sex', col = 'day')
```

`<seaborn.axisgrid.FacetGrid at 0x7f0e4837b0d0>`

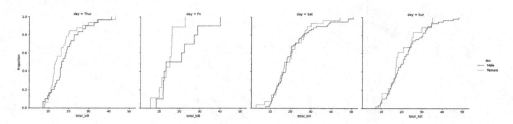

Figure 4.95 An ECDF Distribution Plot with Gender Differentiation in Multicolumns

4.3.1.4 Categorical Plots

```
sns.catplot(data = tips, x = 'day', y = 'total_bill')
```

`<seaborn.axisgrid.FacetGrid at 0x7f0e4159bb50>`

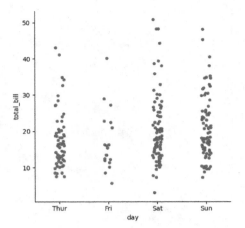

Figure 4.96 A Default Categorical Plot

```
sns.catplot(data = tips, x = 'day', y = 'total_bill', hue = 'sex')
```

<seaborn.axisgrid.FacetGrid at 0x7f0e415ed070>

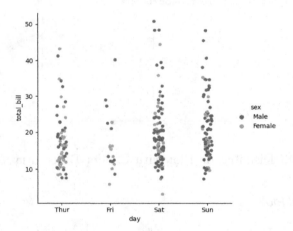

Figure 4.97 A Default Categorical Plot with Gender Differentiation

```
sns.catplot(data = tips, x = 'day', y = 'total_bill'
    , kind = 'box')
```

<seaborn.axisgrid.FacetGrid at 0x7f0e414c6040>

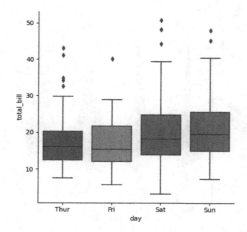

Figure 4.98   A Box Categorical Plot

```
sns.catplot(data = tips, x = 'day', y = 'total_bill'
    , kind = 'box', hue = 'sex')
```

`<seaborn.axisgrid.FacetGrid at 0x7f0e413e08e0>`

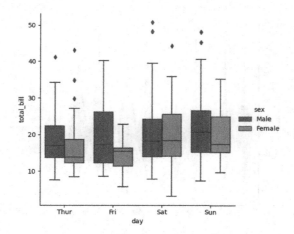

Figure 4.99   A Box Categorical Plot with Gender Differentiation

```
sns.catplot(data = tips, x = 'day', y = 'total_bill', kind = 'violin')
```

`<seaborn.axisgrid.FacetGrid at 0x7f0e4b585eb0>`

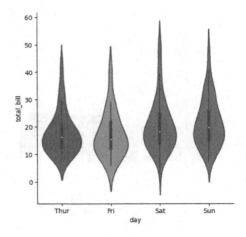

Figure 4.100 A Violin Categorical Plot

```
sns.catplot(data = tips, x = 'day', y = 'total_bill'
    , kind = 'violin', hue = 'sex')
```

<seaborn.axisgrid.FacetGrid at 0x7f0e412877c0>

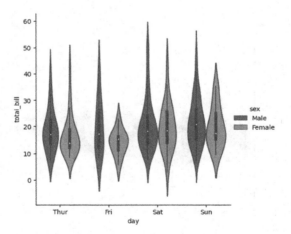

Figure 4.101 A Violin Categorical Plot with Gender Differentiation

```
sns.catplot(data = tips, x = 'day', y = 'total_bill'
    , kind = 'violin', hue = 'sex', split = True)
```

<seaborn.axisgrid.FacetGrid at 0x7f0e412832e0>

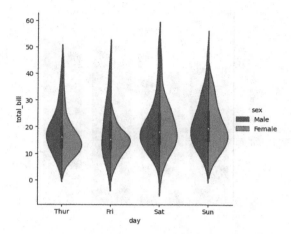

Figure 4.102   Another Violin Categorical Plot with Gender Differentiation

```
sns.violinplot(data = tips, x = 'day', y = 'total_bill'
    , hue = 'sex', split = True, inner = 'quartile')
```

```
<AxesSubplot: xlabel='day', ylabel='total_bill'>
```

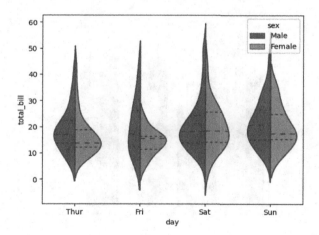

Figure 4.103   A Violin Plot with Gender Differentiation and Quartile

```
sns.catplot(data = tips, x = 'day', y= 'total_bill', kind = 'bar')
```

```
<seaborn.axisgrid.FacetGrid at 0x7f0e410072b0>
```

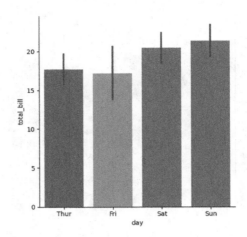

Figure 4.104 A Bar Categorical Plot

```
sns.catplot(data = tips, x = 'day', y= 'total_bill'
    , kind = 'bar', hue = 'sex')
```

<seaborn.axisgrid.FacetGrid at 0x7f0e40f7f0a0>

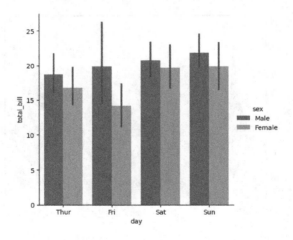

Figure 4.105 A Bar Categorical Plot with Gender Differentiation

4.3.1.5 Joint Plots

```
sns.jointplot(data = tips, x = 'total_bill', y = 'tip'
    , hue = 'sex', kind = 'kde')
```

<seaborn.axisgrid.JointGrid at 0x7f0e40f8ab50>

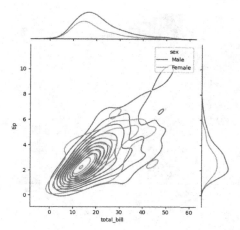

Figure 4.106 A Joint Plot

```
sns.jointplot(data = tips, x = 'total_bill', y = 'tip'
    , hue = 'sex', kind = 'scatter')
```

<seaborn.axisgrid.JointGrid at 0x7f0e4b641130>

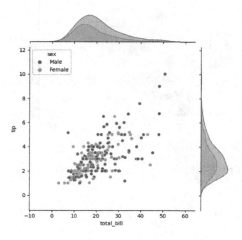

Figure 4.107 Another Joint Plot

```
kind = ['scatter', 'hist', 'hex', 'kde', 'reg', 'resid']
for k in kind:
    sns.jointplot(data = tips, x = 'total_bill', y = 'tip', kind = k)
```

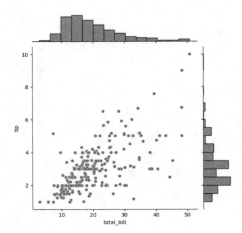

Figure 4.108   Another Joint Plot

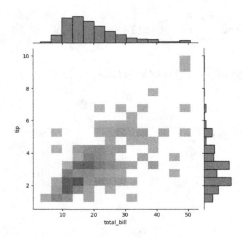

Figure 4.109   Another Joint Plot

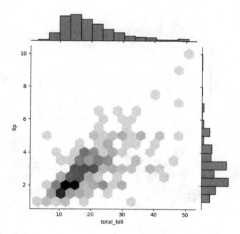

Figure 4.110 Another Joint Plot

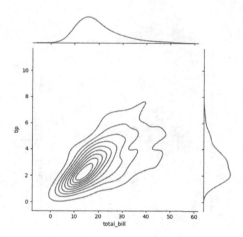

Figure 4.111 Another Joint Plot

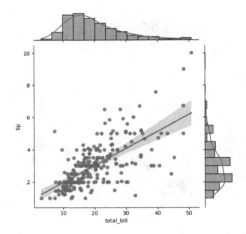

Figure 4.112 Another Joint Plot

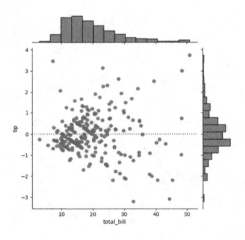

Figure 4.113 Another Joint Plot

4.3.1.6 Pair Plots

```
sns.pairplot(data = tips)
```

```
<seaborn.axisgrid.PairGrid at 0x7f0e40bd8eb0>
```

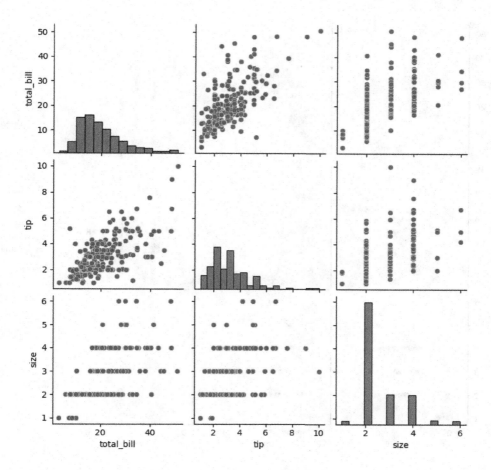

Figure 4.114 A Pair Plot

```
sns.pairplot(data = tips, hue = 'sex')
```

<seaborn.axisgrid.PairGrid at 0x7f0e40766490>

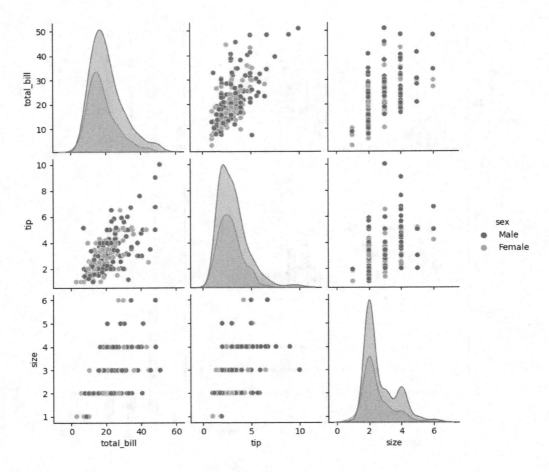

Figure 4.115 A Pair Plot with Gender Differentiation

## CHAPTER 5

Data Preprocessing

D ATA PREPROCESSING is the process of cleaning, transforming, and preparing data for analysis. It is a crucial step in the Data Mining pipeline as it ensures that the data is in a format that can be easily and accurately analyzed.

There are several Python packages that are commonly used for data preprocessing, including:

- Pandas: It is a library for working with data in a tabular format and provides a wide range of tools for reading, writing, and manipulating data, such as DataFrame and series, as well as handling missing values.

- NumPy: It is a library for working with arrays and matrices of numerical data. It provides a wide range of mathematical and statistical functions and is commonly used as the foundation for other libraries.

- Scikit-learn: It is a library for machine learning in Python and provides a wide range of tools for preprocessing data, such as feature scaling, normalization, and one-hot encoding.

- NLTK: It is a library for natural language processing and provides a wide range of tools for text preprocessing, such as tokenization, stemming, and lemmatization.

- SciPy: It is a library for scientific computing in Python and provides a wide range of tools for data preprocessing, such as interpolation and smoothing.

5.1 DEALING WITH MISSING VALUES

Missing values are a common challenge that must be addressed to ensure the accuracy and reliability of your results. This section is dedicated to understanding the importance of handling missing values and equipping you with the knowledge to effectively manage them, whether by dropping them or filling them with appropriate values. We explore several approaches using Pandas to effectively manage missing data:

DOI: 10.1201/9781003462781-5

- Dropping missing values: One straightforward strategy is to remove rows or columns containing missing values using the dropna() method. This approach is appropriate when the missing data doesn't hold critical information.

- Imputing with a constant value: You can replace missing values with a constant value using the fillna() method. This is useful when missing data can be reasonably replaced with a specific constant, such as 0 or a placeholder.

- Imputing with central tendency measures: Imputing missing values with the mean, median, or mode of the respective column is a common technique. Pandas provides these statistics through methods like mean(), median(), and mode(). This approach works well when missing values can be estimated based on the central tendency of the data.

- Forward or backward fill: You can propagate the previous or next valid value to fill missing entries using the fillna() method with the method parameter set to ffill or bfill. This approach is suitable for time series or sequential data.

- Interpolation: Pandas offers interpolation methods, such as linear or polynomial interpolation, to estimate missing values based on the surrounding data points. This is particularly useful for datasets with a temporal or continuous nature.

- Other imputation methods: For more complex scenarios, you can employ machine learning algorithms to predict missing values based on other features in your dataset. This approach requires training a model to impute missing values effectively. In cases where data is grouped by a certain feature, you can use group-wise statistics, such as group means or medians, to impute missing values within each group. Pandas allows you to perform group-wise operations easily. Depending on your dataset's specific characteristics, you may need to develop custom imputation strategies. Pandas provides the flexibility to implement tailored approaches to handle missing values.

5.1.1 Tutorial – Handling Missing Values

5.1.1.1 Setup

```
import numpy as np
import pandas as pd
```

```
df = pd.read_csv('/content/Economy_of_US_na.csv')
```

5.1.1.2 Detect and Report Missing Values

```
df
```

```
     Year  GDP_Nominal  GDP_Growth
0  1980.0       2857.3         NaN
1  1981.0       3207.0       0.025
2  1982.0       3343.8      -0.018
```

3	1983.0	NaN	NaN
4	1984.0	4037.7	0.072
5	1985.0	4339.0	NaN
6	1986.0	NaN	NaN
7	1987.0	4855.3	NaN
8	1988.0	5236.4	0.042
9	1989.0	NaN	NaN
10	1990.0	5963.1	0.019
11	NaN	NaN	NaN
12	1992.0	6520.3	0.035

```
df.isnull()
```

	Year	GDP_Nominal	GDP_Growth
0	False	False	True
1	False	False	False
2	False	False	False
3	False	True	True
4	False	False	False
5	False	False	True
6	False	True	True
7	False	False	True
8	False	False	False
9	False	True	True
10	False	False	False
11	True	True	True
12	False	False	False

```
for c in df.columns:
    miss = df[c].isnull().sum()
    print("{} has {} missing value(s)".format(c,miss))
```

```
Year has 1 missing value(s)
GDP_Nominal has 4 missing value(s)
GDP_Growth has 7 missing value(s)
```

5.1.1.3 Dropping Missing Values

```
df2 = df.dropna()
df2
```

	Year	GDP_Nominal	GDP_Growth
1	1981.0	3207.0	0.025
2	1982.0	3343.8	-0.018
4	1984.0	4037.7	0.072
8	1988.0	5236.4	0.042
10	1990.0	5963.1	0.019
12	1992.0	6520.3	0.035

```
df
```

```
      Year  GDP_Nominal  GDP_Growth
0   1980.0       2857.3         NaN
1   1981.0       3207.0       0.025
2   1982.0       3343.8      -0.018
3   1983.0          NaN         NaN
4   1984.0       4037.7       0.072
5   1985.0       4339.0         NaN
6   1986.0          NaN         NaN
7   1987.0       4855.3         NaN
8   1988.0       5236.4       0.042
9   1989.0          NaN         NaN
10  1990.0       5963.1       0.019
11     NaN          NaN         NaN
12  1992.0       6520.3       0.035
```

```
df2 = df.dropna(axis=1)
df2
```

```
Empty DataFrame
Columns: []
Index: [0, 1, 2, 3, 4, 5, 6, 7, 8, 9, 10, 11, 12]
```

```
df2 = df.dropna(thresh=3)
df2
```

```
      Year  GDP_Nominal  GDP_Growth
1   1981.0       3207.0       0.025
2   1982.0       3343.8      -0.018
4   1984.0       4037.7       0.072
8   1988.0       5236.4       0.042
10  1990.0       5963.1       0.019
12  1992.0       6520.3       0.035
```

```
df2 = df.dropna(thresh=2)
df2
```

```
      Year  GDP_Nominal  GDP_Growth
0   1980.0       2857.3         NaN
1   1981.0       3207.0       0.025
2   1982.0       3343.8      -0.018
4   1984.0       4037.7       0.072
5   1985.0       4339.0         NaN
7   1987.0       4855.3         NaN
8   1988.0       5236.4       0.042
10  1990.0       5963.1       0.019
12  1992.0       6520.3       0.035
```

```
df2 = df.dropna(thresh=1)
df2
```

```
      Year  GDP_Nominal  GDP_Growth
0   1980.0       2857.3         NaN
```

1	1981.0	3207.0	0.025
2	1982.0	3343.8	-0.018
3	1983.0	NaN	NaN
4	1984.0	4037.7	0.072
5	1985.0	4339.0	NaN
6	1986.0	NaN	NaN
7	1987.0	4855.3	NaN
8	1988.0	5236.4	0.042
9	1989.0	NaN	NaN
10	1990.0	5963.1	0.019
12	1992.0	6520.3	0.035

```
df2 = df.dropna(axis = 1, thresh=7)
df2
```

	Year	GDP_Nominal
0	1980.0	2857.3
1	1981.0	3207.0
2	1982.0	3343.8
3	1983.0	NaN
4	1984.0	4037.7
5	1985.0	4339.0
6	1986.0	NaN
7	1987.0	4855.3
8	1988.0	5236.4
9	1989.0	NaN
10	1990.0	5963.1
11	NaN	NaN
12	1992.0	6520.3

```
df2 = df.dropna(axis = 1, thresh=10)
df2
```

	Year
0	1980.0
1	1981.0
2	1982.0
3	1983.0
4	1984.0
5	1985.0
6	1986.0
7	1987.0
8	1988.0
9	1989.0
10	1990.0
11	NaN
12	1992.0

5.1.1.4 Filling with Constant

```
df2 = df.fillna('NA')
df2
```

	Year	GDP_Nominal	GDP_Growth
0	1980.0	2857.3	NA
1	1981.0	3207.0	0.025
2	1982.0	3343.8	-0.018
3	1983.0	NA	NA
4	1984.0	4037.7	0.072
5	1985.0	4339.0	NA
6	1986.0	NA	NA
7	1987.0	4855.3	NA
8	1988.0	5236.4	0.042
9	1989.0	NA	NA
10	1990.0	5963.1	0.019
11	NA	NA	NA
12	1992.0	6520.3	0.035

```
df['Year_filled'] = df['Year'].fillna('YEAR')
df
```

	Year	GDP_Nominal	GDP_Growth	Year_filled
0	1980.0	2857.3	NaN	1980.0
1	1981.0	3207.0	0.025	1981.0
2	1982.0	3343.8	-0.018	1982.0
3	1983.0	NaN	NaN	1983.0
4	1984.0	4037.7	0.072	1984.0
5	1985.0	4339.0	NaN	1985.0
6	1986.0	NaN	NaN	1986.0
7	1987.0	4855.3	NaN	1987.0
8	1988.0	5236.4	0.042	1988.0
9	1989.0	NaN	NaN	1989.0
10	1990.0	5963.1	0.019	1990.0
11	NaN	NaN	NaN	YEAR
12	1992.0	6520.3	0.035	1992.0

5.1.1.5 Filling with ffill

```
df['GDP_filled_ffill'] = df['GDP_Nominal'].fillna(method = 'ffill')
df[['GDP_Nominal', 'GDP_filled_ffill']]
```

	GDP_Nominal	GDP_filled_ffill
0	2857.3	2857.3
1	3207.0	3207.0
2	3343.8	3343.8
3	NaN	3343.8
4	4037.7	4037.7
5	4339.0	4339.0
6	NaN	4339.0
7	4855.3	4855.3

```
8        5236.4           5236.4
9          NaN            5236.4
10       5963.1           5963.1
11         NaN            5963.1
12       6520.3           6520.3
```

5.1.1.6 Filling with bfill

```
df['GDP_filled_bfill'] = df['GDP_Nominal'].fillna(method = 'bfill')
df[['GDP_Nominal', 'GDP_filled_bfill']]
```

```
    GDP_Nominal  GDP_filled_bfill
0       2857.3           2857.3
1       3207.0           3207.0
2       3343.8           3343.8
3         NaN            4037.7
4       4037.7           4037.7
5       4339.0           4339.0
6         NaN            4855.3
7       4855.3           4855.3
8       5236.4           5236.4
9         NaN            5963.1
10      5963.1           5963.1
11        NaN            6520.3
12      6520.3           6520.3
```

5.1.1.7 Filling with mean

```
df['GDP_Nominal_filled_mean'] = df['GDP_Nominal'].fillna(df['GDP_Nominal']
.mean())
df[['GDP_Nominal', 'GDP_Nominal_filled_mean']]
```

```
    GDP_Nominal  GDP_Nominal_filled_mean
0       2857.3             2857.300000
1       3207.0             3207.000000
2       3343.8             3343.800000
3         NaN              4484.433333
4       4037.7             4037.700000
5       4339.0             4339.000000
6         NaN              4484.433333
7       4855.3             4855.300000
8       5236.4             5236.400000
9         NaN              4484.433333
10      5963.1             5963.100000
11        NaN              4484.433333
12      6520.3             6520.300000
```

5.1.1.8 Filling with mode

```
df['GDP_Nominal_filled_mode'] =
    df['GDP_Nominal'].fillna(df['GDP_Nominal'].mode()[0])
df[['GDP_Nominal', 'GDP_Nominal_filled_mode']]
```

	GDP_Nominal	GDP_Nominal_filled_mode
0	2857.3	2857.3
1	3207.0	3207.0
2	3343.8	3343.8
3	NaN	2857.3
4	4037.7	4037.7
5	4339.0	4339.0
6	NaN	2857.3
7	4855.3	4855.3
8	5236.4	5236.4
9	NaN	2857.3
10	5963.1	5963.1
11	NaN	2857.3
12	6520.3	6520.3

5.1.1.9 Summary

```
df['GDP_Growth_fill_NA'] =
    df['GDP_Growth'].fillna('NA')
df['GDP_Growth_fill_0'] = df['GDP_Growth'].fillna(0)
df['GDP_Growth_fill_ffill'] = df['GDP_Growth'].fillna(method = 'ffill')
df['GDP_Growth_fill_bfill'] =
    df['GDP_Growth'].fillna(method = 'bfill')
df['GDP_Growth_fill_mean'] =
    df['GDP_Growth'].fillna(df['GDP_Growth'].mean())
df['GDP_Growth_fill_mode'] =
    df['GDP_Growth'].fillna(df['GDP_Growth'].mode()[0])
df[['GDP_Growth', 'GDP_Growth_fill_NA', 'GDP_Growth_fill_0',
    'GDP_Growth_fill_ffill','GDP_Growth_fill_bfill',
    'GDP_Growth_fill_mean', 'GDP_Growth_fill_mode']]
```

	GDP_Growth	GDP_Growth_fill_NA	GDP_Growth_fill_0	GDP_Growth_fill_ffill \
0	NaN	NA	0.000	NaN
1	0.025	0.025	0.025	0.025
2	-0.018	-0.018	-0.018	-0.018
3	NaN	NA	0.000	-0.018
4	0.072	0.072	0.072	0.072
5	NaN	NA	0.000	0.072
6	NaN	NA	0.000	0.072
7	NaN	NA	0.000	0.072
8	0.042	0.042	0.042	0.042
9	NaN	NA	0.000	0.042
10	0.019	0.019	0.019	0.019
11	NaN	NA	0.000	0.019
12	0.035	0.035	0.035	0.035

	GDP_Growth_fill_bfill	GDP_Growth_fill_mean	GDP_Growth_fill_mode
0	0.025	0.029167	-0.018
1	0.025	0.025000	0.025
2	-0.018	-0.018000	-0.018
3	0.072	0.029167	-0.018
4	0.072	0.072000	0.072
5	0.042	0.029167	-0.018
6	0.042	0.029167	-0.018
7	0.042	0.029167	-0.018
8	0.042	0.042000	0.042
9	0.019	0.029167	-0.018
10	0.019	0.019000	0.019
11	0.035	0.029167	-0.018
12	0.035	0.035000	0.035

5.2 DEALING WITH OUTLIERS

In the world of data analysis, outliers are data points that deviate significantly from the typical distribution of a dataset. Detecting outliers is a crucial step in data preprocessing and analysis, as these unusual data points can distort statistical measures and lead to inaccurate insights. In this section, we explore two fundamental concepts for identifying outliers.

We begin by introducing the Interquartile Range (IQR) as a robust measure of data spread. IQR analysis provides an effective method for identifying outliers by focusing on the middle 50% of the data. You will learn how to calculate the IQR and define bounds to identify potential outliers that fall outside this range. Practical exercises will guide you in applying IQR analysis to your datasets, ensuring accurate identification of outliers.

We follow by introducing a statistical understanding of data distribution; this concept allows you to identify outliers by examining how data points deviate from expected distribution patterns. You will explore various visualization techniques and statistical tests to detect outliers. These methods include visualizing data distributions, applying statistical tests like the Z-score, and interpreting statistical measures such as skewness and kurtosis.

More sophisticated outlier detection methods will be covered in Chapter 10.

5.2.1 Tutorial – Detect Outliers Using IQR

We know that IQR is Q3 - Q1, and we can set the lower and upper bound by Q1 - 1.5IQR and Q3 + 1.5IQR. Boxplot automatically draws the lower/upper bound for us. We can also detect the data by defining a function.

5.2.1.1 Setup

```
import pandas as pd
import matplotlib.pyplot as plt
```

```
df = pd.read_csv('/content/Nov2Temp.csv')
df.info()
```

```
<class 'pandas.core.frame.DataFrame'>
RangeIndex: 118 entries, 0 to 117
Data columns (total 2 columns):
 #   Column  Non-Null Count  Dtype
---  ------  --------------  -----
 0   high    118 non-null    int64
 1   low     118 non-null    int64
dtypes: int64(2)
memory usage: 2.0 KB
```

```
df.describe()
```

```
              high          low
count   118.000000   118.000000
mean     56.830508    29.262712
std      17.205796    12.877084
min      15.000000   -33.000000
25%      48.250000    24.000000
50%      57.500000    31.000000
75%      66.750000    36.750000
max     127.000000    54.000000
```

```
df.shape
```

```
(118, 2)
```

5.2.1.2 Check for Outliers in df['low']

```
df['low'].hist()
```

```
<Axes: >
```

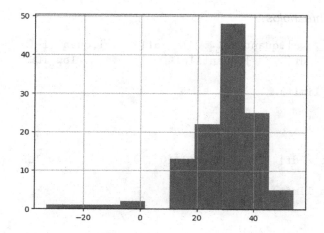

Figure 5.1   The Distribution Plot before Removing Outliers

```
plt.boxplot(df['low'])
```

```
{'whiskers': [<matplotlib.lines.Line2D at 0x7ff0f51fe640>,
  <matplotlib.lines.Line2D at 0x7ff0f51fe8e0>],
 'caps': [<matplotlib.lines.Line2D at 0x7ff0f51feb80>,
  <matplotlib.lines.Line2D at 0x7ff0f51fee20>],
 'boxes': [<matplotlib.lines.Line2D at 0x7ff0f51fe4c0>],
 'medians': [<matplotlib.lines.Line2D at 0x7ff0f5212100>],
 'fliers': [<matplotlib.lines.Line2D at 0x7ff0f52123a0>],
 'means': []}
```

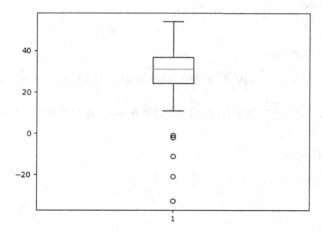

Figure 5.2   The Box Plot before Removing Outliers

5.2.1.3 Setup Thresholds

```
low_IQR = df['low'].quantile(0.75) - df['low'].quantile(0.25)
low_low_limit = df['low'].quantile(0.25) - 1.5 * low_IQR

print(low_low_limit)
```

4.875

```
low_high_limit = df['low'].quantile(0.75) + 1.5 * low_IQR

print(low_high_limit)
```

55.875

```
df[df['low'] < low_low_limit]
```

	high	low
41	41	-2
79	18	-1
109	48	-11
110	43	-21
111	64	-33

```
df[df['low'] > low_high_limit]
```

```
Empty DataFrame
Columns: [high, low]
Index: []
```

5.2.1.4 Remove Outliers

```
df.drop(df[df['low'] < low_low_limit].index, inplace = True)
```

```
df.drop(df[df['low'] > low_high_limit].index, inplace = True)
```

5.2.1.5 Check Results

```
df['low'].hist()
```

```
<Axes: >
```

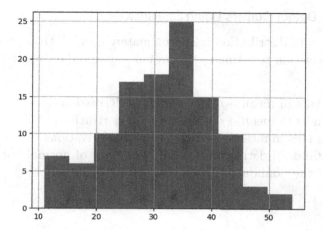

Figure 5.3 The Distribution Plot after Removing Outliers

```
plt.boxplot(df['low'])
```

```
{'whiskers': [<matplotlib.lines.Line2D at 0x7ff0f5106c40>,
  <matplotlib.lines.Line2D at 0x7ff0f5106ee0>],
 'caps': [<matplotlib.lines.Line2D at 0x7ff0f51161c0>,
  <matplotlib.lines.Line2D at 0x7ff0f5116460>],
 'boxes': [<matplotlib.lines.Line2D at 0x7ff0f51069a0>],
 'medians': [<matplotlib.lines.Line2D at 0x7ff0f5116700>],
 'fliers': [<matplotlib.lines.Line2D at 0x7ff0f51169a0>],
 'means': []}
```

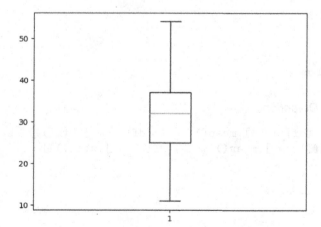

Figure 5.4 The Box Plot after Removing Outliers

5.2.1.6 Practice

Let's do the same thing for df['high'].

5.2.2 Tutorial – Detect Outliers Using Statistics

In statistics, if a data distribution is approximately normal, then we can use the mean and standard derivation to estimate the probability of a data point falls into a certain range:

- 68% data falls in mean +/- one standard derivation
- 95% data falls in mean +/- two standard derivations
- 99.7% data falls in mean +/- three standard derivations. Thus, we can use mean +/-three standard derivations as the boundary of normal data. Any data that falls out of the boundary will be considered as outliers.

5.2.2.1 Setup

```
import numpy as np
import pandas as pd
```

```
df = pd.read_csv('/content/Nov2Temp.csv')
df
```

	high	low
0	58	25
1	26	11
2	53	24
3	60	37
4	67	42
..	...	...
113	119	33
114	127	27
115	18	38
116	15	51
117	30	49

[118 rows x 2 columns]

5.2.2.2 Run the Detection

```
df[(df['low']< (df['low'].mean() - 3 * df['low'].std()))|
(df['low']> (df['low'].mean() + 3 * df['low'].std()))]
```

	high	low
109	48	-11
110	43	-21
111	64	-33

```
df['low'].plot(kind='box')
```

```
<Axes: >
```

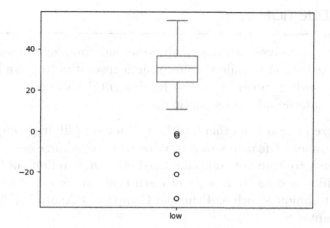

Figure 5.5   The Box Plot before Removing Outliers

5.2.2.3   *Remove the Outliers*

```
df.drop((df[(df['low']< (df['low'].mean() - 3 * df['low'].std())))|
(df['low']> (df['low'].mean() + 3 * df['low'].std()))]).index, inplace
= True)
```

```
df['low'].plot(kind = 'box')
```

```
<Axes: >
```

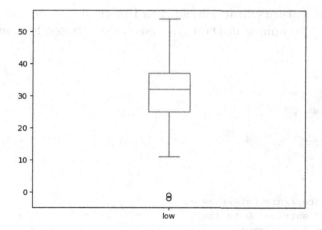

Figure 5.6   The Box Plot after Removing Outliers

5.2.2.4   *Practice*

Play with df['high'].

5.3 DATA REDUCTION

In the field of data analysis, dealing with large and complex datasets is a common challenge. Data reduction techniques offer practical solutions to handle such datasets effectively. This section introduces two fundamental concepts for data reduction: Dimension elimination and data sampling.

Dimensionality reduction is a crucial technique for simplifying complex datasets by reducing the number of features or variables while retaining essential information. This concept aims to improve computational efficiency, reduce noise, and enhance the interpretability of data. Here we will learn basic dimension elimination. We will learn advanced techniques such as Principal Component Analysis (PCA) and Feature Selection in Chapter 8.

Data sampling involves the selection of a subset of data points from a larger dataset. This approach is valuable for reducing the overall dataset size while retaining its statistical characteristics and patterns. Data sampling is particularly useful when working with extensive datasets, as it can significantly improve analysis efficiency.

5.3.1 Tutorial – Dimension Elimination

Sometimes we have our data collected with as much information as possible. However, some attributes do not contribute to our analysis, and we may need to do dimension elimination to focus in the attributes we need. Dimension elimination is one way of reducing the complexity of your data, and you can use your domain knowledge to justify the reasons.

We could also do feature extraction, such as Principal Component Analysis (PCA). We will learn that technique in Data Analysis, unsupervised learning course.

5.3.1.1 Setup

```
import numpy as np
import pandas as pd
```

```
df = pd.read_csv('/content/sample_data/california_housing_train.csv')
df.info()
```

```
<class 'pandas.core.frame.DataFrame'>
RangeIndex: 17000 entries, 0 to 16999
Data columns (total 9 columns):
 #   Column              Non-Null Count  Dtype
---  ------              --------------  -----
 0   longitude           17000 non-null  float64
 1   latitude            17000 non-null  float64
 2   housing_median_age  17000 non-null  float64
 3   total_rooms         17000 non-null  float64
 4   total_bedrooms      17000 non-null  float64
 5   population          17000 non-null  float64
```

```
6    households            17000 non-null   float64
7    median_income         17000 non-null   float64
8    median_house_value    17000 non-null   float64
dtypes: float64(9)
memory usage: 1.2 MB
```

5.3.1.2 Dimension Elimination

```
df_sample1 = df[df.columns[2:]]
df_sample1.info()
```

```
<class 'pandas.core.frame.DataFrame'>
RangeIndex: 17000 entries, 0 to 16999
Data columns (total 7 columns):
 #   Column              Non-Null Count  Dtype
---  ------              --------------  -----
 0   housing_median_age  17000 non-null  float64
 1   total_rooms         17000 non-null  float64
 2   total_bedrooms      17000 non-null  float64
 3   population          17000 non-null  float64
 4   households          17000 non-null  float64
 5   median_income       17000 non-null  float64
 6   median_house_value  17000 non-null  float64
dtypes: float64(7)
memory usage: 929.8 KB
```

```
df_sample2 = df.drop(df.columns[:2], axis = 1)
df_sample2.info()
```

```
<class 'pandas.core.frame.DataFrame'>
RangeIndex: 17000 entries, 0 to 16999
Data columns (total 7 columns):
 #   Column              Non-Null Count  Dtype
---  ------              --------------  -----
 0   housing_median_age  17000 non-null  float64
 1   total_rooms         17000 non-null  float64
 2   total_bedrooms      17000 non-null  float64
 3   population          17000 non-null  float64
 4   households          17000 non-null  float64
 5   median_income       17000 non-null  float64
 6   median_house_value  17000 non-null  float64
dtypes: float64(7)
memory usage: 929.8 KB
```

```
needed_cols = ['total_rooms', 'total_bedrooms',
    'population', 'households']
df_sample3 = df[needed_cols]
df_sample3.info()
```

```
<class 'pandas.core.frame.DataFrame'>
RangeIndex: 17000 entries, 0 to 16999
Data columns (total 4 columns):
```

```
 #   Column          Non-Null Count  Dtype
---  ------          --------------  -----
 0   total_rooms     17000 non-null  float64
 1   total_bedrooms  17000 non-null  float64
 2   population      17000 non-null  float64
 3   households      17000 non-null  float64
dtypes: float64(4)
memory usage: 531.4 KB
```

```
dontneeded_cols = ['latitude', 'longitude',
    'median_income', 'median_house_value']
df_sample4 = df.drop(dontneeded_cols, axis = 1)
df_sample4.info()
```

```
<class 'pandas.core.frame.DataFrame'>
RangeIndex: 17000 entries, 0 to 16999
Data columns (total 5 columns):
 #   Column             Non-Null Count  Dtype
---  ------             --------------  -----
 0   housing_median_age 17000 non-null  float64
 1   total_rooms        17000 non-null  float64
 2   total_bedrooms     17000 non-null  float64
 3   population         17000 non-null  float64
 4   households         17000 non-null  float64
dtypes: float64(5)
memory usage: 664.2 KB
```

5.3.2   Tutorial – Sampling

While dimension elimination is reducing the number of attributes, sampling is working on the number of records.

5.3.2.1   Setup

```
import numpy as np
import pandas as pd
```

```
df = pd.read_csv('/content/sample_data/california_housing_train.csv')
```

```
df.info()
```

```
<class 'pandas.core.frame.DataFrame'>
RangeIndex: 17000 entries, 0 to 16999
Data columns (total 9 columns):
 #   Column             Non-Null Count  Dtype
---  ------             --------------  -----
 0   longitude          17000 non-null  float64
 1   latitude           17000 non-null  float64
 2   housing_median_age 17000 non-null  float64
 3   total_rooms        17000 non-null  float64
 4   total_bedrooms     17000 non-null  float64
 5   population         17000 non-null  float64
```

```
6    households          17000 non-null  float64
7    median_income       17000 non-null  float64
8    median_house_value  17000 non-null  float64
dtypes: float64(9)
memory usage: 1.2 MB
```

##Sampling by numbers

```
df.sample(n=5)
```

	longitude	latitude	housing_median_age	total_rooms	total_bedrooms \
15268	-122.28	37.90	49.0	3191.0	516.0
762	-117.06	32.77	18.0	2269.0	682.0
11262	-121.10	35.60	20.0	3389.0	704.0
4084	-117.98	34.06	33.0	1353.0	228.0
7767	-118.38	33.80	36.0	4421.0	702.0

	population	households	median_income	median_house_value
15268	1148.0	507.0	6.3538	333700.0
762	1329.0	581.0	1.7951	161800.0
11262	1309.0	520.0	3.2112	204500.0
4084	1079.0	237.0	4.5417	160300.0
7767	1433.0	624.0	8.0838	500001.0

5.3.2.2 Sampling by Percentage

```
df.sample(frac=0.001)
```

	longitude	latitude	housing_median_age	total_rooms	total_bedrooms \
352	-116.90	32.79	21.0	3770.0	491.0
2408	-117.56	33.88	40.0	1196.0	294.0
10461	-120.37	40.17	21.0	789.0	141.0
...					
2349	-117.49	33.99	21.0	2050.0	392.0

	population	households	median_income	median_house_value
352	1410.0	446.0	6.7685	294700.0
2408	1052.0	258.0	2.0682	113000.0
10461	406.0	146.0	2.1198	73500.0
...				
2349	1153.0	336.0	4.8400	116400.0

```
df.loc[:10].sample(frac=0.9)
```

	longitude	latitude	housing_median_age	total_rooms	total_bedrooms \
10	-114.60	33.62	16.0	3741.0	801.0
1	-114.47	34.40	19.0	7650.0	1901.0
4	-114.57	33.57	20.0	1454.0	326.0
...					
3	-114.57	33.64	14.0	1501.0	337.0
9	-114.60	34.83	46.0	1497.0	309.0

	population	households	median_income	median_house_value
10	2434.0	824.0	2.6797	86500.0
1	1129.0	463.0	1.8200	80100.0
4	624.0	262.0	1.9250	65500.0
7	375.0	158.0	1.7083	48500.0
...				
3	515.0	226.0	3.1917	73400.0
9	787.0	271.0	2.1908	48100.0

5.3.2.3 Sampling with Replacement

```
df.loc[:10].sample(15,replace=True)
```

	longitude	latitude	housing_median_age	total_rooms	total_bedrooms \
5	-114.58	33.63	29.0	1387.0	236.0
4	-114.57	33.57	20.0	1454.0	326.0
1	-114.47	34.40	19.0	7650.0	1901.0
...					
3	-114.57	33.64	14.0	1501.0	337.0
1	-114.47	34.40	19.0	7650.0	1901.0

	population	households	median_income	median_house_value
5	671.0	239.0	3.3438	74000.0
4	624.0	262.0	1.9250	65500.0
1	1129.0	463.0	1.8200	80100.0
...				
3	515.0	226.0	3.1917	73400.0
1	1129.0	463.0	1.8200	80100.0

5.4 DATA DISCRETIZATION AND SCALING

In the realm of data analysis, preparing and transforming data to ensure it is suitable for analysis is a critical step. This section introduces two fundamental concepts for data preprocessing: Data scaling and data discretization.

Data scaling is the process of transforming data into a consistent range to ensure that no single feature disproportionately influences an analysis. This concept is vital for algorithms that rely on distance calculations or gradient descent, as well as for visualizing data with varying scales. Within this section, you will explore various data scaling methods, including Min-Max Scaling (Normalization), Z-Score Standardization, and Robust Scaling. These methods allow you to rescale data to specific ranges or standardize it to a mean of zero and a standard deviation of one, making it more amenable to analysis.

Data discretization involves the transformation of continuous data into discrete intervals or categories. This technique is beneficial for simplifying complex data, reducing noise, and making data more interpretable. Discretization can be based on statistical measures like quartiles or domain knowledge. In this section, you will explore techniques for data discretization, including Equal Width Binning and Equal Frequency Binning. These methods enable you to partition continuous data into predefined intervals, allowing you to study data patterns and relationships more effectively.

5.4.1 Tutorial – Data Discretization

Many times we need to convert continuous attributes into multiple intervals, so we can reduce the data or remove some variance. This process is called discretization.

5.4.1.1 Setup

```
import numpy as np
import pandas as pd
```

```
df = pd.read_csv('/content/sample_data/california_housing_train.csv')
df.head()
```

	longitude	latitude	housing_median_age	total_rooms	total_bedrooms \
0	-114.31	34.19	15.0	5612.0	1283.0
1	-114.47	34.40	19.0	7650.0	1901.0
2	-114.56	33.69	17.0	720.0	174.0
3	-114.57	33.64	14.0	1501.0	337.0
4	-114.57	33.57	20.0	1454.0	326.0

	population	households	median_income	median_house_value
0	1015.0	472.0	1.4936	66900.0
1	1129.0	463.0	1.8200	80100.0
2	333.0	117.0	1.6509	85700.0
3	515.0	226.0	3.1917	73400.0
4	624.0	262.0	1.9250	65500.0

```
df.describe()
```

	longitude	latitude	housing_median_age	total_rooms \
count	17000.000000	17000.000000	17000.000000	17000.000000
mean	-119.562108	35.625225	28.589353	2643.664412
std	2.005166	2.137340	12.586937	2179.947071
min	-124.350000	32.540000	1.000000	2.000000
25%	-121.790000	33.930000	18.000000	1462.000000
50%	-118.490000	34.250000	29.000000	2127.000000
75%	-118.000000	37.720000	37.000000	3151.250000
max	-114.310000	41.950000	52.000000	37937.000000

	total_bedrooms	population	households	median_income \
count	17000.000000	17000.000000	17000.000000	17000.000000
mean	539.410824	1429.573941	501.221941	3.883578
std	421.499452	1147.852959	384.520841	1.908157
min	1.000000	3.000000	1.000000	0.499900
25%	297.000000	790.000000	282.000000	2.566375
50%	434.000000	1167.000000	409.000000	3.544600
75%	648.250000	1721.000000	605.250000	4.767000
max	6445.000000	35682.000000	6082.000000	15.000100

```
       median_house_value
count        17000.000000
mean        207300.912353
std         115983.764387
min          14999.000000
25%         119400.000000
50%         180400.000000
75%         265000.000000
max         500001.000000
```

5.4.1.2 Discretize Population

```
df['popular'] = np.select([df['population'] <1429.573941
    , df['population'] >= 1429.573941], ['not popular', 'popular'])
df['popular']
```

```
0          not popular
1          not popular
2          not popular
3          not popular
4          not popular
              ...
16995      not popular
16996      not popular
16997      not popular
16998      not popular
16999      not popular
Name: popular, Length: 17000, dtype: object
```

```
df['popular'].value_counts()
```

```
not popular    10862
popular         6138
Name: popular, dtype: int64
```

5.4.1.3 Discretize rooms

```
conditions = [
    (df['total_rooms'] < 1462) & (df['total_bedrooms'] < 297),
    (df['total_rooms'] > 3151) & (df['total_bedrooms'] > 648),
    (df['total_rooms'] < 2127) & (df['total_bedrooms'] > 434),
    (df['total_rooms'] > 2127) & (df['total_bedrooms'] < 434),
]

values = ['LL', 'HH', 'LH', 'HL']
df['rooms'] = np.select(conditions, values)
df['rooms']
```

```
0          HH
1          HH
2          LL
```

```
3         0
4         0
          ..
16995     HL
16996     0
16997     0
16998     0
16999     0
Name: rooms, Length: 17000, dtype: object
```

```
df['rooms'].value_counts()
```

```
0     7970
LL    3424
HH    3394
HL    1110
LH    1102
Name: rooms, dtype: int64
```

5.4.1.4 Discretize house value

```python
def house_value(value):
    if value < 119400:
        return "Low"
    elif value > 265000:
        return "High"
    else:
        return "Medium"
```

```
df['house_value_category'] = df['median_house_value'].apply(house_value)
df['house_value_category']
```

```
0         Low
1         Low
2         Low
3         Low
4         Low
          ...
16995     Low
16996     Low
16997     Low
16998     Low
16999     Low
Name: house_value_category, Length: 17000, dtype: object
```

```
df['house_value_category'].value_counts()
```

```
Medium    8510
High      4247
Low       4243
Name: house_value_category, dtype: int64
```

5.4.2 Tutorial – Data Scaling

1. Min-Max Scaling
2. Z-Score Standardization
3. Decimal Scaling

5.4.2.1 Setup

```python
import numpy as np
import pandas as pd
```

```python
df = pd.read_csv('/content/sample_data/california_housing_train.csv')
```

```python
df.info()
```

```
<class 'pandas.core.frame.DataFrame'>
RangeIndex: 17000 entries, 0 to 16999
Data columns (total 9 columns):
 #   Column              Non-Null Count  Dtype
---  ------              --------------  -----
 0   longitude           17000 non-null  float64
 1   latitude            17000 non-null  float64
 2   housing_median_age  17000 non-null  float64
 3   total_rooms         17000 non-null  float64
 4   total_bedrooms      17000 non-null  float64
 5   population          17000 non-null  float64
 6   households          17000 non-null  float64
 7   median_income       17000 non-null  float64
 8   median_house_value  17000 non-null  float64
dtypes: float64(9)
memory usage: 1.2 MB
```

```python
df['population'].describe()
```

```
count    17000.000000
mean      1429.573941
std       1147.852959
min          3.000000
25%        790.000000
50%       1167.000000
75%       1721.000000
max      35682.000000
Name: population, dtype: float64
```

5.4.2.2 MinMaxScalar Scaling

It is the process of performing a linear transformation on original data.

$$v_i' = \frac{v_i - min}{max - min}(max' - min') + min'$$

where v_i is the current value, min and max are the current min and max, and max' and min' are the new boundary. v_i' is the min_max scaled value.

Normally, we use a special case of [0, 1] as the new scale; in this case, the formular can be as simple as:

$$v_i' = \frac{v_i - min}{max - min}$$

```
df['population_MinMax'] = (df['population'] - df['population'].min())
    / (df['population'].max() - df['population'].min())
df['population_MinMax']
```

```
0        0.028364
1        0.031559
2        0.009249
3        0.014350
4        0.017405
            ...
16995    0.025337
16996    0.033381
16997    0.034782
16998    0.036296
16999    0.022506
Name: population_MinMax, Length: 17000, dtype: float64
```

```
df['population_MinMax'].describe()
```

```
count    17000.000000
mean         0.039984
std          0.032172
min          0.000000
25%          0.022058
50%          0.032624
75%          0.048152
max          1.000000
Name: population_MinMax, dtype: float64
```

5.4.2.3 Z-score Normalization/standardization

In this technique, the values are normalized based on the mean and standard deviation of attribute A. Each value is subtracted with the mean; thus, we leave with the variance in terms of standard deviation.

$$v_i' = \frac{v_i - mean}{std}$$

where v_i is the current value, *mean* and *std* are current mean and standard deviation, and v_i' is the Z-score scaled value.

```
df['population_Z'] = (df['population'] - df['population'].mean())
    /(df['population'].std())
df['population_Z']
```

```
0        -0.361173
1        -0.261858
```

```
2        -0.955326
3        -0.796769
4        -0.701809
           ...
16995    -0.455262
16996    -0.205230
16997    -0.161670
16998    -0.114626
16999    -0.543252
Name: population_Z, Length: 17000, dtype: float64
```

```
df['population_Z'] .describe()
```

```
count    1.700000e+04
mean     6.687461e-17
std      1.000000e+00
min     -1.242819e+00
25%     -5.571915e-01
50%     -2.287522e-01
75%      2.538880e-01
max      2.984043e+01
Name: population_Z, dtype: float64
```

5.4.2.4 Decimal Scaling

It normalizes by moving the decimal point of the values of the data.

$$v_i' = \frac{v_i}{10^t}$$

where v_i is the current value, t is the number of digits of the max absolute value $+ 1$, and v_i' is the decimal scaled value.

Let's understand it by an example: Suppose we have a dataset in which the value ranges from -1234 to 999. In this case, the maximum absolute value is 1234 with four digits, and t is $4 + 1 = 5$.

So to perform decimal scaling, we divide each of the values in the dataset by 10^5.

```
df['population'].max()
```

```
35682.0
```

```
df['population_decimal'] = df['population']/100000
df['population_decimal']
```

```
0        0.01015
1        0.01129
2        0.00333
3        0.00515
4        0.00624
           ...
16995    0.00907
```

```
16996      0.01194
16997      0.01244
16998      0.01298
16999      0.00806
Name: population_decimal, Length: 17000, dtype: float64
```

```
df['population_decimal'].describe()
```

```
count    17000.000000
mean         0.014296
std          0.011479
min          0.000030
25%          0.007900
50%          0.011670
75%          0.017210
max          0.356820
Name: population_decimal, dtype: float64
```

```
df[['population','population_MinMax',
    'population_Z', 'population_decimal']].describe()
```

	population	population_MinMax	population_Z	population_decimal
count	17000.000000	17000.000000	1.700000e+04	17000.000000
mean	1429.573941	0.039984	6.687461e-17	0.014296
std	1147.852959	0.032172	1.000000e+00	0.011479
min	3.000000	0.000000	-1.242819e+00	0.000030
25%	790.000000	0.022058	-5.571915e-01	0.007900
50%	1167.000000	0.032624	-2.287522e-01	0.011670
75%	1721.000000	0.048152	2.538880e-01	0.017210
max	35682.000000	1.000000	2.984043e+01	0.356820

5.5 DATA WAREHOUSE

In the field of data management and analytics, a Data Warehouse serves as a central repository for storing, organizing, and retrieving large volumes of data from various sources. This section introduces the concept of a Data Warehouse, including the essential components of Data Cubes and their dimensions, as well as the versatile built-in PivotTable tool within Pandas.

A Data Warehouse is a dedicated storage system designed to consolidate data from multiple sources, making it accessible for analytical purposes. This centralized repository ensures data consistency and provides a platform for efficient querying and reporting. As the bricks of a Data Warehouse, Data Cubes are multidimensional data structures that allow you to store and analyze data in a way that provides different perspectives or dimensions. Each dimension represents a characteristic or attribute of the data, creating a comprehensive view for analysis. Within this section, you will explore the concept of Data Cubes and their dimensions. You'll learn how to structure data into cubes to facilitate multidimensional analysis and gain insights from complex datasets.

Pandas includes a built-in PivotTable tool. This tool enables you to summarize, analyze, and present data in a dynamic and interactive format, all within the Pandas framework. You will discover how to use Pandas to create PivotTables, arrange data fields, and apply filters and calculations to gain valuable insights from your data. This practical skill is invaluable for data analysts and professionals who need to present data in a meaningful and customizable manner.

5.5.1 Tutorial – Data Cube

5.5.1.1 Setup

```
!pip install atoti
```

```
import pandas as pd
import atoti as tt
```

5.5.1.2 Create Session

```
session = tt.Session()
```

```
df = pd.read_csv('/content/Spotify_Youtube_Sample.csv')
df.head()
```

```
      Artist                                       Track  \
0  Gorillaz                              Feel Good Inc.
1  Gorillaz                             Rhinestone Eyes
2  Gorillaz  New Gold (feat. Tame Impala and Bootie Brown)
3  Gorillaz                            On Melancholy Hill
4  Gorillaz                               Clint Eastwood

                                        Album Album_type       Views  \
0                                  Demon Days      album  693555221.0
1                               Plastic Beach      album   72011645.0
2  New Gold (feat. Tame Impala and Bootie Brown)     single    8435055.0
3                               Plastic Beach      album  211754952.0
4                                    Gorillaz      album  618480958.0

       Likes  Comments Licensed official_video        Stream
0  6220896.0  169907.0     True           True  1.040235e+09
1  1079128.0   31003.0     True           True  3.100837e+08
2   282142.0    7399.0     True           True  6.306347e+07
3  1788577.0   55229.0     True           True  4.346636e+08
4  6197318.0  155930.0     True           True  6.172597e+08
```

```
views = session.read_csv(
    '/content/Spotify_Youtube_Sample.csv',
    keys = ['Artist', 'Track', 'Album'],
)
views.head()
```

```
                                                              Album_type  \
Artist       Track                                  Album
Ryan Castro  Wasa Wasa                              Wasa Wasa        single
             Avemaría                               Avemaría         single
Omar Apollo  Invincible (feat. Daniel Caesar)       Ivory            album
             Useless                                Apolonio         album
             Endlessly                              Ivory (Marfil)   album


                                                                  Views  \
Artist       Track                                  Album
Ryan Castro  Wasa Wasa                              Wasa Wasa      115121545.0
             Avemaría                               Avemaría        10838443.0
Omar Apollo  Invincible (feat. Daniel Caesar)       Ivory            1967236.0
             Useless                                Apolonio          469551.0
             Endlessly                              Ivory (Marfil)    210243.0


                                                                  Likes  \
Artist       Track                                  Album
Ryan Castro  Wasa Wasa                              Wasa Wasa       761203.0
             Avemaría                               Avemaría         96423.0
Omar Apollo  Invincible (feat. Daniel Caesar)       Ivory            38113.0
             Useless                                Apolonio         13611.0
             Endlessly                              Ivory (Marfil)    4704.0


                                                               Comments  \
Artist       Track                                  Album
Ryan Castro  Wasa Wasa                              Wasa Wasa        17238.0
             Avemaría                               Avemaría          6616.0
Omar Apollo  Invincible (feat. Daniel Caesar)       Ivory              764.0
             Useless                                Apolonio           405.0
             Endlessly                              Ivory (Marfil)     123.0


                                                               Licensed  \
Artist       Track                                  Album
Ryan Castro  Wasa Wasa                              Wasa Wasa          True
             Avemaría                               Avemaría          False
Omar Apollo  Invincible (feat. Daniel Caesar)       Ivory              True
             Useless                                Apolonio           True
             Endlessly                              Ivory (Marfil)     True


                                                         official_video  \
Artist       Track                                  Album
Ryan Castro  Wasa Wasa                              Wasa Wasa          True
             Avemaría                               Avemaría           True
Omar Apollo  Invincible (feat. Daniel Caesar)       Ivory              True
             Useless                                Apolonio           True
             Endlessly                              Ivory (Marfil)     True


                                                                 Stream
Artist       Track                                  Album
Ryan Castro  Wasa Wasa                              Wasa Wasa       96300795.0
             Avemaría                               Avemaría         9327917.0
Omar Apollo  Invincible (feat. Daniel Caesar)       Ivory           29596755.0
             Useless                                Apolonio         25646394.0
             Endlessly                              Ivory (Marfil)   10150327.0
```

5.5.1.3 Create a Data Cube

```
cube = session.create_cube(views, name = 'Views')
cube
```

```
m= cube.measures
m
```

```
l = cube.levels
l
```

5.5.1.4 Play with the Cube

Apex or 0-D

```
cube.query(m['Views.SUM'])
```

```
            Views.SUM
0   1,902,053,002,307.00
```

1D

```
cube.query(m['Views.SUM'], levels = [l['Artist']])
```

```
                    Views.SUM
Artist
$NOT               110,784,903.00
$uicideboy$        334,135,108.00
(G)I-DLE         1,754,953,941.00
*NSYNC           1,027,832,862.00
070 Shake           96,099,359.00
...                        ...
will.i.am        2,831,320,166.00
Ángela Aguilar   1,385,295,291.00
Ñejo               626,680,824.00
Ñengo Flow         812,726,315.00
Øneheart            34,623,310.00
```

```
[2063 rows x 1 columns]
```

```
cube.query(m['Views.SUM'], levels = [l['Album']])
```

```
                                              Views.SUM
Album
!Volare! The Very Best of the Gipsy Kings    5,760,198.00
"Awaken, My Love!"                         694,453,372.00
"Heroes" (2017 Remaster)                    29,328,667.00
"Let Go" Dj Pack                                    56.00
"Let's Rock"                                14,005,512.00
...                                                  ...
```

```
[11727 rows x 1 columns]
```

2D

```
cube.query(m['Views.SUM'], levels = [l['Album'], l['Artist']])
```

```
                                              Views.SUM
Album                              Artist
!Volare! The Very Best of the Gipsy Kings Gipsy Kings      5,760,198.00
"Awaken, My Love!"                 Childish Gambino 694,453,372.00
"Heroes" (2017 Remaster)           David Bowie      29,328,667.00
"Let Go" Dj Pack                   Dina Rae                 56.00
"Let's Rock"                       The Black Keys   14,005,512.00
...                                                       ...

[13955 rows x 1 columns]
```

2D with slicing

```
cube.query(m['Views.SUM'], levels = [l['Album'], l['Track']],
    filter=l['Artist'] == 'The Beatles')
```

```
cube.query(m['Views.SUM'], levels = [l['Album'], l['Track']],
    filter=l['Artist'] == 'Michael Jackson')
```

```
cube.query(m['Views.SUM'], levels = [l['Album'], l['Track']],
    filter=l['official_video'] == 'True')
```

```
cube.query(m['Views.SUM'], levels = [l['Album'], l['Track']],
    filter=l['official_video'] == 'False')
```

```
                                      Views.SUM
Album                  Track
"Miguel"               Te Amaré       30,083,671.00
...
#1s ... and then some  Brand New Man     33,246.00
$outh $ide $uicide     Cold Turkey      214,405.00
                       Muddy Blunts      31,879.00
...                                         ...

[4237 rows x 1 columns]
```

3D

```
cube.query(m['Views.SUM']
    , levels = [l['Album'], l['Track'], l['official_video']])
```

3D with slicing

```
cube.query(m['Views.SUM']
    , levels = [l['Album'], l['Track'], l['official_video']]
    ,filter=l['Artist'] == 'Michael Jackson')
```

Exercise You can play with other interests in measure and try different dimension of the cube.

5.5.2 Tutorial – Pivot Table

- OLTP: Online Transaction Processing
- OLAP: Online Analytical Processing

5.5.2.1 *Setup*

```
import numpy as np
import pandas as pd
```

```
df = pd.read_csv('/content/Spotify_Youtube_Sample.csv')
```

```
df.info()
```

```
<class 'pandas.core.frame.DataFrame'>
RangeIndex: 20718 entries, 0 to 20717
Data columns (total 10 columns):
 #   Column          Non-Null Count  Dtype
---  ------          --------------  -----
 0   Artist          20718 non-null  object
 1   Track           20718 non-null  object
 2   Album           20718 non-null  object
 3   Album_type      20718 non-null  object
 4   Views           20248 non-null  float64
 5   Likes           20177 non-null  float64
 6   Comments        20149 non-null  float64
 7   Licensed        20248 non-null  object
 8   official_video  20248 non-null  object
 9   Stream          20142 non-null  float64
dtypes: float64(4), object(6)
memory usage: 1.6+ MB
```

```
df['Artist'].unique()[:100]
```

```
array(['Gorillaz', 'Red Hot Chili Peppers', '50 Cent', 'Metallica',
       'Coldplay', 'Daft Punk', 'Linkin Park', 'Radiohead', 'AC/DC',
       'Black Eyed Peas', 'Michael Jackson', 'P!nk', 'Eminem',
       'Pharrell Williams', 'Khalid', 'Shakira', 'Machine Gun Kelly',
       ...
       'Udit Narayan', 'Vishal-Shekhar', 'Bibi und Tina',
       'Yuvan Shankar Raja', 'Bibi Blocksberg'], dtype=object)
```

5.5.2.2 *Create Pivot Table*

```
df_pivot = df.pivot_table(values=['Views','Likes','Comments'],
                          index=['Artist','Album'],
                          aggfunc='mean')
df_pivot
```

```
                                                       Comments        Likes  \
Artist    Album
$NOT      - TRAGEDY +                                     3404.0  165966.666667
          Beautiful Havoc                                13900.5  371387.500000
          EAT YOUR HEART OUT                               735.0   19033.000000
          Ethereal                                        8183.0  388334.000000
          Fast & Furious: Drift Tape (Phonk Vol 1)          32.0    1725.000000
...                                                          ...            ...
Øneheart  snowfall (Slowed + Reverb)                     11423.0  561165.000000
          snowfall (Sped Up)                              1361.0   66128.000000
          this feeling                                     516.0   32838.000000
          watching the stars                               216.0   13429.000000
          watching the stars (Remixes)                      16.0    2145.000000

                                                          Views
Artist    Album
$NOT      - TRAGEDY +                                  9158825.0
          Beautiful Havoc                             14683693.5
          EAT YOUR HEART OUT                            681136.0
          Ethereal                                    10114989.0
          Fast & Furious: Drift Tape (Phonk Vol 1)       76559.0
...                                                          ...
Øneheart  snowfall (Slowed + Reverb)                  15361992.0
          snowfall (Sped Up)                           1707355.0
          this feeling                                  856049.0
          watching the stars                            323775.0
          watching the stars (Remixes)                  139020.0

[13955 rows x 3 columns]
```

5.5.2.3 Play with the Pivot Table

```
df_pivot.loc['Michael Jackson']
```

```
                                       Comments       Likes         Views
Album
Bad (Remastered)                        60358.5   1594227.0  2.604891e+08
Dangerous                              127080.0   3085718.0  5.040573e+08
HIStory - PAST, PRESENT AND FUTURE -   335112.0   8312571.0  9.786800e+08
  BOOK I
Off the Wall                            88325.0   2262080.0  3.254739e+08
Thriller                               383891.5   8089856.5  1.103212e+09
XSCAPE                                  27103.5   1064408.0  1.719371e+08
```

```
df_pivot.loc[['Michael Jackson', 'The Beatles', 'Beyoncé']]
```

```
                                                             Comments  \
Artist           Album
Michael Jackson  Bad (Remastered)                            60358.50
                 Dangerous                                  127080.00
                 HIStory - PAST, PRESENT AND FUTURE - BOOK I 335112.00
                 Off the Wall                                88325.00
                 Thriller                                   383891.50
                 XSCAPE                                      27103.50
```

```
The Beatles     1 (Remastered)                             5300.00
                Abbey Road (Remastered)                    20924.00
                Help! (Remastered)                          5938.00
                Let It Be (Remastered)                     15452.00
                Please Please Me (Remastered)               4309.00
                Rubber Soul (Remastered)                    8607.00
                The Beatles (Remastered)                    4522.00
Beyoncé         4                                         166002.00
                BEYONCÉ [Platinum Edition]                129479.00
                Dangerously In Love                        66334.00
                I AM...SASHA FIERCE                       203892.00
                Perfect Duet (Ed Sheeran & Beyoncé)        70570.00
                RENAISSANCE                                 3808.25

                                                         Likes  \
Artist          Album
Michael Jackson Bad (Remastered)                        1594227.0
                Dangerous                                3085718.0
                HIStory - PAST, PRESENT AND FUTURE - BOOK I 8312571.0
                Off the Wall                             2262080.0
                Thriller                                 8089856.5
                XSCAPE                                   1064408.0
The Beatles     1 (Remastered)                           368291.5
                Abbey Road (Remastered)                   728453.0
                Help! (Remastered)                        475089.0
                Let It Be (Remastered)                   1075941.0
                Please Please Me (Remastered)             490790.0
                Rubber Soul (Remastered)                  463315.0
                The Beatles (Remastered)                  365297.0
Beyoncé         4                                        2623723.5
                BEYONCÉ [Platinum Edition]               2906283.0
                Dangerously In Love                      3218858.0
                I AM...SASHA FIERCE                      6931695.0
                Perfect Duet (Ed Sheeran & Beyoncé)      1998224.0
                RENAISSANCE                                112728.5

                                                            Views
Artist          Album
Michael Jackson Bad (Remastered)                        2.604891e+08
                Dangerous                                5.040573e+08
                HIStory - PAST, PRESENT AND FUTURE - BOOK I 9.786800e+08
                Off the Wall                             3.254739e+08
                Thriller                                 1.103212e+09
                XSCAPE                                   1.719371e+08
The Beatles     1 (Remastered)                           4.284411e+07
                Abbey Road (Remastered)                  8.114310e+07
                Help! (Remastered)                       4.285668e+07
                Let It Be (Remastered)                   1.319251e+08
                Please Please Me (Remastered)            5.322836e+07
                Rubber Soul (Remastered)                 6.322312e+07
                The Beatles (Remastered)                 3.385295e+07
Beyoncé         4                                        5.347308e+08
                BEYONCÉ [Platinum Edition]               6.870312e+08
                Dangerously In Love                      6.690844e+08
                I AM...SASHA FIERCE                      1.357274e+09
```

```
        Perfect Duet (Ed Sheeran & Beyoncé)        2.315809e+08
        RENAISSANCE                                 7.965112e+06
```

5.5.2.4 Sort the Values

```
df_pivot.sort_values(by = 'Views', ascending= False)
```

```
                                                            Comments   \
Artist          Album
Daddy Yankee    VIDA                                        4252791.0
Charlie Puth    See You Again (feat. Charlie Puth)          2127346.0
Wiz Khalifa     See You Again (feat. Charlie Puth)          2127345.0
Mark Ronson     Uptown Special                              598916.0
...                                                         ...
Camila          Resistiré                                         1.0
Peter Groeger   Der Kaiser von Dallas (Die einzige Wahrheit übe...   0.0
Deep Purple     Machine Head (2016 Version)                       0.0
Christian Rode  Auf dem hohen Küstensande (Von Meer und Strand ...   0.0
Maroon 5        Hands All Over                                    0.0


                                                              Likes   \
Artist          Album
Daddy Yankee    VIDA                                        50788626.0
Charlie Puth    See You Again (feat. Charlie Puth)          40147674.0
Wiz Khalifa     See You Again (feat. Charlie Puth)          40147618.0
Mark Ronson     Uptown Special                              20067879.0
...                                                         ...
Camila          Resistiré                                         9.0
Peter Groeger   Der Kaiser von Dallas (Die einzige Wahrheit übe...   0.0
Deep Purple     Machine Head (2016 Version)                       1.0
Christian Rode  Auf dem hohen Küstensande (Von Meer und Strand ...   0.0
Maroon 5        Hands All Over                                    0.0


                                                                Views
Artist          Album
Daddy Yankee    VIDA                                        8.079647e+09
Charlie Puth    See You Again (feat. Charlie Puth)          5.773798e+09
Wiz Khalifa     See You Again (feat. Charlie Puth)          5.773797e+09
Mark Ronson     Uptown Special                              4.821016e+09
...                                                         ...
Camila          Resistiré                                   4.900000e+01
Peter Groeger   Der Kaiser von Dallas (Die einzige Wahrheit übe...   3.688889e+01
Deep Purple     Machine Head (2016 Version)                       3.100000e+01
Christian Rode  Auf dem hohen Küstensande (Von Meer und Strand ...   2.800000e+01
Maroon 5        Hands All Over                                    2.600000e+01

[13955 rows x 3 columns]
```

```
df_pivot.sort_values(by = ['Artist','Views'], ascending= False)
```

```
                                    Comments        Likes   \
Artist     Album
Øneheart   snowfall                 11423.0    561165.000000
           snowfall (Slowed + Reverb)   11423.0    561165.000000
```

```
            snowfall (Sped Up)                          1361.0    66128.000000
            this feeling                                 516.0    32838.000000
            apathy                                        419.0    23615.000000
...                                                        ...             ...
$NOT        Ethereal                                     8183.0   388334.000000
            - TRAGEDY +                                  3404.0   165966.666667
            SIMPLE                                       2317.0    95313.000000
            EAT YOUR HEART OUT                            735.0    19033.000000
            Fast & Furious: Drift Tape (Phonk Vol 1)      32.0     1725.000000

                                                            Views
Artist     Album
Øneheart   snowfall                                     15361992.0
           snowfall (Slowed + Reverb)                   15361992.0
           snowfall (Sped Up)                            1707355.0
           this feeling                                   856049.0
           apathy                                         597163.0
...                                                            ...
$NOT       Ethereal                                     10114989.0
           - TRAGEDY +                                    9158825.0
           SIMPLE                                         1967700.0
           EAT YOUR HEART OUT                              681136.0
           Fast & Furious: Drift Tape (Phonk Vol 1)        76559.0

[13955 rows x 3 columns]
```

```
df_pivot.sort_values(by = ['Artist','Views'], ascending= False
    ).loc['Daddy Yankee']
```

```
                                      Comments          Likes         Views
Album
VIDA                                 4252791.0   5.078863e+07   8.079647e+09
Con Calma                             384865.0   1.303660e+07   2.626439e+09
LEGENDADDY                             16214.0   8.849240e+05   8.708415e+07
Barrio Fino (Bonus Track Version)       4184.0   1.790017e+05   2.172502e+07
ULALA (OOH LA LA)                       3837.0   2.278240e+05   9.058435e+06
Talento de Barrio                       1675.0   3.271800e+04   3.647171e+06
El Cartel: The Big Boss                  193.0   1.036000e+04   8.649900e+05
YHLQMDLG                                   1.0   1.180000e+02   1.084500e+04
```

```
df_pivot.sort_values(by = ['Artist','Views'], ascending= False
    ).loc[['Coldplay', 'The Beatles']]
```

```
                                                         Comments        Likes  \
Artist     Album
Coldplay   Memories...Do Not Open                        270444.0   10282499.0
           A Head Full of Dreams                         377666.0   13515772.0
           Mylo Xyloto                                   343020.0    8497224.0
           A Rush of Blood to the Head                   124357.0    5532787.0
           Viva La Vida or Death and All His Friends     261790.0    4370461.0
           Ghost Stories                                  79974.0    3741300.0
           X&Y                                           114460.0    2962029.0
           Parachutes                                     59966.5    2694138.0
```

```
              Music Of The Spheres                      432726.0   8867547.0
The Beatles   Let It Be (Remastered)                     15452.0   1075941.0
              Abbey Road (Remastered)                     20924.0    728453.0
              Rubber Soul (Remastered)                     8607.0    463315.0
              Please Please Me (Remastered)                4309.0    490790.0
              Help! (Remastered)                           5938.0    475089.0
              1 (Remastered)                               5300.0    368291.5
              The Beatles (Remastered)                     4522.0    365297.0

                                                          Views
Artist        Album
Coldplay      Memories...Do Not Open                      2.118019e+09
              A Head Full of Dreams                       1.828242e+09
              Mylo Xyloto                                 1.665814e+09
              A Rush of Blood to the Head                 1.082588e+09
              Viva La Vida or Death and All His Friends   7.895815e+08
              Ghost Stories                               7.864046e+08
              X&Y                                         5.662392e+08
              Parachutes                                  4.528667e+08
              Music Of The Spheres                        2.546560e+08
The Beatles   Let It Be (Remastered)                      1.319251e+08
              Abbey Road (Remastered)                     8.114310e+07
              Rubber Soul (Remastered)                     6.322312e+07
              Please Please Me (Remastered)               5.322836e+07
              Help! (Remastered)                          4.285668e+07
              1 (Remastered)                              4.284411e+07
              The Beatles (Remastered)                    3.385295e+07
```

II

Data Analysis

## CHAPTER 6

Classification

C LASSIFICATION is a method of supervised learning in which an algorithm is trained to assign one or more predefined labels to a given input. The goal of classification is to learn a function that can accurately predict the class label of an unseen input, based on the class labels of a set of labeled training data. Classification algorithms typically take as input a set of feature values for a given input and use these features to predict the class label. Common examples of classification problems include image recognition, spam detection, and natural language processing.

There are many different classification methods we use with Scikit-learn, but some of the most common include:

- Logistic Regression: A linear model that is often used for binary classification, where the goal is to predict one of two possible classes.

- Decision Trees: A tree-based model that uses a series of if-then rules to make predictions.

- Random Forest: An ensemble method that combines many decision trees to improve the accuracy of predictions.

- Naive Bayes: A probabilistic model that makes predictions based on the probability of each class given the input features.

- Support Vector Machines (SVMs): A linear model that finds the best boundary between classes by maximizing the margin between them.

- K-Nearest Neighbors: A simple method that uses the k closest labeled examples to the input in question to make a prediction.

- Gradient Boosting: An ensemble method that combines many weak models to improve the accuracy of predictions.

DOI: 10.1201/9781003462781-6

6.1 NEAREST NEIGHBOR CLASSIFIERS

In the field of machine learning and pattern recognition, Nearest Neighbor Classifiers are fundamental algorithms that leverage the proximity of data points to make predictions or classifications. This section introduces two essential Nearest Neighbor Classifiers, K-Nearest Neighbors (KNN) and Radius Neighbors (RNN), and demonstrates their practical implementation using the Scikit-learn package. K-Nearest Neighbors (KNN) is a supervised machine learning algorithm used for classification and regression tasks. It operates on the principle that data points with similar features tend to belong to the same class or category. Throughout this section, you will explore the KNN algorithm's core concepts and practical implementation using Scikit-learn.

Radius Neighbors (RNN) is an extension of the KNN algorithm that focuses on data points within a specific radius or distance from a query point. This approach is useful when you want to identify data points that are similar to a given reference point. Within this section, you will delve into the RNN algorithm's fundamental concepts and practical implementation using Scikit-learn

6.1.1 Tutorial – Iris Binary Classification Using KNN

Documentation: https://scikit-learn.org/stable/modules/generated/sklearn.neighbors .KNeighborsClassifier.html

6.1.1.1 Setup

Environment

```
import numpy as np
import pandas as pd
import matplotlib.pyplot as plt
import seaborn as sns
from sklearn import datasets
```

Load the dataset iris

```
iris = datasets.load_iris()
```

```
df = pd.DataFrame({'Sepal length': iris.data[:,0],
                   'Sepal width': iris.data[:,1],
                   'Petal length':iris.data[:,2],
                   'Petal width':iris.data[:,3],
                   'Species':iris.target})
df.head()
```

	Sepal length	Sepal width	Petal length	Petal width	Species
0	5.1	3.5	1.4	0.2	0
1	4.9	3.0	1.4	0.2	0
2	4.7	3.2	1.3	0.2	0
3	4.6	3.1	1.5	0.2	0
4	5.0	3.6	1.4	0.2	0

```
df = df[df['Species'] != 0]
```

```
df.info()
```

```
<class 'pandas.core.frame.DataFrame'>
Int64Index: 100 entries, 50 to 149
Data columns (total 5 columns):
 #   Column        Non-Null Count  Dtype
---  ------        --------------  -----
 0   Sepal length  100 non-null    float64
 1   Sepal width   100 non-null    float64
 2   Petal length  100 non-null    float64
 3   Petal width   100 non-null    float64
 4   Species       100 non-null    int64
dtypes: float64(4), int64(1)
memory usage: 4.7 KB
```

A simple visualization

```
sns.relplot(data = df, x = 'Sepal length', y = 'Sepal width'
    , hue = 'Species')
```

```
<seaborn.axisgrid.FacetGrid at 0x7c8ff7e55ed0>
```

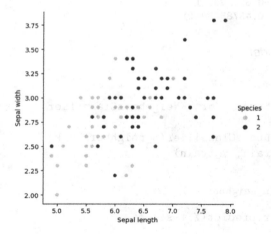

Figure 6.1   A Scatter Plot of Sepal Length VS Sepal Width with Species Differentiation

Train-test split

```
from sklearn.model_selection import train_test_split

X = df[df.columns[:2]]
y = df[df.columns[-1]]
X_train, X_test, y_train, y_test = train_test_split(X, y, test_size = 0.50)
```

```
X_train[:5]
```

```
     Sepal length  Sepal width
99             5.7          2.8
51             6.4          3.2
57             4.9          2.4
134            6.1          2.6
59             5.2          2.7
```

Scaling

```
from sklearn.preprocessing import StandardScaler

scaler = StandardScaler()
scaler.fit(X_train)
X_train = scaler.transform(X_train)
X_test = scaler.transform(X_test)
```

```
X_train[:5]
```

```
array([[-0.83327391, -0.12378458],
       [ 0.1454035 ,  1.33250465],
       [-1.95176237, -1.58007382],
       [-0.27402967, -0.8519292 ],
       [-1.5323292 , -0.48785689]])
```

6.1.1.2 Train your model

```
k = 1
```

```
from sklearn.neighbors import KNeighborsClassifier

classifier = KNeighborsClassifier(n_neighbors = k)
classifier.fit(X_train, y_train)
```

```
KNeighborsClassifier(n_neighbors=1)
```

```
y_pred = classifier.predict(X_test)
```

```
from sklearn.metrics
    import classification_report, confusion_matrix, accuracy_score

result = confusion_matrix(y_test, y_pred)
print("Confusion Matrix:")
print(result)
result1 = classification_report(y_test, y_pred)
print("Classification Report:",)
print (result1)
result2 = accuracy_score(y_test,y_pred)
print("Accuracy:",result2)
```

```
Confusion Matrix:
[[13  9]
 [14 14]]
Classification Report:
              precision    recall  f1-score   support

           1       0.48      0.59      0.53        22
           2       0.61      0.50      0.55        28

    accuracy                           0.54        50
   macro avg       0.55      0.55      0.54        50
weighted avg       0.55      0.54      0.54        50
```

```
Accuracy: 0.54
```

6.1.1.3 Best k

```
def knn_tuning(k):
  classifier = KNeighborsClassifier(n_neighbors = k)
  classifier.fit(X_train, y_train)
  y_pred = classifier.predict(X_test)
  accuracy = accuracy_score(y_test,y_pred)
  return accuracy
```

```
knn_tuning(1)
```

```
0.54
```

```
knn_tuning(5)
```

```
0.6
```

```
knn_results = pd.DataFrame({'K':np.arange(1, len(X_train), 5)})
```

```
knn_results['K']
```

```
0     1
1     6
2    11
3    16
4    21
5    26
6    31
7    36
8    41
9    46
Name: K, dtype: int64
```

```
knn_results['Accuracy'] = knn_results['K'].apply(knn_tuning)
knn_results['Accuracy']
```

```
0    0.54
1    0.54
2    0.66
3    0.66
4    0.64
5    0.58
6    0.62
7    0.58
8    0.60
9    0.44
Name: Accuracy, dtype: float64
```

```
knn_results
```

```
     K   Accuracy
0    1   0.54
1    6   0.54
2    11  0.66
3    16  0.66
4    21  0.64
5    26  0.58
6    31  0.62
7    36  0.58
8    41  0.60
9    46  0.44
```

6.1.1.4 Optimize weights

```
def knn_tuning_uniform(k):
  classifier = KNeighborsClassifier(n_neighbors = k, weights= 'uniform')
  classifier.fit(X_train, y_train)
  y_pred = classifier.predict(X_test)
  accuracy = accuracy_score(y_test,y_pred)
  return accuracy
```

```
def knn_tuning_distance(k):
  classifier = KNeighborsClassifier(n_neighbors = k, weights= 'distance')
  classifier.fit(X_train, y_train)
  y_pred = classifier.predict(X_test)
  accuracy = accuracy_score(y_test,y_pred)
  return accuracy
```

```
knn_results['Uniform'] = knn_results['K'].apply(knn_tuning_uniform)
knn_results['Distance'] = knn_results['K'].apply(knn_tuning_distance)
knn_results
```

	K	Accuracy	Uniform	Distance
0	1	0.54	0.54	0.54
1	6	0.54	0.54	0.60
2	11	0.66	0.66	0.58
3	16	0.66	0.66	0.60
4	21	0.64	0.64	0.58

```
5  26     0.58      0.58      0.56
6  31     0.62      0.62      0.58
7  36     0.58      0.58      0.58
8  41     0.60      0.60      0.58
9  46     0.44      0.44      0.56
```

6.1.2   Tutorial – Iris Multiclass Classification Using KNN

Documentation: https://scikit-learn.org/stable/modules/generated/sklearn.neighbors
.KNeighborsClassifier.html

6.1.2.1   Setup

Environment

```
import numpy as np
import pandas as pd
import matplotlib.pyplot as plt
import seaborn as sns
from sklearn import datasets
```

Load the dataset irist

```
iris = datasets.load_iris()
```

```
df = pd.DataFrame({'Sepal length': iris.data[:,0],
                   'Sepal width': iris.data[:,1],
                   'Petal length':iris.data[:,2],
                   'Petal width':iris.data[:,3],
                   'Species':iris.target})
df.head()
```

```
   Sepal length  Sepal width  Petal length  Petal width  Species
0           5.1          3.5           1.4          0.2        0
1           4.9          3.0           1.4          0.2        0
2           4.7          3.2           1.3          0.2        0
3           4.6          3.1           1.5          0.2        0
4           5.0          3.6           1.4          0.2        0
```

```
df.info()
```

```
<class 'pandas.core.frame.DataFrame'>
RangeIndex: 150 entries, 0 to 149
Data columns (total 5 columns):
 #   Column        Non-Null Count   Dtype
---  ------        --------------   -----
 0   Sepal length  150 non-null     float64
 1   Sepal width   150 non-null     float64
 2   Petal length  150 non-null     float64
 3   Petal width   150 non-null     float64
 4   Species       150 non-null     int64
dtypes: float64(4), int64(1)
memory usage: 6.0 KB
```

A simple visualization

```
sns.relplot(data = df, x = 'Sepal length', y = 'Sepal width'
    , hue = 'Species')
```

```
<seaborn.axisgrid.FacetGrid at 0x7e6a2a8a3430>
```

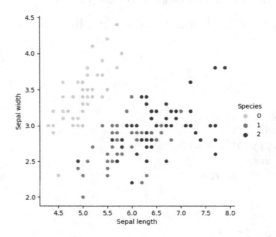

Figure 6.2   A Scatter Plot of Sepal Length VS Sepal Width with Species Differentiation

Train-test split

```
from sklearn.model_selection import train_test_split

X = df[df.columns[:4]]
y = df[df.columns[-1]]
X_train, X_test, y_train, y_test = train_test_split(X, y, test_size = 0.20)
```

```
X_train[:5]
```

	Sepal length	Sepal width	Petal length	Petal width
118	7.7	2.6	6.9	2.3
120	6.9	3.2	5.7	2.3
93	5.0	2.3	3.3	1.0
69	5.6	2.5	3.9	1.1
24	4.8	3.4	1.9	0.2

Scaling

```
from sklearn.preprocessing import StandardScaler

scaler = StandardScaler()
scaler.fit(X_train)
X_train = scaler.transform(X_train)
X_test = scaler.transform(X_test)
```

```
X_train[:5]
```

```
array([[ 2.27184218, -1.02396111,  1.80797693,  1.54156604],
       [ 1.30809119,  0.34894764,  1.12998558,  1.54156604],
       [-0.98081741, -1.71041548, -0.22599712, -0.2074107 ],
       [-0.25800417, -1.25277923,  0.11299856, -0.07287403],
       [-1.22175516,  0.80658389, -1.01698703, -1.28370408]])
```

6.1.2.2 K-Nearest Neighbors

```
k = 1
```

```
from sklearn.neighbors import KNeighborsClassifier

classifier = KNeighborsClassifier(n_neighbors = k)
classifier.fit(X_train, y_train)
```

```
KNeighborsClassifier(n_neighbors=1)
```

```
y_pred = classifier.predict(X_test)
```

```
from sklearn.metrics
    import classification_report, confusion_matrix, accuracy_score

result = confusion_matrix(y_test, y_pred)
print("Confusion Matrix:")
print(result)
result1 = classification_report(y_test, y_pred)
print("Classification Report:",)
print (result1)
result2 = accuracy_score(y_test,y_pred)
print("Accuracy:",result2)
```

```
Confusion Matrix:
[[ 8  0  0]
 [ 0  8  2]
 [ 0  0 12]]
Classification Report:
              precision    recall  f1-score   support

           0       1.00      1.00      1.00         8
           1       1.00      0.80      0.89        10
           2       0.86      1.00      0.92        12

    accuracy                           0.93        30
   macro avg       0.95      0.93      0.94        30
weighted avg       0.94      0.93      0.93        30

Accuracy: 0.9333333333333333
```

6.1.2.3 Best k

```
def knn_tuning(k):
  classifier = KNeighborsClassifier(n_neighbors = k)
  classifier.fit(X_train, y_train)
  y_pred = classifier.predict(X_test)
  accuracy = accuracy_score(y_test,y_pred)
  return accuracy
```

```
knn_tuning(1)
```

0.9333333333333333

```
knn_tuning(5)
```

0.9333333333333333

```
knn_results = pd.DataFrame({'K':np.arange(1, len(X_train), 5)})
```

```
knn_results['K']
```

```
0        1
1        6
2       11
3       16
4       21
5       26
6       31
7       36
8       41
9       46
10      51
11      56
12      61
13      66
14      71
15      76
16      81
17      86
18      91
19      96
20     101
21     106
22     111
23     116
Name: K, dtype: int64
```

```
knn_results['Accuracy'] = knn_results['K'].apply(knn_tuning)
knn_results['Accuracy']
```

```
0      0.933333
1      1.000000
2      1.000000
3      0.966667
4      0.966667
5      0.966667
6      0.966667
7      0.933333
8      0.933333
9      0.933333
10     0.933333
11     0.933333
12     0.833333
13     0.833333
14     0.866667
15     0.666667
16     0.600000
17     0.633333
18     0.633333
19     0.600000
20     0.600000
21     0.600000
22     0.600000
23     0.566667
Name: Accuracy, dtype: float64
```

knn_results

```
     K    Accuracy
0    1    0.933333
1    6    1.000000
2    11   1.000000
3    16   0.966667
4    21   0.966667
5    26   0.966667
6    31   0.966667
7    36   0.933333
8    41   0.933333
9    46   0.933333
10   51   0.933333
11   56   0.933333
12   61   0.833333
13   66   0.833333
14   71   0.866667
15   76   0.666667
16   81   0.600000
17   86   0.633333
18   91   0.633333
19   96   0.600000
20   101  0.600000
21   106  0.600000
22   111  0.600000
23   116  0.566667
```

6.1.2.4 Optimize weights

```
def knn_tuning_uniform(k):
  classifier = KNeighborsClassifier(n_neighbors = k, weights= 'uniform')
  classifier.fit(X_train, y_train)
  y_pred = classifier.predict(X_test)
  accuracy = accuracy_score(y_test,y_pred)
  return accuracy
```

```
def knn_tuning_distance(k):
  classifier = KNeighborsClassifier(n_neighbors = k, weights= 'distance')
  classifier.fit(X_train, y_train)
  y_pred = classifier.predict(X_test)
  accuracy = accuracy_score(y_test,y_pred)
  return accuracy
```

```
knn_results['Uniform'] = knn_results['K'].apply(knn_tuning_uniform)
knn_results['Distance'] = knn_results['K'].apply(knn_tuning_distance)
knn_results
```

	K	Accuracy	Uniform	Distance
0	1	0.933333	0.933333	0.933333
1	6	1.000000	1.000000	0.966667
2	11	1.000000	1.000000	1.000000
3	16	0.966667	0.966667	0.966667
4	21	0.966667	0.966667	0.966667
5	26	0.966667	0.966667	0.966667
6	31	0.966667	0.966667	0.966667
7	36	0.933333	0.933333	0.966667
8	41	0.933333	0.933333	0.966667
9	46	0.933333	0.933333	0.933333
10	51	0.933333	0.933333	0.933333
11	56	0.933333	0.933333	0.933333
12	61	0.833333	0.833333	0.933333
13	66	0.833333	0.833333	0.966667
14	71	0.866667	0.866667	0.966667
15	76	0.666667	0.666667	0.966667
16	81	0.600000	0.600000	0.966667
17	86	0.633333	0.633333	0.966667
18	91	0.633333	0.633333	0.966667
19	96	0.600000	0.600000	0.966667
20	101	0.600000	0.600000	0.966667
21	106	0.600000	0.600000	0.966667
22	111	0.600000	0.600000	0.966667
23	116	0.566667	0.566667	0.966667

6.1.3 Tutorial – Iris Binary Classification Using RNN

Documentation: https://scikit-learn.org/stable/modules/generated/sklearn.neighbors
.RadiusNeighborsClassifier.html

6.1.3.1 Setup

```
import numpy as np
import pandas as pd
import matplotlib.pyplot as plt
import seaborn as sns
from sklearn import datasets
```

```
iris = datasets.load_iris()
```

```
df = pd.DataFrame({'Sepal length': iris.data[:,0],
                   'Sepal width': iris.data[:,1],
                   'Petal length':iris.data[:,2],
                   'Petal width':iris.data[:,3],
                   'Species':iris.target})
df.head()
```

	Sepal length	Sepal width	Petal length	Petal width	Species
0	5.1	3.5	1.4	0.2	0
1	4.9	3.0	1.4	0.2	0
2	4.7	3.2	1.3	0.2	0
3	4.6	3.1	1.5	0.2	0
4	5.0	3.6	1.4	0.2	0

```
df = df[df['Species'] != 0]
```

```
df.info()
```

```
<class 'pandas.core.frame.DataFrame'>
Int64Index: 100 entries, 50 to 149
Data columns (total 5 columns):
 #   Column        Non-Null Count  Dtype
---  ------        --------------  -----
 0   Sepal length  100 non-null    float64
 1   Sepal width   100 non-null    float64
 2   Petal length  100 non-null    float64
 3   Petal width   100 non-null    float64
 4   Species       100 non-null    int64
dtypes: float64(4), int64(1)
memory usage: 4.7 KB
```

```
sns.relplot(data = df, x = 'Sepal length', y = 'Sepal width'
    , hue = 'Species')
```

```
<seaborn.axisgrid.FacetGrid at 0x7b63ed91fb20>
```

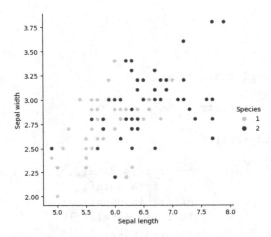

Figure 6.3 A Scatter Plot of Sepal Length VS Sepal Width with Species Differentiation

```
from sklearn.model_selection import train_test_split

X = df[df.columns[:2]]
y = df[df.columns[-1]]
X_train, X_test, y_train, y_test = train_test_split(X, y, test_size = 0.20)
```

```
X_train[:5]
```

	Sepal length	Sepal width
113	5.7	2.5
53	5.5	2.3
70	5.9	3.2
94	5.6	2.7
71	6.1	2.8

```
from sklearn.preprocessing import StandardScaler

scaler = StandardScaler()
scaler.fit(X_train)
X_train = scaler.transform(X_train)
X_test = scaler.transform(X_test)
```

```
X_train[:5]
```

```
array([[-0.85622399, -1.19846152],
       [-1.1718826 , -1.83551748],
       [-0.54056538,  1.03123433],
       [-1.0140533 , -0.56140556],
       [-0.22490676, -0.24287758]])
```

6.1.3.2 R-Nearest Neighbors

```
r = 1
```

```
from sklearn.neighbors import RadiusNeighborsClassifier

classifier = RadiusNeighborsClassifier(radius = r)
classifier.fit(X_train, y_train)
```

```
RadiusNeighborsClassifier(radius=1)
```

```
y_pred = classifier.predict(X_test)
```

```
from sklearn.metrics
    import classification_report, confusion_matrix, accuracy_score

result = confusion_matrix(y_test, y_pred)
print("Confusion Matrix:")
print(result)
result1 = classification_report(y_test, y_pred)
print("Classification Report:",)
print (result1)
result2 = accuracy_score(y_test,y_pred)
print("Accuracy:",result2)
```

```
Confusion Matrix:
[[4 4]
 [4 8]]
Classification Report:
              precision    recall  f1-score   support

           1       0.50      0.50      0.50         8
           2       0.67      0.67      0.67        12

    accuracy                           0.60        20
   macro avg       0.58      0.58      0.58        20
weighted avg       0.60      0.60      0.60        20

Accuracy: 0.6
```

6.1.3.3 Best r

```
def rnn_tuning(r):
  classifier = RadiusNeighborsClassifier(radius = r)
  classifier.fit(X_train, y_train)
  y_pred = classifier.predict(X_test)
  accuracy = accuracy_score(y_test,y_pred)
  return accuracy
```

```
rnn_tuning(1)
```

0.6

```
rnn_tuning(5)
```

0.45

```
rnn_results = pd.DataFrame({'R':np.arange(1, 10, 0.5)})
```

```
rnn_results['R']
```

```
0      1.0
1      1.5
2      2.0
3      2.5
4      3.0
5      3.5
6      4.0
7      4.5
8      5.0
9      5.5
10     6.0
11     6.5
12     7.0
13     7.5
14     8.0
15     8.5
16     9.0
17     9.5
Name: R, dtype: float64
```

```
rnn_results['Accuracy'] = rnn_results['R'].apply(rnn_tuning)
rnn_results['Accuracy']
```

```
0      0.60
1      0.55
2      0.55
3      0.60
4      0.55
5      0.50
6      0.45
7      0.45
8      0.45
9      0.45
10     0.40
11     0.40
12     0.40
13     0.40
14     0.40
15     0.40
16     0.40
17     0.40
Name: Accuracy, dtype: float64
```

```
rnn_results
```

```
      R  Accuracy
0   1.0      0.60
1   1.5      0.55
2   2.0      0.55
3   2.5      0.60
4   3.0      0.55
5   3.5      0.50
6   4.0      0.45
7   4.5      0.45
8   5.0      0.45
9   5.5      0.45
10  6.0      0.40
11  6.5      0.40
12  7.0      0.40
13  7.5      0.40
14  8.0      0.40
15  8.5      0.40
16  9.0      0.40
17  9.5      0.40
```

6.1.3.4 Optimize weights

```
def rnn_tuning_uniform(r):
  classifier = RadiusNeighborsClassifier(radius = r, weights= 'uniform')
  classifier.fit(X_train, y_train)
  y_pred = classifier.predict(X_test)
  accuracy = accuracy_score(y_test,y_pred)
  return accuracy
```

```
def rnn_tuning_distance(k):
  classifier = RadiusNeighborsClassifier(radius = k, weights= 'distance')
  classifier.fit(X_train, y_train)
  y_pred = classifier.predict(X_test)
  accuracy = accuracy_score(y_test,y_pred)
  return accuracy
```

```
rnn_results['Uniform'] = rnn_results['R'].apply(rnn_tuning_uniform)
rnn_results['Distance'] = rnn_results['R'].apply(rnn_tuning_distance)
rnn_results
```

```
     R  Accuracy  Uniform  Distance
0  1.0      0.60     0.60      0.50
1  1.5      0.55     0.55      0.45
2  2.0      0.55     0.55      0.45
3  2.5      0.60     0.60      0.45
4  3.0      0.55     0.55      0.45
5  3.5      0.50     0.50      0.45
6  4.0      0.45     0.45      0.45
7  4.5      0.45     0.45      0.45
8  5.0      0.45     0.45      0.45
```

```
9    5.5    0.45    0.45    0.45
10   6.0    0.40    0.40    0.45
11   6.5    0.40    0.40    0.45
12   7.0    0.40    0.40    0.45
13   7.5    0.40    0.40    0.45
14   8.0    0.40    0.40    0.45
15   8.5    0.40    0.40    0.45
16   9.0    0.40    0.40    0.45
17   9.5    0.40    0.40    0.45
```

6.1.4   Tutorial – Iris Multiclass Classification Using RNN

Documentation: https://scikit-learn.org/stable/modules/generated/sklearn.neighbors
.RadiusNeighborsClassifier.html

6.1.4.1   Setup

```python
import numpy as np
import pandas as pd
import matplotlib.pyplot as plt
import seaborn as sns
from sklearn import datasets
```

```python
iris = datasets.load_iris()
```

```python
df = pd.DataFrame({'Sepal length': iris.data[:,0],
                   'Sepal width': iris.data[:,1],
                   'Petal length':iris.data[:,2],
                   'Petal width':iris.data[:,3],
                   'Species':iris.target})
df.head()
```

	Sepal length	Sepal width	Petal length	Petal width	Species
0	5.1	3.5	1.4	0.2	0
1	4.9	3.0	1.4	0.2	0
2	4.7	3.2	1.3	0.2	0
3	4.6	3.1	1.5	0.2	0
4	5.0	3.6	1.4	0.2	0

```python
df.info()
```

```
<class 'pandas.core.frame.DataFrame'>
RangeIndex: 150 entries, 0 to 149
Data columns (total 5 columns):
 #   Column        Non-Null Count   Dtype
---  ------        --------------   -----
 0   Sepal length  150 non-null     float64
 1   Sepal width   150 non-null     float64
 2   Petal length  150 non-null     float64
 3   Petal width   150 non-null     float64
 4   Species       150 non-null     int64
dtypes: float64(4), int64(1)
```

memory usage: 6.0 KB

```
sns.relplot(data = df, x = 'Sepal length', y = 'Sepal width'
    , hue = 'Species')
```

<seaborn.axisgrid.FacetGrid at 0x79783b73e890>

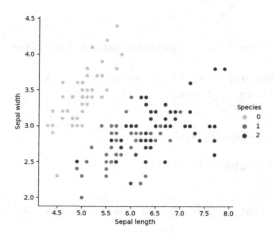

Figure 6.4 A Scatter Plot of Sepal Length VS Sepal Width with Species Differentiation

```
from sklearn.model_selection import train_test_split

X = df[df.columns[:4]]
y = df[df.columns[-1]]
X_train, X_test, y_train, y_test = train_test_split(X, y, test_size = 0.20)
```

```
X_train[:5]
```

	Sepal length	Sepal width	Petal length	Petal width
71	6.1	2.8	4.0	1.3
97	6.2	2.9	4.3	1.3
95	5.7	3.0	4.2	1.2
129	7.2	3.0	5.8	1.6
148	6.2	3.4	5.4	2.3

```
from sklearn.preprocessing import StandardScaler

scaler = StandardScaler()
scaler.fit(X_train)
X_train = scaler.transform(X_train)
X_test = scaler.transform(X_test)
```

```
X_train[:5]
```

```
array([[ 0.3344104 , -0.62374154,  0.16477965,  0.15444797],
       [ 0.46020741, -0.40163773,  0.33475294,  0.15444797],
       [-0.16877766, -0.17953392,  0.27809517,  0.02300289],
       [ 1.71817755, -0.17953392,  1.18461934,  0.54878321],
       [ 0.46020741,  0.70888134,  0.9579883 ,  1.46889877]])
```

6.1.4.2 R-Nearest Neighbors

```
r = 1
```

```
from sklearn.neighbors import RadiusNeighborsClassifier

classifier = RadiusNeighborsClassifier(radius = r)
classifier.fit(X_train, y_train)
```

```
RadiusNeighborsClassifier(radius=1)
```

```
y_pred = classifier.predict(X_test)
```

```
from sklearn.metrics
    import classification_report, confusion_matrix, accuracy_score

result = confusion_matrix(y_test, y_pred)
print("Confusion Matrix:")
print(result)
result1 = classification_report(y_test, y_pred)
print("Classification Report:",)
print (result1)
result2 = accuracy_score(y_test,y_pred)
print("Accuracy:",result2)
```

```
Confusion Matrix:
[[ 8  0  0]
 [ 0 12  0]
 [ 0  0 10]]
Classification Report:
              precision    recall  f1-score   support

           0       1.00      1.00      1.00         8
           1       1.00      1.00      1.00        12
           2       1.00      1.00      1.00        10

    accuracy                           1.00        30
   macro avg       1.00      1.00      1.00        30
weighted avg       1.00      1.00      1.00        30

Accuracy: 1.0
```

6.1.4.3 Best r

```
def rnn_tuning(r):
  classifier = RadiusNeighborsClassifier(radius = r)
  classifier.fit(X_train, y_train)
  y_pred = classifier.predict(X_test)
  accuracy = accuracy_score(y_test,y_pred)
  return accuracy
```

```
rnn_tuning(1)
```

1.0

```
rnn_tuning(5)
```

0.4

```
rnn_results = pd.DataFrame({'R':np.arange(1, 10, 0.5)})
```

```
rnn_results['R']
```

```
0     1.0
1     1.5
2     2.0
3     2.5
4     3.0
5     3.5
6     4.0
7     4.5
8     5.0
9     5.5
10    6.0
11    6.5
12    7.0
13    7.5
14    8.0
15    8.5
16    9.0
17    9.5
Name: R, dtype: float64
```

```
rnn_results['Accuracy'] = rnn_results['R'].apply(rnn_tuning)
rnn_results['Accuracy']
```

```
0     1.000000
1     0.933333
2     0.866667
3     0.900000
4     0.866667
5     0.700000
```

```
6      0.600000
7      0.500000
8      0.400000
9      0.366667
10     0.300000
11     0.266667
12     0.266667
13     0.266667
14     0.266667
15     0.266667
16     0.266667
17     0.266667
Name: Accuracy, dtype: float64
```

```
rnn_results
```

```
      R   Accuracy
0    1.0  1.000000
1    1.5  0.933333
2    2.0  0.866667
3    2.5  0.900000
4    3.0  0.866667
5    3.5  0.700000
6    4.0  0.600000
7    4.5  0.500000
8    5.0  0.400000
9    5.5  0.366667
10   6.0  0.300000
11   6.5  0.266667
12   7.0  0.266667
13   7.5  0.266667
14   8.0  0.266667
15   8.5  0.266667
16   9.0  0.266667
17   9.5  0.266667
```

6.1.4.4 *Optimize Weights*

```python
def rnn_tuning_uniform(r):
    classifier = RadiusNeighborsClassifier(radius = r, weights= 'uniform')
    classifier.fit(X_train, y_train)
    y_pred = classifier.predict(X_test)
    accuracy = accuracy_score(y_test,y_pred)
    return accuracy
```

```python
def rnn_tuning_distance(k):
    classifier = RadiusNeighborsClassifier(radius = k, weights= 'distance')
    classifier.fit(X_train, y_train)
    y_pred = classifier.predict(X_test)
    accuracy = accuracy_score(y_test,y_pred)
    return accuracy
```

```
rnn_results['Uniform'] = rnn_results['R'].apply(rnn_tuning_uniform)
rnn_results['Distance'] = rnn_results['R'].apply(rnn_tuning_distance)
rnn_results
```

```
      R   Accuracy   Uniform   Distance
0   1.0   1.000000   1.000000  1.000000
1   1.5   0.933333   0.933333  0.966667
2   2.0   0.866667   0.866667  1.000000
3   2.5   0.900000   0.900000  1.000000
4   3.0   0.866667   0.866667  0.966667
5   3.5   0.700000   0.700000  0.966667
6   4.0   0.600000   0.600000  0.966667
7   4.5   0.500000   0.500000  0.966667
8   5.0   0.400000   0.400000  0.966667
9   5.5   0.366667   0.366667  0.966667
10  6.0   0.300000   0.300000  0.966667
11  6.5   0.266667   0.266667  0.966667
12  7.0   0.266667   0.266667  0.966667
13  7.5   0.266667   0.266667  0.966667
14  8.0   0.266667   0.266667  0.966667
15  8.5   0.266667   0.266667  0.966667
16  9.0   0.266667   0.266667  0.966667
17  9.5   0.266667   0.266667  0.966667
```

6.1.5   Case Study – Breast Cancer Classification Using Nearest Neighbor Classifiers

We will create a tutorial for the Nearest Neighbor algorithm, including K-Nearest Neighbors (KNN) and Radius Neighbors (RNN), using the Breast Cancer dataset. We will demonstrate how the choices of k and radius affect the classification results and compare the performance of different models. To aid understanding, we will visualize the prediction results.

6.1.5.1   Setup

Import necessary libraries and load the Breast Cancer dataset.

```
import numpy as np
import pandas as pd
import matplotlib.pyplot as plt
from sklearn.datasets import load_breast_cancer
from sklearn.model_selection import train_test_split
from sklearn.neighbors
    import KNeighborsClassifier, RadiusNeighborsClassifier
from sklearn.metrics
    import accuracy_score, classification_report, confusion_matrix

# Load the Breast Cancer dataset
data = load_breast_cancer()
X = pd.DataFrame(data.data, columns=data.feature_names)
y = pd.Series(data.target)
```

6.1.5.2 Split the Dataset into Training and Testing Set

```
# Split the dataset into training and testing sets (80% train, 20% test)
X_train, X_test, y_train, y_test =
    train_test_split(X, y, test_size=0.2, random_state=42)
```

6.1.5.3 Create and Train the K-Nearest Neighbors (KNN) Model

```
# Create a list of k values for KNN
k_values = [1, 5, 11, 15, 21]

# Train KNN models with different k values and store the results
knn_results = {}
for k in k_values:
    knn_model = KNeighborsClassifier(n_neighbors=k)
    knn_model.fit(X_train, y_train)
    y_pred_knn = knn_model.predict(X_test)
    knn_results[k] = {
        'model': knn_model,
        'y_pred': y_pred_knn,
        'accuracy': accuracy_score(y_test, y_pred_knn)
    }
```

6.1.5.4 Create and Train the Radius Neighbors (RNN) Model

```
# Create a list of radius values for RNN
radius_values = [350, 400, 450, 500, 550, 600]

# Train RNN models with different radius values and store the results
rnn_results = {}
for radius in radius_values:
    rnn_model = RadiusNeighborsClassifier(radius=radius)
    rnn_model.fit(X_train, y_train)
    y_pred_rnn = rnn_model.predict(X_test)
    rnn_results[radius] = {
        'model': rnn_model,
        'y_pred': y_pred_rnn,
        'accuracy': accuracy_score(y_test, y_pred_rnn)
    }
```

6.1.5.5 Compare the Performance of KNN and RNN Models

```
# Print the accuracy of KNN models
print("KNN Accuracy:")
for k, result in knn_results.items():
    print(f"K = {k}: {result['accuracy']:.2f}")

# Print the accuracy of RNN models
print("\nRNN Accuracy:")
```

```
for radius, result in rnn_results.items():
    print(f"Radius = {radius}: {result['accuracy']:.2f}")
```

```
KNN Accuracy:
K = 1: 0.93
K = 5: 0.96
K = 11: 0.98
K = 15: 0.96
K = 21: 0.96

RNN Accuracy:
Radius = 350: 0.94
Radius = 400: 0.94
Radius = 450: 0.94
Radius = 500: 0.91
Radius = 550: 0.90
Radius = 600: 0.90
```

6.1.5.6   Visualize the Prediction Results for KNN and RNN

```
# Visualize the accuracy of KNN models
k_values = [k for k in knn_results.keys()]
k_accuracies = [result['accuracy'] for result in knn_results.values()]

plt.figure(figsize=(8, 4))
plt.plot(k_values, k_accuracies, marker='o')
plt.xlabel('K Value')
plt.ylabel('Accuracy')
plt.title('Accuracy of KNN models')
plt.grid(True)
plt.show()

# Visualize the accuracy of RNN models
radius_values = [radius for radius in rnn_results.keys()]
radius_accuracies = [result['accuracy'] for result in rnn_results.values()]

plt.figure(figsize=(8, 4))
plt.plot(radius_values, radius_accuracies, marker='o')
plt.xlabel('Radius Value')
plt.ylabel('Accuracy')
plt.title('Accuracy of RNN models')
plt.grid(True)
plt.show()
```

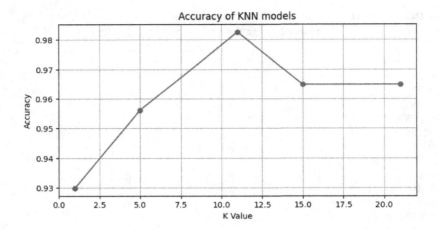

Figure 6.5 Accuracy of KNN Models

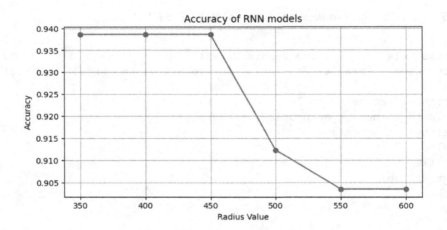

Figure 6.6 Accuracy of RNN Models

6.1.5.7 K and R

Feel free to experiment with different values of k and radius to observe how they affect the accuracy of the models.

6.2 DECISION TREE CLASSIFIERS

Decision Trees are powerful machine learning algorithms that are widely used for classification tasks due to their interpretability and simplicity. This section introduces Decision Tree Classifiers using the Scikit-learn package, covering classification, visualization, and model tuning aspects.

Decision Tree Classifiers are versatile algorithms used for both classification and regression tasks. They operate by recursively splitting the dataset based on the most informative features to make predictions. Visualizing Decision Trees is essential for interpreting model decisions and gaining insights into how the algorithm works. Decision Trees can be fine-tuned by selecting different splitting criteria and applying pruning techniques to improve model generalization and prevent overfitting. In this section, you will learn how to implement Decision Tree classification, visualize the result, and tune your decision tree model using Scikit-learn.

6.2.1   Tutorial – Iris Binary Classification Using Decision Tree

Documentation: https://scikit-learn.org/stable/modules/generated/sklearn.tree.DecisionTreeClassifier.html

6.2.1.1   Setup

```
import numpy as np
import pandas as pd
import matplotlib.pyplot as plt
import seaborn as sns
from sklearn import datasets
```

6.2.1.2   Load the Dataset iris

```
iris = datasets.load_iris()
```

```
df = pd.DataFrame({'Sepal length': iris.data[:,0],
    'Sepal width': iris.data[:,1],
    'Petal length':iris.data[:,2],
    'Petal width':iris.data[:,3],
    'Species':iris.target})
df.head()
```

	Sepal length	Sepal width	Petal length	Petal width	Species
0	5.1	3.5	1.4	0.2	0
1	4.9	3.0	1.4	0.2	0
2	4.7	3.2	1.3	0.2	0
3	4.6	3.1	1.5	0.2	0
4	5.0	3.6	1.4	0.2	0

```
df = df[df['Species'] !=0]
```

```
df.info()
```

```
<class 'pandas.core.frame.DataFrame'>
Int64Index: 100 entries, 50 to 149
Data columns (total 5 columns):
 #   Column        Non-Null Count   Dtype
---  ------        --------------   -----
 0   Sepal length  100 non-null     float64
 1   Sepal width   100 non-null     float64
 2   Petal length  100 non-null     float64
```

```
3    Petal width     100 non-null    float64
4    Species         100 non-null    int64
dtypes: float64(4), int64(1)
memory usage: 4.7 KB
```

```
sns.relplot(data = df, x = 'Sepal length', y = 'Sepal width'
    , hue = 'Species')
```

```
<seaborn.axisgrid.FacetGrid at 0x7efc06708a90>
```

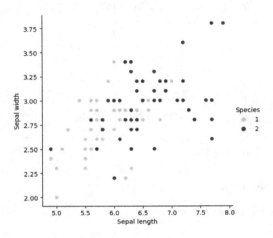

Figure 6.7   A Scatter Plot of Sepal Length VS Sepal Width with Species Differentiation

6.2.1.3 Train-test Split

Training and testing datasets are split with test_size as ratio. Here we use 80% for training and 20% for testing.

```
from sklearn.model_selection import train_test_split

X = df[df.columns[:4]]
y = df[df.columns[-1]]
X_train, X_test, y_train, y_test = train_test_split(X, y, test_size = 0.20)
```

```
X_train
```

	Sepal length	Sepal width	Petal length	Petal width
76	6.8	2.8	4.8	1.4
51	6.4	3.2	4.5	1.5
67	5.8	2.7	4.1	1.0
109	7.2	3.6	6.1	2.5
104	6.5	3.0	5.8	2.2
..	...	...	...	...
58	6.6	2.9	4.6	1.3
108	6.7	2.5	5.8	1.8
117	7.7	3.8	6.7	2.2

| 55 | 5.7 | 2.8 | 4.5 | 1.3 |
| 66 | 5.6 | 3.0 | 4.5 | 1.5 |

[80 rows x 4 columns]

6.2.1.4 Train Your Model

```
from sklearn.tree import DecisionTreeClassifier
classifier = DecisionTreeClassifier()
classifier.fit(X_train, y_train)
```

```
DecisionTreeClassifier()
```

6.2.1.5 Evaluate Your Model

```
y_pred = classifier.predict(X_test)
```

```
from sklearn.metrics
    import classification_report, confusion_matrix, accuracy_score
print(confusion_matrix(y_test, y_pred))
print('Accuracy:', accuracy_score(y_test,y_pred))
```

```
[[10  0]
 [ 1  9]]
Accuracy: 0.95
```

6.2.1.6 Visualize the Result

```
from sklearn import tree

text_representation = tree.export_text(classifier)
print(text_representation)
```

```
|--- feature_3 <= 1.75
|   |--- feature_2 <= 4.95
|   |   |--- feature_3 <= 1.65
|   |   |   |--- class: 1
|   |   |--- feature_3 >  1.65
|   |   |   |--- class: 2
|   |--- feature_2 >  4.95
|   |   |--- feature_3 <= 1.55
|   |   |   |--- class: 2
|   |   |--- feature_3 >  1.55
|   |   |   |--- class: 1
|--- feature_3 >  1.75
|   |--- feature_2 <= 4.85
|   |   |--- feature_1 <= 3.10
|   |   |   |--- class: 2
|   |   |--- feature_1 >  3.10
|   |   |   |--- class: 1
```

```
|   |--- feature_2 >  4.85
|   |   |--- class: 2
```

```
import matplotlib.pyplot as plt

fig = plt.figure(figsize=(10,8))
_ = tree.plot_tree(classifier,
                   feature_names=iris.feature_names,
                   class_names=iris.target_names,
                   filled=True)
```

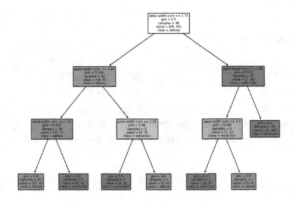

Figure 6.8   A Default Decision Tree

6.2.1.7   Tune the Model

Change hyperparameters, such as criterion, max_depth.

```
classifier = DecisionTreeClassifier(criterion= 'entropy')
classifier.fit(X_train, y_train)

y_pred = classifier.predict(X_test)

print(confusion_matrix(y_test, y_pred))
print('Accuracy:', accuracy_score(y_test,y_pred))

text_representation = tree.export_text(classifier)
print(text_representation)

fig = plt.figure(figsize=(10,8))
_ = tree.plot_tree(classifier,
                   feature_names=iris.feature_names,
                   class_names=iris.target_names,
                   filled=True)
```

```
[[10  0]
 [ 1  9]]
Accuracy: 0.95
|--- feature_3 <= 1.75
|   |--- feature_2 <= 4.95
|   |   |--- feature_3 <= 1.65
|   |   |   |--- class: 1
|   |   |--- feature_3 >  1.65
|   |   |   |--- class: 2
|   |--- feature_2 >  4.95
|   |   |--- feature_3 <= 1.55
|   |   |   |--- class: 2
|   |   |--- feature_3 >  1.55
|   |   |   |--- class: 1
|--- feature_3 >  1.75
|   |--- feature_2 <= 4.85
|   |   |--- feature_1 <= 3.10
|   |   |   |--- class: 2
|   |   |--- feature_1 >  3.10
|   |   |   |--- class: 1
|   |--- feature_2 >  4.85
|   |   |--- class: 2
```

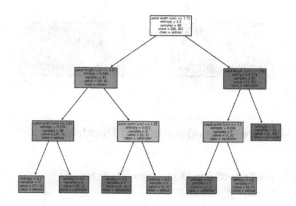

Figure 6.9 A Decision Tree Trained with Entropy

```
classifier = DecisionTreeClassifier(max_depth=1)
classifier.fit(X_train, y_train)

y_pred = classifier.predict(X_test)

print(confusion_matrix(y_test, y_pred))
print('Accuracy:', accuracy_score(y_test,y_pred))

text_representation = tree.export_text(classifier)
print(text_representation)
```

```
fig = plt.figure()
_ = tree.plot_tree(classifier,
                   feature_names=iris.feature_names,
                   class_names=iris.target_names,
                   filled=True)
```

```
[[10  0]
 [ 1  9]]
Accuracy: 0.95
|--- feature_3 <= 1.75
|    |--- class: 1
|--- feature_3 >  1.75
|    |--- class: 2
```

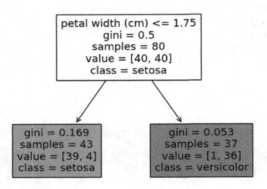

Figure 6.10 A Decision Tree Trained with Max Depth as 1

```
classifier = DecisionTreeClassifier(max_depth=2)
classifier.fit(X_train, y_train)

y_pred = classifier.predict(X_test)

print(confusion_matrix(y_test, y_pred))
print('Accuracy:', accuracy_score(y_test,y_pred))

text_representation = tree.export_text(classifier)
print(text_representation)

fig = plt.figure(figsize=(10,8))
_ = tree.plot_tree(classifier,
                   feature_names=iris.feature_names,
                   class_names=iris.target_names,
                   filled=True)
```

```
[[10  0]
 [ 0 10]]
Accuracy: 1.0
|--- feature_3 <= 1.75
|    |--- feature_2 <= 4.95
|    |    |--- class: 1
|    |--- feature_2 >  4.95
|    |    |--- class: 2
|--- feature_3 >  1.75
|    |--- feature_2 <= 4.85
|    |    |--- class: 2
|    |--- feature_2 >  4.85
|    |    |--- class: 2
```

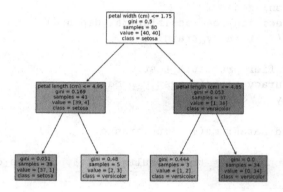

Figure 6.11   A Decision Tree Trained with Max Depth as 3

```
classifier = DecisionTreeClassifier(max_depth=3)
classifier.fit(X_train, y_train)

y_pred = classifier.predict(X_test)

print(confusion_matrix(y_test, y_pred))
print('Accuracy:', accuracy_score(y_test,y_pred))

text_representation = tree.export_text(classifier)
print(text_representation)
```

```
[[10  0]
 [ 1  9]]
Accuracy: 0.95
|--- feature_3 <= 1.75
|    |--- feature_2 <= 4.95
|    |    |--- feature_3 <= 1.65
|    |    |    |--- class: 1
|    |    |--- feature_3 >  1.65
```

```
|   |   |   |--- class: 2
|   |--- feature_2 >  4.95
|   |   |--- feature_3 <= 1.55
|   |   |   |--- class: 2
|   |   |--- feature_3 >  1.55
|   |   |   |--- class: 1
|--- feature_3 >  1.75
|   |--- feature_2 <= 4.85
|   |   |--- feature_1 <= 3.10
|   |   |   |--- class: 2
|   |   |--- feature_1 >  3.10
|   |   |   |--- class: 1
|   |--- feature_2 >  4.85
|   |   |--- class: 2
```

```python
def tree_depth_tuning(d):
    classifier = DecisionTreeClassifier(max_depth=d)
    classifier.fit(X_train, y_train)

    y_pred = classifier.predict(X_test)
    accuracy = accuracy_score(y_test,y_pred)
    return accuracy
```

```python
tree_results = pd.DataFrame({'D':np.arange(1, 10)})
```

```python
tree_results['Accuracy'] = tree_results['D'].apply(tree_depth_tuning)
tree_results
```

```
    D  Accuracy
0   1     0.95
1   2     1.00
2   3     0.95
3   4     0.95
4   5     0.95
5   6     0.95
6   7     0.95
7   8     0.95
8   9     0.95
```

6.2.2 Tutorial – Iris Multiclass Classification Using Decision Tree

Documentation: https://scikit-learn.org/stable/modules/generated/sklearn.tree.DecisionTreeClassifier.html

6.2.2.1 Setup

```python
import numpy as np
import pandas as pd
import matplotlib.pyplot as plt
import seaborn as sns
from sklearn import datasets
```

6.2.2.2 Load the Dataset iris

```
iris = datasets.load_iris()
```

```
df = pd.DataFrame({'Sepal length': iris.data[:,0],
    'Sepal width': iris.data[:,1],
    'Petal length':iris.data[:,2],
    'Petal width':iris.data[:,3],
    'Species':iris.target})
df.head()
```

	Sepal length	Sepal width	Petal length	Petal width	Species
0	5.1	3.5	1.4	0.2	0
1	4.9	3.0	1.4	0.2	0
2	4.7	3.2	1.3	0.2	0
3	4.6	3.1	1.5	0.2	0
4	5.0	3.6	1.4	0.2	0

```
df.info()
```

```
<class 'pandas.core.frame.DataFrame'>
RangeIndex: 150 entries, 0 to 149
Data columns (total 5 columns):
 #   Column        Non-Null Count  Dtype
---  ------        --------------  -----
 0   Sepal length  150 non-null    float64
 1   Sepal width   150 non-null    float64
 2   Petal length  150 non-null    float64
 3   Petal width   150 non-null    float64
 4   Species       150 non-null    int64
dtypes: float64(4), int64(1)
memory usage: 6.0 KB
```

```
sns.relplot(data = df, x = 'Sepal length', y = 'Sepal width'
    , hue = 'Species')
```

```
<seaborn.axisgrid.FacetGrid at 0x7f10608b6b20>
```

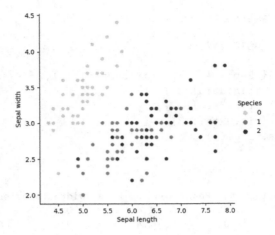

Figure 6.12 A Scatter Plot of Sepal Length VS Sepal Width with Species Differentiation

6.2.2.3 *Train-test Split*

Training and testing datasets are split with test_size as ratio. Here we use 80% for training and 20% for testing.

```
from sklearn.model_selection import train_test_split

X = df[df.columns[:4]]
y = df[df.columns[-1]]
X_train, X_test, y_train, y_test = train_test_split(X, y, test_size = 0.20)
```

```
X_train
```

	Sepal length	Sepal width	Petal length	Petal width
21	5.1	3.7	1.5	0.4
66	5.6	3.0	4.5	1.5
34	4.9	3.1	1.5	0.2
80	5.5	2.4	3.8	1.1
79	5.7	2.6	3.5	1.0
..	...	...	...	...
93	5.0	2.3	3.3	1.0
115	6.4	3.2	5.3	2.3
8	4.4	2.9	1.4	0.2
149	5.9	3.0	5.1	1.8
43	5.0	3.5	1.6	0.6

[120 rows x 4 columns]

6.2.2.4 *Train Your Model*

```
from sklearn.tree import DecisionTreeClassifier
classifier = DecisionTreeClassifier()
classifier.fit(X_train, y_train)
```

```
DecisionTreeClassifier()
```

6.2.2.5 *Evaluate Your Model*

```
y_pred = classifier.predict(X_test)
```

```
from sklearn.metrics
    import classification_report, confusion_matrix, accuracy_score
print(confusion_matrix(y_test, y_pred))
print('Accuracy:', accuracy_score(y_test,y_pred))
```

```
[[12  0  0]
 [ 0  9  1]
 [ 0  1  7]]
Accuracy: 0.9333333333333333
```

6.2.2.6 *Visualize the Result*

```
from sklearn import tree

text_representation = tree.export_text(classifier)
print(text_representation)
```

```
|--- feature_3 <= 0.80
|   |--- class: 0
|--- feature_3 >  0.80
|   |--- feature_3 <= 1.75
|   |   |--- feature_2 <= 5.35
|   |   |   |--- feature_0 <= 4.95
|   |   |   |   |--- class: 2
|   |   |   |--- feature_0 >  4.95
|   |   |   |   |--- feature_2 <= 4.95
|   |   |   |   |   |--- class: 1
|   |   |   |   |--- feature_2 >  4.95
|   |   |   |   |   |--- feature_1 <= 2.45
|   |   |   |   |   |   |--- class: 2
|   |   |   |   |   |--- feature_1 >  2.45
|   |   |   |   |   |   |--- class: 1
|   |   |--- feature_2 >  5.35
|   |   |   |--- class: 2
|   |--- feature_3 >  1.75
|   |   |--- feature_2 <= 4.85
|   |   |   |--- feature_0 <= 5.95
|   |   |   |   |--- class: 1
```

```
|   |   |   |--- feature_0 >  5.95
|   |   |   |   |--- class: 2
|   |   |--- feature_2 >  4.85
|   |   |   |--- class: 2
```

```python
import matplotlib.pyplot as plt

fig = plt.figure(figsize=(10,8))
_ = tree.plot_tree(classifier,
                   feature_names=iris.feature_names,
                   class_names=iris.target_names,
                   filled=True)
```

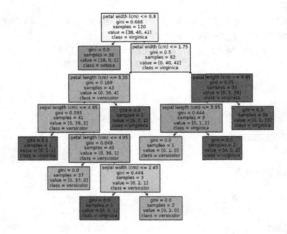

Figure 6.13 A Default Decision Tree

6.2.2.7 Tune the Model

Change hyperparameters, such as criterion, max_depth.

```python
classifier = DecisionTreeClassifier(criterion= 'entropy')
classifier.fit(X_train, y_train)

y_pred = classifier.predict(X_test)

print(confusion_matrix(y_test, y_pred))
print('Accuracy:', accuracy_score(y_test,y_pred))

text_representation = tree.export_text(classifier)
print(text_representation)

fig = plt.figure(figsize=(10,8))
_ = tree.plot_tree(classifier,
                   feature_names=iris.feature_names,
                   class_names=iris.target_names,
                   filled=True)
```

```
[[12  0  0]
 [ 0  9  1]
 [ 0  1  7]]
Accuracy: 0.9333333333333333
|--- feature_2 <= 2.45
|   |--- class: 0
|--- feature_2 >  2.45
|   |--- feature_3 <= 1.75
|   |   |--- feature_2 <= 4.95
|   |   |   |--- feature_0 <= 4.95
|   |   |   |   |--- class: 2
|   |   |   |--- feature_0 >  4.95
|   |   |   |   |--- class: 1
|   |   |--- feature_2 >  4.95
|   |   |   |--- feature_1 <= 2.65
|   |   |   |   |--- class: 2
|   |   |   |--- feature_1 >  2.65
|   |   |   |   |--- feature_2 <= 5.45
|   |   |   |   |   |--- class: 1
|   |   |   |   |--- feature_2 >  5.45
|   |   |   |   |   |--- class: 2
|   |--- feature_3 >  1.75
|   |   |--- feature_2 <= 4.85
|   |   |   |--- feature_0 <= 5.95
|   |   |   |   |--- class: 1
|   |   |   |--- feature_0 >  5.95
|   |   |   |   |--- class: 2
|   |   |--- feature_2 >  4.85
|   |   |   |--- class: 2
```

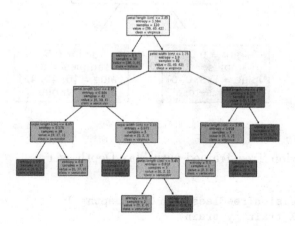

Figure 6.14   A Decision Tree Trained with Entropy

```
classifier = DecisionTreeClassifier(max_depth=1)
classifier.fit(X_train, y_train)
```

```
y_pred = classifier.predict(X_test)

print(confusion_matrix(y_test, y_pred))
print('Accuracy:', accuracy_score(y_test,y_pred))

text_representation = tree.export_text(classifier)
print(text_representation)

fig = plt.figure()
_ = tree.plot_tree(classifier,
                   feature_names=iris.feature_names,
                   class_names=iris.target_names,
                   filled=True)
```

```
[[12  0  0]
 [ 0  0 10]
 [ 0  0  8]]
Accuracy: 0.6666666666666666
|--- feature_3 <= 0.80
|   |--- class: 0
|--- feature_3 >  0.80
|   |--- class: 2
```

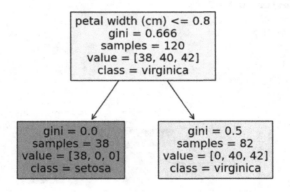

Figure 6.15 A Decision Tree Trained with Max Depth as 1

```
classifier = DecisionTreeClassifier(max_depth=2)
classifier.fit(X_train, y_train)

y_pred = classifier.predict(X_test)

print(confusion_matrix(y_test, y_pred))
print('Accuracy:', accuracy_score(y_test,y_pred))

text_representation = tree.export_text(classifier)
```

```
print(text_representation)

fig = plt.figure(figsize=(10,8))
_ = tree.plot_tree(classifier,
                   feature_names=iris.feature_names,
                   class_names=iris.target_names,
                   filled=True)
```

```
[[12  0  0]
 [ 0 10  0]
 [ 0  1  7]]
Accuracy: 0.9666666666666667
|--- feature_2 <= 2.45
|   |--- class: 0
|--- feature_2 >  2.45
|   |--- feature_3 <= 1.75
|   |   |--- class: 1
|   |--- feature_3 >  1.75
|   |   |--- class: 2
```

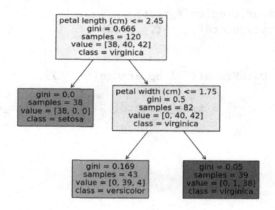

Figure 6.16   A Decision Tree Trained with Max Depth as 3

```
classifier = DecisionTreeClassifier(max_depth=3)
classifier.fit(X_train, y_train)

y_pred = classifier.predict(X_test)

print(confusion_matrix(y_test, y_pred))
print('Accuracy:', accuracy_score(y_test,y_pred))

text_representation = tree.export_text(classifier)
print(text_representation)
```

```
[[12  0  0]
 [ 0 10  0]
 [ 0  1  7]]
Accuracy: 0.9666666666666667
|--- feature_2 <= 2.45
|   |--- class: 0
|--- feature_2 >  2.45
|   |--- feature_3 <= 1.75
|   |   |--- feature_2 <= 5.35
|   |   |   |--- class: 1
|   |   |--- feature_2 >  5.35
|   |   |   |--- class: 2
|   |--- feature_3 >  1.75
|   |   |--- feature_2 <= 4.85
|   |   |   |--- class: 2
|   |   |--- feature_2 >  4.85
|   |   |   |--- class: 2
```

```python
def tree_depth_tuning(d):
    classifier = DecisionTreeClassifier(max_depth=d)
    classifier.fit(X_train, y_train)

    y_pred = classifier.predict(X_test)
    accuracy = accuracy_score(y_test,y_pred)
    return accuracy
```

```python
tree_results = pd.DataFrame({'D':np.arange(1, 10)})
```

```python
tree_results['Accuracy'] = tree_results['D'].apply(tree_depth_tuning)
tree_results
```

	D	Accuracy
0	1	0.666667
1	2	0.966667
2	3	0.966667
3	4	0.933333
4	5	0.933333
5	6	0.933333
6	7	0.933333
7	8	0.966667
8	9	0.933333

6.2.3 Case Study – Breast Cancer Classification Using Decision Tree

Let's prepare a step-by-step tutorial for the Decision Tree algorithm using the Breast Cancer dataset. We'll demonstrate how the choices of different splitting criteria (Information and Gini Index) and tree pruning (max depth) affect the classification results. We'll print the results of the classification and visualize the accuracy vs hyperparameters for comparison.

6.2.3.1 Setup

Import necessary libraries and load the Breast Cancer dataset.

```
import numpy as np
import pandas as pd
import matplotlib.pyplot as plt
from sklearn.datasets import load_breast_cancer
from sklearn.model_selection import train_test_split
from sklearn.tree import DecisionTreeClassifier
from sklearn.metrics import accuracy_score

# Load the Breast Cancer dataset
data = load_breast_cancer()
X = pd.DataFrame(data.data, columns=data.feature_names)
y = pd.Series(data.target)
```

6.2.3.2 Split the Dataset into Training and Testing Sets

```
# Split the dataset into training and testing sets (80% train, 20% test)
X_train, X_test, y_train, y_test =
    train_test_split(X, y, test_size=0.2, random_state=42)
```

6.2.3.3 Create and Train Decision Tree Models with Different Splitting Criteria and Max Depth

```
# Create a list of splitting criteria
splitting_criteria = ['entropy', 'gini']

# Create a list of max depth values
max_depth_values = range(1, 20, 2)

# Create an empty dictionary to store the results
results = {}

# Train Different Decision Tree models
for criterion in splitting_criteria:
    for max_depth in max_depth_values:
        dt_model =
        DecisionTreeClassifier(criterion=criterion, max_depth=max_depth)
        dt_model.fit(X_train, y_train)
        y_pred = dt_model.predict(X_test)
        accuracy = accuracy_score(y_test, y_pred)
        results[(criterion, max_depth)] = {
            'model': dt_model,
            'accuracy': accuracy
        }
```

6.2.3.4 *Print the Results of the Classification*

```
# Print the results of the classification
print("Results of Decision Tree Classification:")
for (criterion, max_depth), result in results.items():
    print(f"Criterion: {criterion}
        , Max Depth: {max_depth}
        , Accuracy: {result['accuracy']:.2f}")
```

```
Results of Decision Tree Classification:
Criterion: entropy, Max Depth: 1, Accuracy: 0.89
Criterion: entropy, Max Depth: 3, Accuracy: 0.96
Criterion: entropy, Max Depth: 5, Accuracy: 0.96
Criterion: entropy, Max Depth: 7, Accuracy: 0.95
Criterion: entropy, Max Depth: 9, Accuracy: 0.95
Criterion: entropy, Max Depth: 11, Accuracy: 0.95
Criterion: entropy, Max Depth: 13, Accuracy: 0.96
Criterion: entropy, Max Depth: 15, Accuracy: 0.95
Criterion: entropy, Max Depth: 17, Accuracy: 0.96
Criterion: entropy, Max Depth: 19, Accuracy: 0.94
Criterion: gini, Max Depth: 1, Accuracy: 0.89
Criterion: gini, Max Depth: 3, Accuracy: 0.95
Criterion: gini, Max Depth: 5, Accuracy: 0.94
Criterion: gini, Max Depth: 7, Accuracy: 0.93
Criterion: gini, Max Depth: 9, Accuracy: 0.93
Criterion: gini, Max Depth: 11, Accuracy: 0.95
Criterion: gini, Max Depth: 13, Accuracy: 0.94
Criterion: gini, Max Depth: 15, Accuracy: 0.95
Criterion: gini, Max Depth: 17, Accuracy: 0.94
Criterion: gini, Max Depth: 19, Accuracy: 0.94
```

6.2.3.5 *Visualize the Accuracy vs Hyperparameters for Comparison*

```
# Visualize the accuracy vs max depth for each splitting criterion
plt.figure(figsize=(10, 6))
for criterion in splitting_criteria:
    accuracies = [result['accuracy'] for (c, md),
    result in results.items() if c == criterion]
    plt.plot(max_depth_values, accuracies, marker='o',
      label=f'Splitting Criterion: {criterion}')
plt.xlabel('Max Depth')
plt.ylabel('Accuracy')
plt.title('Accuracy vs Max Depth for Different Splitting Criteria')
plt.legend()
plt.grid(True)
plt.show()
```

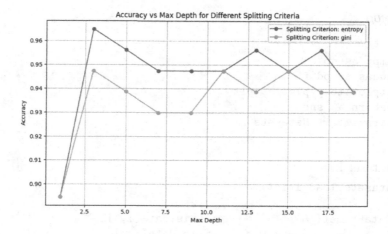

Figure 6.17 Accuracy VS Max Depth for Different Splitting Criteria

6.2.3.6 Conclusion

This tutorial covers the Decision Tree algorithm using the Breast Cancer dataset. It demonstrates how different splitting criteria (Information Gain and Gini Index) and tree pruning (max depth) affect the classification results. The tutorial prints the accuracy of the models with different hyperparameters and visualizes the accuracy vs max depth for each splitting criterion for comparison.

Feel free to adjust the max_depth_values and add other hyperparameters to explore their effects on the decision tree's performance.

6.3 SUPPORT VECTOR MACHINE CLASSIFIERS

Support Vector Machines (SVMs) are powerful and versatile machine learning algorithms used for classification and regression tasks. This section introduces SVM Classifiers using the Scikit-learn package, covering their theory, implementation, and practical applications.

Support Vector Machine Classifiers (SVMs) are supervised learning algorithms that excel in both linear and non-linear classification tasks. They work by finding the optimal hyperplane that best separates data into distinct classes. Scikit-learn provides a robust library for implementing SVM Classifiers with ease. You will explore practical implementation steps, including using the SVC (Support Vector Classification) class in Scikit-learn to create SVM Classifier models and understanding the role of hyperparameters such as the kernel type, regularization parameter (C), and gamma in SVM model performance.

6.3.1 Tutorial – Iris Binary Classification Using SVM

https://scikit-learn.org/stable/modules/svm.html

6.3.1.1 Setup

Environment

```
import numpy as np
import pandas as pd
import matplotlib.pyplot as plt
import seaborn as sns
from sklearn import datasets
```

Load the dataset iris

```
iris = datasets.load_iris()
```

```
df = pd.DataFrame({'Sepal length': iris.data[:,0],
                   'Sepal width': iris.data[:,1],
                   'Petal length':iris.data[:,2],
                   'Petal width':iris.data[:,3],
                   'Species':iris.target})
df.head()
```

	Sepal length	Sepal width	Petal length	Petal width	Species
0	5.1	3.5	1.4	0.2	0
1	4.9	3.0	1.4	0.2	0
2	4.7	3.2	1.3	0.2	0
3	4.6	3.1	1.5	0.2	0
4	5.0	3.6	1.4	0.2	0

```
df = df[df['Species'] !=0]
```

```
df.info()
```

```
<class 'pandas.core.frame.DataFrame'>
Int64Index: 100 entries, 50 to 149
Data columns (total 5 columns):
 #   Column        Non-Null Count  Dtype
---  ------        --------------  -----
 0   Sepal length  100 non-null    float64
 1   Sepal width   100 non-null    float64
 2   Petal length  100 non-null    float64
 3   Petal width   100 non-null    float64
 4   Species       100 non-null    int64
dtypes: float64(4), int64(1)
memory usage: 4.7 KB
```

A simple visualization

```
sns.relplot(data = df, x = 'Sepal length', y = 'Sepal width'
    , hue = 'Species')
```

```
<seaborn.axisgrid.FacetGrid at 0x7f8358fbf880>
```

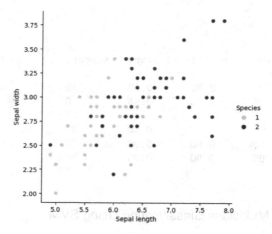

Figure 6.18   A Scatter Plot of Sepal Length VS Sepal Width with Species Differentiation

Train-test split

```
from sklearn.model_selection import train_test_split

X = df[df.columns[:2]]
y = df[df.columns[-1]]
X_train, X_test, y_train, y_test = train_test_split(X, y, test_size = 0.20)
```

```
X_train[:5]
```

	Sepal length	Sepal width
131	7.9	3.8
86	6.7	3.1
64	5.6	2.9
138	6.0	3.0
94	5.6	2.7

6.3.1.2   Train Your Model

```
from sklearn import svm

model = svm.SVC(kernel='linear')
classifier = model.fit(X_train, y_train)
```

6.3.1.3   Evaluate Your Model

```
y_pred = classifier.predict(X_test)
```

```
from sklearn.metrics
    import classification_report, confusion_matrix, accuracy_score
print(confusion_matrix(y_test, y_pred))
print(classification_report(y_test, y_pred))
print(accuracy_score(y_test,y_pred))
```

```
[[11  1]
 [ 1  7]]
              precision    recall  f1-score   support

           1       0.92      0.92      0.92        12
           2       0.88      0.88      0.88         8

    accuracy                           0.90        20
   macro avg       0.90      0.90      0.90        20
weighted avg       0.90      0.90      0.90        20
```

0.9

6.3.2   Tutorial – Iris Multiclass Classification Using SVM

https://scikit-learn.org/stable/modules/svm.html

6.3.2.1   Setup

Environment

```
import numpy as np
import pandas as pd
import matplotlib.pyplot as plt
import seaborn as sns
from sklearn import datasets
```

Load the dataset iris

```
iris = datasets.load_iris()
```

```
df = pd.DataFrame({'Sepal length': iris.data[:,0],
                   'Sepal width': iris.data[:,1],
                   'Petal length':iris.data[:,2],
                   'Petal width':iris.data[:,3],
                   'Species':iris.target})
df.head()
```

```
   Sepal length  Sepal width  Petal length  Petal width  Species
0           5.1          3.5           1.4          0.2        0
1           4.9          3.0           1.4          0.2        0
2           4.7          3.2           1.3          0.2        0
3           4.6          3.1           1.5          0.2        0
4           5.0          3.6           1.4          0.2        0
```

```
df.info()
```

```
<class 'pandas.core.frame.DataFrame'>
RangeIndex: 150 entries, 0 to 149
Data columns (total 5 columns):
 #   Column        Non-Null Count  Dtype
---  ------        --------------  -----
 0   Sepal length  150 non-null    float64
```

```
1    Sepal width    150 non-null    float64
2    Petal length   150 non-null    float64
3    Petal width    150 non-null    float64
4    Species        150 non-null    int64
dtypes: float64(4), int64(1)
memory usage: 6.0 KB
```

A simple visualization

```
sns.relplot(data = df, x = 'Sepal length', y = 'Sepal width'
    , hue = 'Species')
```

```
<seaborn.axisgrid.FacetGrid at 0x7aaccd3501f0>
```

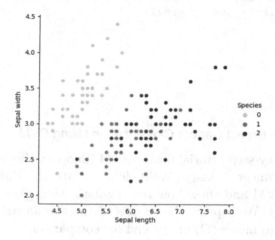

Figure 6.19 A Scatter Plot of Sepal Length VS Sepal Width with Species Differentiation

Train-test split

```
from sklearn.model_selection import train_test_split

X = df[df.columns[:4]]
y = df[df.columns[-1]]
X_train, X_test, y_train, y_test = train_test_split(X, y, test_size = 0.20)
```

```
X_train[:5]
```

	Sepal length	Sepal width	Petal length	Petal width
51	6.4	3.2	4.5	1.5
8	4.4	2.9	1.4	0.2
99	5.7	2.8	4.1	1.3
117	7.7	3.8	6.7	2.2
144	6.7	3.3	5.7	2.5

6.3.2.2 Train Your Model

```
from sklearn import svm

model = svm.SVC(kernel='linear')
classifier = model.fit(X_train, y_train)
```

6.3.2.3 Evaluate Your Model

```
y_pred = classifier.predict(X_test)
```

```
from sklearn.metrics
    import classification_report, confusion_matrix, accuracy_score
print(confusion_matrix(y_test, y_pred))
print(accuracy_score(y_test,y_pred))
```

```
[[12  0  0]
 [ 0  8  1]
 [ 0  0  9]]
0.9666666666666667
```

6.3.3 Case Study – Breast Cancer Classification Using SVM

Let's prepare a step-by-step tutorial for the SVM (Support Vector Machine) algorithm using the Breast Cancer dataset. We'll demonstrate the difference between soft and hard margin SVM and show how the regularization parameter (C) affects the classification results. We'll print the results of the classification and visualize the accuracy vs hyperparameter (C) at the end for comparison.

6.3.3.1 Setup

```
import numpy as np
import pandas as pd
import matplotlib.pyplot as plt
from sklearn.datasets import load_breast_cancer
from sklearn.model_selection import train_test_split
from sklearn.svm import SVC
from sklearn.metrics import accuracy_score

# Load the Breast Cancer dataset
data = load_breast_cancer()
X = pd.DataFrame(data.data, columns=data.feature_names)
y = pd.Series(data.target)

# Split the dataset into training and testing sets (80% train, 20% test)
X_train, X_test, y_train, y_test = train_test_split(X, y, test_size=0.2
    , random_state=42)
```

6.3.3.2 Create and Train SVM Models with Different Regularization Parameters (C)

```
# Create a list of regularization parameter values
C_values = [0.01, 0.1, 1, 10, 100]

# Create an empty dictionary to store the results
results = {}

# Train SVM models with different C values
for C in C_values:
    svm_model = SVC(C=C, kernel='linear')
    svm_model.fit(X_train, y_train)
    y_pred = svm_model.predict(X_test)
    accuracy = accuracy_score(y_test, y_pred)
    results[C] = {
        'model': svm_model,
        'accuracy': accuracy
    }
```

6.3.3.3 Print the Results of the Classification

```
# Print the results of the classification
print("Results of SVM Classification:")
for C, result in results.items():
    print(f"C = {C}, Accuracy: {result['accuracy']:.4f}")
```

```
Results of SVM Classification:
C = 0.01, Accuracy: 0.9561
C = 0.1, Accuracy: 0.9649
C = 1, Accuracy: 0.9561
C = 10, Accuracy: 0.9561
C = 100, Accuracy: 0.9561
```

6.3.3.4 Visualize the Accuracy vs Regularization Parameter (C) for Comparison

```
# Visualize the accuracy vs regularization parameter (C)
accuracies = [result['accuracy'] for C, result in results.items()]

plt.figure(figsize=(8, 4))
plt.plot(C_values, accuracies, marker='o')
plt.xscale('log')
plt.xlabel('Regularization Parameter (C)')
plt.ylabel('Accuracy')
plt.title('Accuracy vs Regularization Parameter (C) for SVM')
plt.grid(True)
plt.show()
```

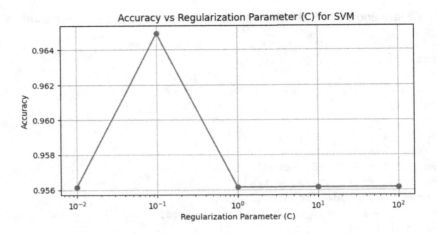

Figure 6.20 Accuracy VS Regularization Parameter (C) for SVM

6.3.3.5 Conclusion

This tutorial covers the SVM algorithm using the Breast Cancer dataset. It demonstrates the difference between soft and hard margin SVM and shows how the regularization parameter (C) affects the classification results. The tutorial prints the accuracy of the models with different values of C and visualizes the accuracy vs regularization parameter (C) for comparison.

Feel free to adjust the C_values list and try other kernel types (e.g., 'rbf', 'poly') to explore their effects on SVM's performance.

6.4 NAIVE BAYES CLASSIFIERS

Naive Bayes classifiers are probabilistic machine learning algorithms commonly used for classification tasks, particularly in natural language processing and text analysis. This section introduces Naive Bayes classifiers using the Scikit-learn package, covering their theory, implementation, and practical applications.

Naive Bayes classifiers are based on Bayes' theorem and assume that features are conditionally independent, hence the term "naive". They are known for their simplicity, efficiency, and effectiveness in various classification tasks. Scikit-learn provides a user-friendly environment for implementing Naive Bayes classifiers. You will explore practical implementation steps, including using the MultinomialNB, GaussianNB, and BernoulliNB classes in Scikit-learn for different types of Naive Bayes models and understanding the Laplace smoothing technique to handle unseen features and improve model performance.

6.4.1 Tutorial – Iris Binary Classification Using Naive Bayes

Documentation: https://scikit-learn.org/stable/modules/naive_bayes.html

6.4.1.1 Setup

Environment

```
import numpy as np
import pandas as pd
import matplotlib.pyplot as plt
import seaborn as sns
from sklearn import datasets
```

Load the dataset iris

```
iris = datasets.load_iris()
```

```
df = pd.DataFrame({'Sepal length': iris.data[:,0],
                   'Sepal width': iris.data[:,1],
                   'Petal length':iris.data[:,2],
                   'Petal width':iris.data[:,3],
                   'Species':iris.target})
df.head()
```

```
   Sepal length  Sepal width  Petal length  Petal width  Species
0           5.1          3.5           1.4          0.2        0
1           4.9          3.0           1.4          0.2        0
2           4.7          3.2           1.3          0.2        0
3           4.6          3.1           1.5          0.2        0
4           5.0          3.6           1.4          0.2        0
```

```
df = df[df['Species'] != 0]
```

```
df.info()
```

```
<class 'pandas.core.frame.DataFrame'>
Int64Index: 100 entries, 50 to 149
Data columns (total 5 columns):
 #   Column        Non-Null Count  Dtype
---  ------        --------------  -----
 0   Sepal length  100 non-null    float64
 1   Sepal width   100 non-null    float64
 2   Petal length  100 non-null    float64
 3   Petal width   100 non-null    float64
 4   Species       100 non-null    int64
dtypes: float64(4), int64(1)
memory usage: 4.7 KB
```

A simple visualization

```
sns.relplot(data = df, x = 'Sepal length', y = 'Sepal width'
    , hue = 'Species')
```

```
<seaborn.axisgrid.FacetGrid at 0x79b596653b80>
```

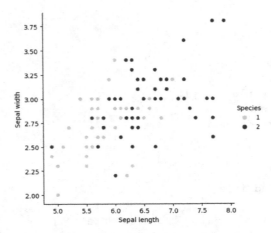

Figure 6.21   A Scatter Plot of Sepal Length VS Sepal Width with Species Differentiation

Train-test split

```
from sklearn.model_selection import train_test_split

X = df[df.columns[:2]]
y = df[df.columns[-1]]
X_train, X_test, y_train, y_test = train_test_split(X, y, test_size = 0.20)
```

```
X_train[:5]
```

	Sepal length	Sepal width
76	6.8	2.8
109	7.2	3.6
88	5.6	3.0
62	6.0	2.2
51	6.4	3.2

6.4.1.2   Train the Model

```
from sklearn.naive_bayes import GaussianNB

classifier = GaussianNB()
classifier.fit(X_train, y_train)
y_pred = classifier.predict(X_test)
```

```
from sklearn.metrics
    import classification_report, confusion_matrix, accuracy_score

result = confusion_matrix(y_test, y_pred)
print("Confusion Matrix:")
print(result)
result1 = classification_report(y_test, y_pred)
print("Classification Report:",)
```

```
print (result1)
result2 = accuracy_score(y_test,y_pred)
print("Accuracy:",result2)
```

```
Confusion Matrix:
[[9 2]
 [1 8]]
Classification Report:
              precision    recall  f1-score   support

           1       0.90      0.82      0.86        11
           2       0.80      0.89      0.84         9

    accuracy                           0.85        20
   macro avg       0.85      0.85      0.85        20
weighted avg       0.86      0.85      0.85        20

Accuracy: 0.85
```

6.4.2   Tutorial – Iris Multiclass Classification Using Naive Bayes

Documentation: https://scikit-learn.org/stable/modules/naive_bayes.html

6.4.2.1   Setup

Environment

```
import numpy as np
import pandas as pd
import matplotlib.pyplot as plt
import seaborn as sns
from sklearn import datasets
```

Load the dataset iris

```
iris = datasets.load_iris()
```

```
df = pd.DataFrame({'Sepal length': iris.data[:,0],
                   'Sepal width': iris.data[:,1],
                   'Petal length':iris.data[:,2],
                   'Petal width':iris.data[:,3],
                   'Species':iris.target})
df.head()
```

```
   Sepal length  Sepal width  Petal length  Petal width  Species
0           5.1          3.5           1.4          0.2        0
1           4.9          3.0           1.4          0.2        0
2           4.7          3.2           1.3          0.2        0
3           4.6          3.1           1.5          0.2        0
4           5.0          3.6           1.4          0.2        0
```

```
df.info()
```

```
<class 'pandas.core.frame.DataFrame'>
RangeIndex: 150 entries, 0 to 149
Data columns (total 5 columns):
 #   Column        Non-Null Count  Dtype
---  ------        --------------  -----
 0   Sepal length  150 non-null    float64
 1   Sepal width   150 non-null    float64
 2   Petal length  150 non-null    float64
 3   Petal width   150 non-null    float64
 4   Species       150 non-null    int64
dtypes: float64(4), int64(1)
memory usage: 6.0 KB
```

A simple visualization

```
sns.relplot(data = df, x = 'Sepal length', y = 'Sepal width'
    , hue = 'Species')
```

```
<seaborn.axisgrid.FacetGrid at 0x7e90b4584700>
```

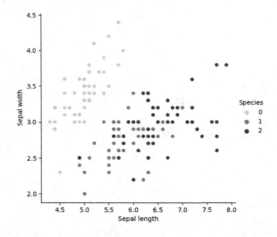

Figure 6.22   A Scatter Plot of Sepal Length VS Sepal Width with Species Differentiation

Train-test split

```
from sklearn.model_selection import train_test_split

X = df[df.columns[:4]]
y = df[df.columns[-1]]
X_train, X_test, y_train, y_test = train_test_split(X, y, test_size = 0.20)
```

```
X_train[:5]
```

	Sepal length	Sepal width	Petal length	Petal width
59	5.2	2.7	3.9	1.4
146	6.3	2.5	5.0	1.9
89	5.5	2.5	4.0	1.3
65	6.7	3.1	4.4	1.4
129	7.2	3.0	5.8	1.6

6.4.2.2 Train the Model

```
from sklearn.naive_bayes import GaussianNB

classifier = GaussianNB()
classifier.fit(X_train, y_train)
y_pred = classifier.predict(X_test)
```

```
from sklearn.metrics
    import classification_report, confusion_matrix, accuracy_score

result = confusion_matrix(y_test, y_pred)
print("Confusion Matrix:")
print(result)
result1 = classification_report(y_test, y_pred)
print("Classification Report:",)
print (result1)
result2 = accuracy_score(y_test,y_pred)
print("Accuracy:",result2)
```

```
Confusion Matrix:
[[ 7  0  0]
 [ 0  8  2]
 [ 0  0 13]]
Classification Report:
```

	precision	recall	f1-score	support
0	1.00	1.00	1.00	7
1	1.00	0.80	0.89	10
2	0.87	1.00	0.93	13
accuracy			0.93	30
macro avg	0.96	0.93	0.94	30
weighted avg	0.94	0.93	0.93	30

```
Accuracy: 0.9333333333333333
```

6.4.3 Case Study – Breast Cancer Classification Using Naive Bayes

Let's prepare a step-by-step tutorial for the Naive Bayes algorithm using the Breast Cancer dataset. We'll demonstrate how the Naive Bayes algorithm works for classification.

6.4.3.1   Setup

```
import numpy as np
import pandas as pd
import matplotlib.pyplot as plt
from sklearn.datasets import load_breast_cancer
from sklearn.model_selection import train_test_split
from sklearn.naive_bayes import GaussianNB
from sklearn.metrics import accuracy_score

# Load the Breast Cancer dataset
data = load_breast_cancer()
X = pd.DataFrame(data.data, columns=data.feature_names)
y = pd.Series(data.target)

# Split the dataset into training and testing sets (80% train, 20% test)
X_train, X_test, y_train, y_test = train_test_split(X, y, test_size=0.2
    , random_state=42)
```

6.4.3.2   Create and Train the Naive Bayes Model

```
# Create the Naive Bayes model
nb_model = GaussianNB()

# Train the model
nb_model.fit(X_train, y_train)

# Make predictions on the test set
y_pred = nb_model.predict(X_test)

# Calculate the accuracy of the model
accuracy = accuracy_score(y_test, y_pred)
```

6.4.3.3   Print the Results of the Classification

```
# Print the accuracy of the Naive Bayes model
print("Accuracy of Naive Bayes model:", accuracy)
```

```
Accuracy of Naive Bayes model: 0.9736842105263158
```

6.4.3.4   Conclusion

This tutorial covers the Naive Bayes algorithm using the Breast Cancer dataset. It demonstrates how to create and train the Naive Bayes model for classification and prints the accuracy of the model on the test set.

Naive Bayes is a simple yet powerful algorithm for classification tasks, especially when dealing with text or categorical data.

6.5 LOGISTIC REGRESSION CLASSIFIERS

Logistic Regression is a widely used statistical and machine learning technique for binary classification tasks. This section introduces Logistic Regression classifiers using the Scikit-learn package, covering their theory, implementation, and practical applications.

Logistic Regression is a fundamental classification algorithm that models the probability of a binary outcome based on one or more predictor variables. Despite its name, it is used for classification rather than regression tasks. Scikit-learn offers a convenient environment for implementing Logistic Regression classifiers. You will explore practical implementation steps, including using the LogisticRegression class in Scikit-learn to create Logistic Regression models and training Logistic Regression models on labeled datasets and making binary classification predictions.

6.5.1 Tutorial – Iris Binary Classification Using Logistic Regression

Documentation: https://scikit-learn.org/stable/modules/generated/sklearn.linear_model.LogisticRegression.html

6.5.1.1 Setup

Environment

```
import numpy as np
import pandas as pd
import matplotlib.pyplot as plt
import seaborn as sns
from sklearn import datasets
```

Load the dataset iris

```
iris = datasets.load_iris()
```

```
df = pd.DataFrame({'Sepal length': iris.data[:,0],
                   'Sepal width': iris.data[:,1],
                   'Petal length':iris.data[:,2],
                   'Petal width':iris.data[:,3],
                   'Species':iris.target})
df.head()
```

```
   Sepal length  Sepal width  Petal length  Petal width  Species
0           5.1          3.5           1.4          0.2        0
1           4.9          3.0           1.4          0.2        0
2           4.7          3.2           1.3          0.2        0
3           4.6          3.1           1.5          0.2        0
4           5.0          3.6           1.4          0.2        0
```

```
df = df[df['Species'] != 0]
```

```
df.info()
```

```
<class 'pandas.core.frame.DataFrame'>
Int64Index: 100 entries, 50 to 149
Data columns (total 5 columns):
 #   Column        Non-Null Count   Dtype
---  ------        --------------   -----
 0   Sepal length  100 non-null     float64
 1   Sepal width   100 non-null     float64
 2   Petal length  100 non-null     float64
 3   Petal width   100 non-null     float64
 4   Species       100 non-null     int64
dtypes: float64(4), int64(1)
memory usage: 4.7 KB
```

A simple visualization

```
sns.relplot(data = df, x = 'Sepal length', y = 'Sepal width'
    , hue = 'Species')
```

```
<seaborn.axisgrid.FacetGrid at 0x77fc4c650100>
```

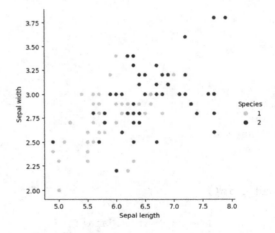

Figure 6.23   A Scatter Plot of Sepal Length VS Sepal Width with Species Differentiation

Train-test split

```
from sklearn.model_selection import train_test_split

X = df[df.columns[:2]]
y = df[df.columns[-1]]
X_train, X_test, y_train, y_test = train_test_split(X, y, test_size = 0.20)
```

```
X_train[:5]
```

	Sepal length	Sepal width
107	7.3	2.9
52	6.9	3.1

```
146        6.3        2.5
77         6.7        3.0
71         6.1        2.8
```

6.5.1.2   Train the Model

```python
from sklearn.linear_model import LogisticRegression

classifier = LogisticRegression().fit(X, y)
classifier.fit(X_train, y_train)
```

```
LogisticRegression()
```

```python
y_pred = classifier.predict(X_test)
```

```python
from sklearn.metrics
    import classification_report, confusion_matrix, accuracy_score

result = confusion_matrix(y_test, y_pred)
print("Confusion Matrix:")
print(result)
report = classification_report(y_test, y_pred)
print("Classification Report:",)
print (report)
accuracy = accuracy_score(y_test,y_pred)
print("Accuracy:",accuracy)
```

```
Confusion Matrix:
[[6 1]
 [4 9]]
Classification Report:
              precision    recall  f1-score   support

           1       0.60      0.86      0.71         7
           2       0.90      0.69      0.78        13

    accuracy                           0.75        20
   macro avg       0.75      0.77      0.74        20
weighted avg       0.80      0.75      0.76        20

Accuracy: 0.75
```

6.5.2   Tutorial – Iris Multiclass Classification Using Logistic Regression

Documentation: https://scikit-learn.org/stable/modules/generated/sklearn.linear_model.LogisticRegression.html

6.5.2.1   Setup

Environment

```
import numpy as np
import pandas as pd
import matplotlib.pyplot as plt
import seaborn as sns
from sklearn import datasets
```

Load the dataset iris

```
iris = datasets.load_iris()
```

```
df = pd.DataFrame({'Sepal length': iris.data[:,0],
                   'Sepal width': iris.data[:,1],
                   'Petal length':iris.data[:,2],
                   'Petal width':iris.data[:,3],
                   'Species':iris.target})
df.head()
```

	Sepal length	Sepal width	Petal length	Petal width	Species
0	5.1	3.5	1.4	0.2	0
1	4.9	3.0	1.4	0.2	0
2	4.7	3.2	1.3	0.2	0
3	4.6	3.1	1.5	0.2	0
4	5.0	3.6	1.4	0.2	0

```
df.info()
```

```
<class 'pandas.core.frame.DataFrame'>
RangeIndex: 150 entries, 0 to 149
Data columns (total 5 columns):
 #   Column        Non-Null Count  Dtype
---  ------        --------------  -----
 0   Sepal length  150 non-null    float64
 1   Sepal width   150 non-null    float64
 2   Petal length  150 non-null    float64
 3   Petal width   150 non-null    float64
 4   Species       150 non-null    int64
dtypes: float64(4), int64(1)
memory usage: 6.0 KB
```

A simple visualization

```
sns.relplot(data = df, x = 'Sepal length', y = 'Sepal width'
    , hue = 'Species')
```

```
<seaborn.axisgrid.FacetGrid at 0x7e3b5deaa890>
```

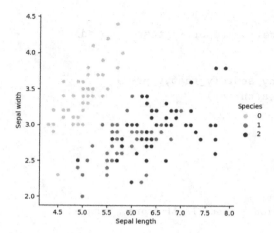

Figure 6.24 A Scatter Plot of Sepal Length VS Sepal Width with Species Differentiation

Train-test split

```
from sklearn.model_selection import train_test_split

X = df[df.columns[:4]]
y = df[df.columns[-1]]
X_train, X_test, y_train, y_test = train_test_split(X, y, test_size = 0.20)
```

```
X_train[:5]
```

	Sepal length	Sepal width	Petal length	Petal width
5	5.4	3.9	1.7	0.4
76	6.8	2.8	4.8	1.4
24	4.8	3.4	1.9	0.2
99	5.7	2.8	4.1	1.3
15	5.7	4.4	1.5	0.4

6.5.2.2 Train the Model

```
from sklearn.linear_model import LogisticRegression

classifier = LogisticRegression().fit(X, y)
classifier.fit(X_train, y_train)
```

```
LogisticRegression()
```

```
y_pred = classifier.predict(X_test)
```

```
from sklearn.metrics
    import classification_report, confusion_matrix, accuracy_score

result = confusion_matrix(y_test, y_pred)
print("Confusion Matrix:")
```

```
print(result)
report = classification_report(y_test, y_pred)
print("Classification Report:")
print(report)
accuracy = accuracy_score(y_test,y_pred)
print("Accuracy:",accuracy)
```

```
Confusion Matrix:
[[11  0  0]
 [ 0  9  1]
 [ 0  1  8]]
Classification Report:
              precision    recall  f1-score   support

           0       1.00      1.00      1.00        11
           1       0.90      0.90      0.90        10
           2       0.89      0.89      0.89         9

    accuracy                           0.93        30
   macro avg       0.93      0.93      0.93        30
weighted avg       0.93      0.93      0.93        30

Accuracy: 0.9333333333333333
```

6.5.3 Case Study – Breast Cancer Classification Using Logistic Regression

Let's prepare a step-by-step tutorial for the Logistic Regression algorithm using the Breast Cancer dataset. We'll demonstrate how the Logistic Regression algorithm works for classification and visualize the accuracy vs hyperparameter for comparison.

6.5.3.1 Setup

```
import numpy as np
import pandas as pd
import matplotlib.pyplot as plt
from sklearn.datasets import load_breast_cancer
from sklearn.model_selection import train_test_split
from sklearn.linear_model import LogisticRegression
from sklearn.metrics import accuracy_score

# Load the Breast Cancer dataset
data = load_breast_cancer()
X = pd.DataFrame(data.data, columns=data.feature_names)
y = pd.Series(data.target)

# Split the dataset into training and testing sets (80% train, 20% test)
X_train, X_test, y_train, y_test =
     train_test_split(X, y, test_size=0.2, random_state=42)
```

6.5.3.2 Create and Train the Logistic Regression Model with Different Regularization Parameters

```
# Create a list of regularization parameter values
C_values = [0.001, 0.01, 0.1, 1, 10, 100, 1000]

# Create an empty dictionary to store the results
results = {}

# Train Logistic Regression models with different C values
for C in C_values:
    lr_model = LogisticRegression(C=C, random_state=42, max_iter=2000)
    lr_model.fit(X_train, y_train)
    y_pred = lr_model.predict(X_test)
    accuracy = accuracy_score(y_test, y_pred)
    results[C] = {
        'model': lr_model,
        'accuracy': accuracy
    }
```

6.5.3.3 Print the Results of the Classification

```
# Print the results of the classification
print("Results of Logistic Regression Classification:")
for C, result in results.items():
    print(f"C = {C}, Accuracy: {result['accuracy']:.4f}")
```

```
Results of Logistic Regression Classification:
C = 0.001, Accuracy: 0.9649
C = 0.01, Accuracy: 0.9649
C = 0.1, Accuracy: 0.9649
C = 1, Accuracy: 0.9561
C = 10, Accuracy: 0.9561
C = 100, Accuracy: 0.9649
C = 1000, Accuracy: 0.9649
```

6.5.3.4 Visualize the Accuracy vs Regularization Parameter (C) for Comparison

```
# Visualize the accuracy vs regularization parameter (C)
accuracies = [result['accuracy'] for C, result in results.items()]

plt.figure(figsize=(8, 4))
plt.plot(C_values, accuracies, marker='o')
plt.xscale('log')
plt.xlabel('Regularization Parameter (C)')
plt.ylabel('Accuracy')
plt.title('Accuracy vs Regularization Parameter (C)')
plt.grid(True)
plt.show()
```

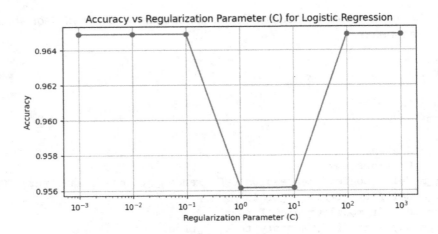

Figure 6.25 Accuracy VS Regularization Parameter (C)

6.5.3.5 Conclusion

This tutorial covers the Logistic Regression algorithm using the Breast Cancer dataset. It demonstrates how to create and train the Logistic Regression model for classification and prints the accuracy of the model with different values of the regularization parameter (C). The tutorial also visualizes the accuracy vs regularization parameter (C) for comparison.

Feel free to experiment with different values of C to observe how it affects the model's performance.

6.6 CLASSIFICATION METHODS' COMPARISON

In this section, we will conduct a comprehensive case study to explore and compare the performance of various classification methods we have introduced using a single dataset. This hands-on approach will provide you with a practical understanding of how different classifiers behave and perform in real-world scenarios.

The case study aims to demonstrate the strengths and weaknesses of different classification methods, allowing you to make informed choices when selecting the most appropriate algorithm for a specific task. You will work with a dataset that is suitable for classification and apply all classifiers we have covered. Based on the case study results, you will gain insights into which classifier(s) perform best for the given dataset and classification task. You will also learn how to choose the most suitable classifier based on the specific requirements and characteristics of a problem.

6.6.1 Case Study – Wine Classification Using Multiple Classifiers

Let's proceed with the Wine Dataset and apply the same classification methods we used before, including K-Nearest Neighbors (KNN), Decision Trees, SVM, Naive Bayes, and Logistic Regression. We will explore each method with different hyperparameters and summarize their performance in terms of accuracy. At the end, we will visualize the results for comparison.

The Wine Dataset is a popular dataset for classification tasks, where the target class represents the origin of different wines. It contains 13 features that describe various properties of the wines.

6.6.1.1 Setup

```python
import numpy as np
import pandas as pd
import matplotlib.pyplot as plt
from sklearn.datasets import load_wine
from sklearn.model_selection import train_test_split
from sklearn.neighbors import KNeighborsClassifier
from sklearn.tree import DecisionTreeClassifier
from sklearn.svm import SVC
from sklearn.naive_bayes import GaussianNB
from sklearn.linear_model import LogisticRegression
from sklearn.metrics import accuracy_score

# Load the Wine dataset
data = load_wine()
X = pd.DataFrame(data.data, columns=data.feature_names)
y = pd.Series(data.target, name='target')

# Split the dataset into training and testing sets (80% train, 20% test)
X_train, X_test, y_train, y_test =
    train_test_split(X, y, test_size=0.2, random_state=42)
```

6.6.1.2 Apply K-Nearest Neighbors (KNN) with Different Values of k

```python
# Create a list of k values
k_values = range(1, 51, 4)

# Create an empty dictionary to store the results
knn_results = {}

# Train KNN models with different k values
for k in k_values:
    knn_model = KNeighborsClassifier(n_neighbors=k)
    knn_model.fit(X_train, y_train)
    y_pred = knn_model.predict(X_test)
    accuracy = accuracy_score(y_test, y_pred)
    knn_results[k] = accuracy
```

6.6.1.3 Apply Decision Trees with Different Values of max depth

```python
# Create a list of max depth values
max_depth_values = range(1, 21, 2)

# Create an empty dictionary to store the results
dt_results = {}

# Train Decision Tree models with different max depth values
for max_depth in max_depth_values:
    dt_model = DecisionTreeClassifier(max_depth=max_depth)
    dt_model.fit(X_train, y_train)
    y_pred = dt_model.predict(X_test)
    accuracy = accuracy_score(y_test, y_pred)
    dt_results[max_depth] = accuracy
```

6.6.1.4 Apply SVM with Different Values of C

```python
# Create a list of C values
C_values = [0.001, 0.01, 0.1, 1, 10, 100, 200]

# Create an empty dictionary to store the results
svm_results = {}

# Train SVM models with different C values
for C in C_values:
    svm_model = SVC(C=C)
    svm_model.fit(X_train, y_train)
    y_pred = svm_model.predict(X_test)
    accuracy = accuracy_score(y_test, y_pred)
    svm_results[C] = accuracy
```

6.6.1.5 Apply Naive Bayes (GaussianNB)

```python
# Train Naive Bayes model
nb_model = GaussianNB()
nb_model.fit(X_train, y_train)
y_pred = nb_model.predict(X_test)
nb_accuracy = accuracy_score(y_test, y_pred)
```

6.6.1.6 Apply Logistic Regression with Different Values of C

```python
# Create an empty dictionary to store the results
logreg_results = {}

# Train Logistic Regression models with different C values
for C in C_values:
    lr_model = LogisticRegression(C=C, random_state=42)
    lr_model.fit(X_train, y_train)
    y_pred = lr_model.predict(X_test)
```

```
    accuracy = accuracy_score(y_test, y_pred)
    logreg_results[C] = accuracy
```

6.6.1.7 Summarize the Performance of each Method in Terms of Accuracy

```
# Print the results of each method
print("Results of Classification Methods:")
print("KNN:")
for k, accuracy in knn_results.items():
    print(f"k = {k}, Accuracy: {accuracy:.2f}")

print("\nDecision Trees:")
for max_depth, accuracy in dt_results.items():
    print(f"Max Depth = {max_depth}, Accuracy: {accuracy:.2f}")

print("\nSVM:")
for C, accuracy in svm_results.items():
    print(f"C = {C}, Accuracy: {accuracy:.2f}")

print("\nNaive Bayes:")
print(f"Accuracy: {nb_accuracy:.2f}")

print("\nLogistic Regression:")
for C, accuracy in logreg_results.items():
    print(f"C = {C}, Accuracy: {accuracy:.2f}")
```

```
Results of Classification Methods:
KNN:
k = 1, Accuracy: 0.78
k = 5, Accuracy: 0.72
k = 9, Accuracy: 0.72
k = 13, Accuracy: 0.72
k = 17, Accuracy: 0.78
k = 21, Accuracy: 0.78
k = 25, Accuracy: 0.78
k = 29, Accuracy: 0.78
k = 33, Accuracy: 0.78
k = 37, Accuracy: 0.81
k = 41, Accuracy: 0.81
k = 45, Accuracy: 0.81
k = 49, Accuracy: 0.75

Decision Trees:
Max Depth = 1, Accuracy: 0.67
Max Depth = 3, Accuracy: 0.94
Max Depth = 5, Accuracy: 0.94
Max Depth = 7, Accuracy: 0.94
Max Depth = 9, Accuracy: 0.94
Max Depth = 11, Accuracy: 0.94
Max Depth = 13, Accuracy: 0.94
Max Depth = 15, Accuracy: 0.94
Max Depth = 17, Accuracy: 0.94
```

```
Max Depth = 19, Accuracy: 0.94

SVM:
C = 0.001, Accuracy: 0.39
C = 0.01, Accuracy: 0.39
C = 0.1, Accuracy: 0.78
C = 1, Accuracy: 0.81
C = 10, Accuracy: 0.78
C = 100, Accuracy: 0.83
C = 200, Accuracy: 0.83

Naive Bayes:
Accuracy: 1.00

Logistic Regression:
C = 0.001, Accuracy: 0.89
C = 0.01, Accuracy: 1.00
C = 0.1, Accuracy: 1.00
C = 1, Accuracy: 0.97
C = 10, Accuracy: 0.94
C = 100, Accuracy: 0.94
C = 200, Accuracy: 0.94
```

6.6.1.8 Visualize the Accuracy for each Method

```python
# Visualize the accuracy vs hyperparameter for each method
plt.figure(figsize=(12, 6))
plt.subplot(2, 2, 1)
plt.plot(list(knn_results.keys()), list(knn_results.values()), marker='o')
plt.xlabel('k Value')
plt.ylabel('Accuracy')
plt.title('Accuracy vs k for KNN')

plt.subplot(2, 2, 2)
plt.plot(list(dt_results.keys()), list(dt_results.values()), marker='o')
plt.xlabel('Max Depth')
plt.ylabel('Accuracy')
plt.title('Accuracy vs Max Depth for Decision Trees')

plt.subplot(2, 2, 3)
plt.plot(C_values, list(svm_results.values()), marker='o')
plt.xscale('log')
plt.xlabel('C Value')
plt.ylabel('Accuracy')
plt.title('Accuracy vs C for SVM')

plt.subplot(2, 2, 4)
plt.plot(C_values, list(logreg_results.values()), marker='o')
plt.xscale('log')
plt.xlabel('C Value')
plt.ylabel('Accuracy')
plt.title('Accuracy vs C for Logistic Regression')
```

```
plt.tight_layout()
plt.show()
```

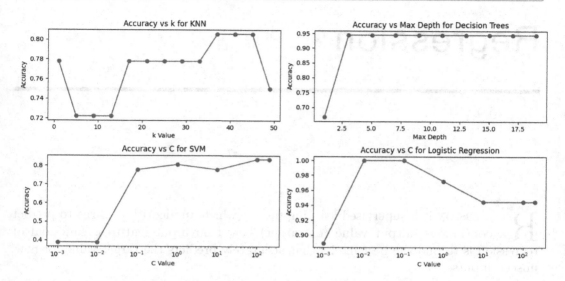

Figure 6.26 Accuracy Comparison Among Classification Methods

6.6.1.9 Conclusion

This tutorial covers various classification methods (KNN, Decision Trees, SVM, Naive Bayes, and Logistic Regression) using the Wine Dataset. It demonstrates how to apply each method with different hyperparameters, summarizes their performance in terms of accuracy, and visualizes the accuracy for comparison.

Feel free to experiment with other classification algorithms, hyperparameters, or additional datasets to further explore different classification techniques.

## CHAPTER 7

Regression

REGRESSION is a supervised learning task in which an algorithm learns to predict a continuous output value (or target) based on input features. The goal of regression is to find the best model that accurately predicts the target value for new, unseen inputs.

There are many different regression methods we use with Scikit-learn, but some of the most common include:

- Linear Regression: A simple model that finds the best linear relationship between the input features and the target value.

- Polynomial Regression: A non-linear extension of Linear Regression that uses polynomial functions of the input features to fit the data.

- Ridge Regression: A Linear Regression model that includes a regularization term to prevent overfitting.

- Lasso Regression: A Linear Regression model that includes a regularization term to shrink the coefficient of less important features to zero.

- Decision Tree Regression: A tree-based model that uses a series of if-then rules to make predictions.

- Random Forest Regression: An ensemble method that combines many decision trees to improve the accuracy of predictions.

- Gradient Boosting Regression: An ensemble method that combines many weak models to improve the accuracy of predictions.

7.1 SIMPLE REGRESSION

Simple Regression, also known as Linear Regression, is a fundamental statistical and machine learning technique used for modeling and analyzing the linear relationship

DOI: 10.1201/9781003462781-7

between two variables: one independent variable (predictor) and one dependent variable (outcome). Simple Regression is a powerful method for modeling linear relationships between variables. It is commonly used for making predictions and understanding how changes in one variable affect another. Scikit-learn provides a user-friendly environment for implementing Simple Regression models. You will explore practical implementation steps, including data preparation and exploration, which involve cleaning and visualizing the dataset to identify trends and relationships, using the LinearRegression class in Scikit-learn to fit a Linear Regression model to the data, and assessing the goodness of fit and model performance using metrics like R-squared and residual analysis.

7.1.1 Tutorial – California Housing Price

Documentation: https://scikit-learn.org/stable/modules/generated/sklearn.linear_model.LinearRegression.html

7.1.1.1 Setup

```
import numpy as np
import pandas as pd
import seaborn as sns
import matplotlib.pyplot as plt
```

```
df = pd.read_csv('/content/sample_data/california_housing_train.csv')
df.head()
```

```
   longitude  latitude  housing_median_age  total_rooms  total_bedrooms  \
0   -114.31     34.19                15.0       5612.0          1283.0
1   -114.47     34.40                19.0       7650.0          1901.0
2   -114.56     33.69                17.0        720.0           174.0
3   -114.57     33.64                14.0       1501.0           337.0
4   -114.57     33.57                20.0       1454.0           326.0

   population  households  median_income  median_house_value
0      1015.0       472.0         1.4936             66900.0
1      1129.0       463.0         1.8200             80100.0
2       333.0       117.0         1.6509             85700.0
3       515.0       226.0         3.1917             73400.0
4       624.0       262.0         1.9250             65500.0
```

7.1.1.2 Try total_rooms with total_bedrooms

Simple visualization

```
sns.relplot(data = df, x = 'total_rooms', y = 'total_bedrooms')
```

```
<seaborn.axisgrid.FacetGrid at 0x7f840ad533d0>
```

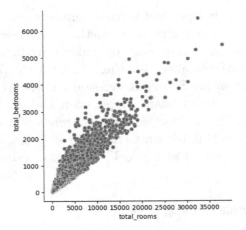

Figure 7.1   A Scatter Plot of Total Rooms VS Total Bedrooms

Prepare independent

```
x = np.array(df['total_rooms']).reshape(-1,1)
```

Prepare dependent

```
y = np.array(df['total_bedrooms']).reshape(-1, 1)
```

Split train and test data

```
from sklearn.model_selection import train_test_split


x_train, x_test, y_train, y_test = train_test_split(x, y, test_size = 0.20)
```

Train the model

```
from sklearn.linear_model import LinearRegression

reg = LinearRegression()
model = reg.fit(x_train, y_train)
```

```
model.coef_, model.intercept_
```

```
(array([[0.18070511]]), array([61.86755768]))
```

Evaluate the model

```
from sklearn.metrics
    import mean_absolute_error,mean_squared_error, r2_score

y_pred = model.predict(x_test)
mae = mean_absolute_error(y_true=y_test,y_pred=y_pred)
mse = mean_squared_error(y_true=y_test,y_pred=y_pred)
```

```
rmse = mean_squared_error(y_true=y_test,y_pred=y_pred,squared=False)
mse = mean_squared_error(y_test, y_pred)
r2 = r2_score(y_test, y_pred)

print('MAE: {} MSE: {} RMSE: {} R^2 {}'.format(mae, mse, rmse, r2))
```

```
MAE: 101.35888011777651
MSE: 23752.731604495282
RMSE: 154.1192123146731
R^2 0.8637647401970822
```

Visualize your result

```
plt.scatter(x_test, y_test)
plt.scatter(x_test, y_pred)
```

```
<matplotlib.collections.PathCollection at 0x7f840540fbe0>
```

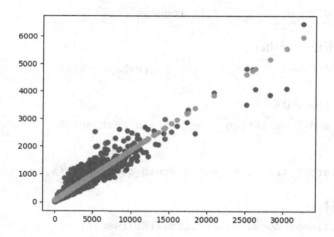

Figure 7.2 A Comparison with Predicted and True Values

7.1.1.3 *Try Median Income with Median House Value*

Simple visualization

```
sns.relplot(data = df, x = 'median_income', y = 'median_house_value')
```

```
<seaborn.axisgrid.FacetGrid at 0x7f84053cedc0>
```

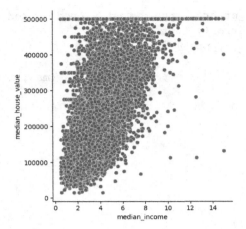

Figure 7.3 A Scatter Plot of Median Income VS Median House Value

Prepare independent variable

```
x = np.array(df['median_income']).reshape(-1,1)
```

Prepare dependent variable

```
y = np.array(df['median_house_value']).reshape(-1,1)
```

Split train and test data

```
from sklearn.model_selection import train_test_split

x_train, x_test, y_train, y_test = train_test_split(x, y, test_size = 0.20)
```

Train the model

```
from sklearn.linear_model import LinearRegression

reg = LinearRegression()
model = reg.fit(x_train, y_train)
```

Evaluate the model

```
from sklearn.metrics
    import mean_absolute_error,mean_squared_error, r2_score

y_pred = model.predict(x_test)
mae = mean_absolute_error(y_true=y_test,y_pred=y_pred)
mse = mean_squared_error(y_true=y_test,y_pred=y_pred)
rmse = mean_squared_error(y_true=y_test,y_pred=y_pred,squared=False)
mse = mean_squared_error(y_test, y_pred)
r2 = r2_score(y_test, y_pred)

print('MAE: {} MSE: {} RMSE: {} R^2 {}'.format(mae, mse, rmse, r2))
```

```
MAE: 61776.93574574111
MSE: 6756173988.71918
RMSE: 82195.94873665721
R^2 0.4940654658976973
```

Visualize your result

```
model.coef_, model.intercept_
```

```
(array([[41854.98097901]]), array([44955.95374405]))
```

```
plt.scatter(x_test, y_test)
plt.scatter(x_test, y_pred)
```

```
<matplotlib.collections.PathCollection at 0x7f8403b29f40>
```

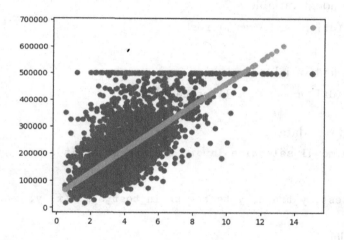

Figure 7.4 A Comparison with Predicted and True Values

7.1.1.4 *Try Households with Population*

Simple visualization

```
sns.relplot(data = df, x = 'households', y = 'population')
```

```
<seaborn.axisgrid.FacetGrid at 0x7f8405370a00>
```

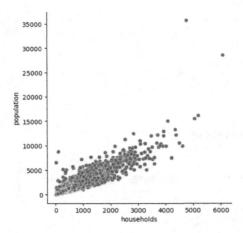

Figure 7.5   A Scatter Plot of Households VS Population

Prepare independent variable

```
x = np.array(df['households']).reshape(-1,1)
```

Prepare dependent variable

```
y = np.array(df['population']).reshape(-1,1)
```

Split train and test data

```
from sklearn.model_selection import train_test_split


x_train, x_test, y_train, y_test = train_test_split(x, y, test_size = 0.20)
```

Train the model

```
from sklearn.linear_model import LinearRegression

reg = LinearRegression()
model = reg.fit(x_train, y_train)
```

```
model.coef_, model.intercept_
```

```
(array([[2.74182763]]), array([55.92258466]))
```

Evaluate the model

```
from sklearn.metrics
    import mean_absolute_error,mean_squared_error, r2_score

y_pred = model.predict(x_test)
mae = mean_absolute_error(y_true=y_test,y_pred=y_pred)
mse = mean_squared_error(y_true=y_test,y_pred=y_pred)
```

```
rmse = mean_squared_error(y_true=y_test,y_pred=y_pred,squared=False)
mse = mean_squared_error(y_test, y_pred)
r2 = r2_score(y_test, y_pred)

print('MAE: {} MSE: {} RMSE: {} R^2 {}'.format(mae, mse, rmse, r2))
```

```
MAE: 270.2469967472556
MSE: 184962.76253804995
RMSE: 430.07297350339275
R^2 0.8435552238188913
```

Visualize your result

```
plt.scatter(x_test, y_test)
plt.scatter(x_test, y_pred)
```

```
<matplotlib.collections.PathCollection at 0x7f84039d3c10>
```

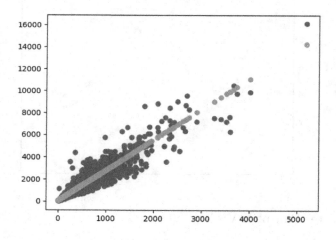

Figure 7.6 A Comparison with Predicted and True Values

7.1.2   Tutorial – California Housing Price

Documentation: https://scikit-learn.org/stable/modules/linear_model.html#polyn omial-regression-extending-linear-models-with-basis-functions

7.1.2.1   *Setup*

```
import numpy as np
import pandas as pd
import seaborn as sns
import matplotlib.pyplot as plt
```

7.1.2.2 *Try Simple Linear Regression first*

Prepare independent variable

```
x = np.random.uniform(-3, 3,(100)).reshape(-1,1)
```

Prepare dependent variable

```
y = x * x - x - 1
error = np.random.rand((100)).reshape(-1, 1)
y = y + error*2
y = y.reshape(-1, 1)
```

Simple visualization

```
plt.scatter(x, y)
```

```
<matplotlib.collections.PathCollection at 0x79d0267957e0>
```

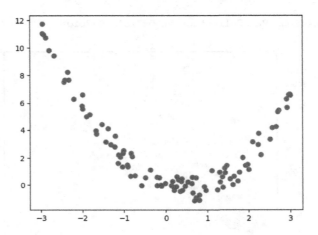

Figure 7.7   A Scatter Plot of X VS Y

Split train and test data

```
from sklearn.model_selection import train_test_split


x_train, x_test, y_train, y_test = train_test_split(x, y, test_size = 0.20)
```

Train the model

```
from sklearn.linear_model import LinearRegression

reg = LinearRegression()
model = reg.fit(x_train, y_train)
```

```
model.coef_, model.intercept_
```

```
(array([[-0.84541517]]), array([2.72343055]))
```

Evaluate the model

```
from sklearn.metrics
     import mean_absolute_error,mean_squared_error, r2_score

y_pred = model.predict(x_test)
mae = mean_absolute_error(y_true=y_test,y_pred=y_pred)
mse = mean_squared_error(y_true=y_test,y_pred=y_pred)
rmse = mean_squared_error(y_true=y_test,y_pred=y_pred,squared=False)
mse = mean_squared_error(y_test, y_pred)
r2 = r2_score(y_test, y_pred)

print('MAE: {} MSE: {} RMSE: {} R^2 {}'.format(mae, mse, rmse, r2))
```

```
MAE: 2.7050964291043655
MSE: 8.22603426094628
RMSE: 2.868106389405086
R^2 0.0913959729699606
```

Visualize your result

```
plt.scatter(x, y)
plt.scatter(x_test, y_pred)
```

```
<matplotlib.collections.PathCollection at 0x79d0266ba2f0>
```

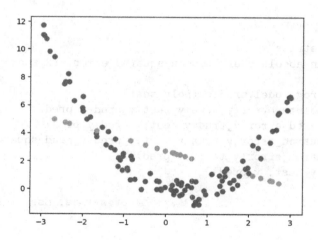

Figure 7.8 A Scatter Plot of X VS Y

Not so good, isn't it?

7.1.2.3 Try polynomial features

```
from sklearn.model_selection import train_test_split


x_train, x_test, y_train, y_test = train_test_split(x, y, test_size = 0.20)
```

```
from sklearn.preprocessing import PolynomialFeatures

poly = PolynomialFeatures(degree=2)
poly_train = poly.fit_transform(x_train.reshape(-1, 1))
poly_test = poly.fit_transform(x_test.reshape(-1, 1))
```

```
poly_train
```

```
array([[ 1.00000000e+00, -1.21969425e+00,  1.48765407e+00],
       [ 1.00000000e+00, -3.69662985e-01,  1.36650722e-01],
       [ 1.00000000e+00, -2.35481836e+00,  5.54516950e+00],
...

       [ 1.00000000e+00,  1.30722306e+00,  1.70883212e+00],
       [ 1.00000000e+00,  2.71660146e+00,  7.37992350e+00]]])
```

Train the model with polynomial features

```
from sklearn.linear_model import LinearRegression

poly_reg_model = LinearRegression()
poly_reg_model.fit(poly_train, y_train)
```

```
LinearRegression()
```

Evaluate the model

```
from sklearn.metrics
    import mean_absolute_error,mean_squared_error, r2_score

y_pred = poly_reg_model.predict(poly_test)
mae = mean_absolute_error(y_true=y_test,y_pred=y_pred)
mse = mean_squared_error(y_true=y_test,y_pred=y_pred)
rmse = mean_squared_error(y_true=y_test,y_pred=y_pred,squared=False)
mse = mean_squared_error(y_test, y_pred)
r2 = r2_score(y_test, y_pred)

print('MAE: {} MSE: {} RMSE: {} R^2 {}'.format(mae, mse, rmse, r2))
```

```
MAE: 0.39897424716689717
MSE: 0.22466684994348615
RMSE: 0.4739903479433797
R^2 0.9596978093663853
```

Visualize the model

```
plt.scatter(x, y)
plt.scatter(x_test, y_pred)
```

```
<matplotlib.collections.PathCollection at 0x79d026554760>
```

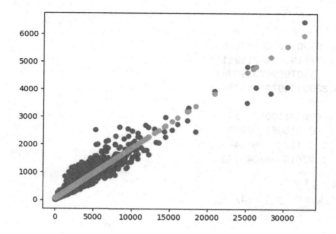

Figure 7.9 A Comparison with Predicted and True Values

Much better! Isn't it? Is the degree higher, the result better? How about we do a degree as 51?

```python
poly = PolynomialFeatures(degree=51)
poly_train = poly.fit_transform(x_train.reshape(-1, 1))
poly_test = poly.fit_transform(x_test.reshape(-1, 1))
poly_reg_model = LinearRegression()
poly_reg_model.fit(poly_train, y_train)
y_pred = poly_reg_model.predict(poly_train)
mae = mean_absolute_error(y_true=y_train,y_pred=y_pred)
mse = mean_squared_error(y_true=y_train,y_pred=y_pred)
rmse = mean_squared_error(y_true=y_train,y_pred=y_pred,squared=False)
mse = mean_squared_error(y_train, y_pred)
r2 = r2_score(y_train, y_pred)

print('''Training:
        MAE: {}
        MSE: {}
        RMSE: {}
        R^2 {}'''.format(mae, mse, rmse, r2))

y_pred = poly_reg_model.predict(poly_test)
mae = mean_absolute_error(y_true=y_test,y_pred=y_pred)
mse = mean_squared_error(y_true=y_test,y_pred=y_pred)
rmse = mean_squared_error(y_true=y_test,y_pred=y_pred,squared=False)
mse = mean_squared_error(y_test, y_pred)
r2 = r2_score(y_test, y_pred)
print('''Testing:
        MAE: {}
        MSE: {}
        RMSE: {}
        R^2 {}'''.format(mae, mse, rmse, r2))
```

```
Training:
        MAE: 0.9300192606660586
        MSE: 1.7181920444211911
        RMSE: 1.3107982470316288
        R^2 0.8398154972074873
Testing:
        MAE: 1.62949110030523
        MSE: 4.890215068197883
        RMSE: 2.2113830668154
        R^2 0.12276163587346123
```

```
plt.scatter(x, y)
plt.scatter(x_test, y_pred)
```

`<matplotlib.collections.PathCollection at 0x79d028a3d270>`

`<matplotlib.collections.PathCollection at 0x79d026554760>`

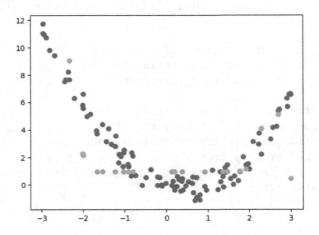

Figure 7.10 A Comparison with Predicted and True Values

Nope! High-degree Polynomial Regression may result in overfitting – Training result is better, but testing result is poor!

7.2 MULTIPLE REGRESSION

Multiple Regression is a powerful statistical and machine learning technique used for modeling and analyzing the relationship between multiple independent variables (predictors) and a single dependent variable (outcome). Multiple Regression extends the concepts of Simple Regression to model complex relationships involving multiple predictors. It allows us to understand how changes in multiple variables affect a single outcome. Scikit-learn provides a versatile environment for implementing Multiple Regression models. You will explore practical implementation steps, including data preparation and exploration, including feature selection and handling multicollinearity, using the LinearRegression class in Scikit-learn to fit a Multiple Regression model to the data, and evaluating model performance and assessing the significance of predictors using hypothesis tests and regression metrics.

7.2.1 Tutorial – California Housing Price

Documentation: https://scikit-learn.org/stable/modules/generated/sklearn.linear_model.LinearRegression.html

7.2.1.1 Setup

```
import numpy as np
import pandas as pd
import seaborn as sns
import matplotlib.pyplot as plt
```

```
df = pd.read_csv('/content/sample_data/california_housing_train.csv')
df.head()
```

```
   longitude  latitude  housing_median_age  total_rooms  total_bedrooms  \
0   -114.31     34.19                15.0       5612.0          1283.0
1   -114.47     34.40                19.0       7650.0          1901.0
2   -114.56     33.69                17.0        720.0           174.0
3   -114.57     33.64                14.0       1501.0           337.0
4   -114.57     33.57                20.0       1454.0           326.0

   population  households  median_income  median_house_value
0      1015.0       472.0         1.4936             66900.0
1      1129.0       463.0         1.8200             80100.0
2       333.0       117.0         1.6509             85700.0
3       515.0       226.0         3.1917             73400.0
4       624.0       262.0         1.9250             65500.0
```

```
df.info()
```

```
<class 'pandas.core.frame.DataFrame'>
RangeIndex: 17000 entries, 0 to 16999
Data columns (total 9 columns):
 #   Column              Non-Null Count  Dtype
---  ------              --------------  -----
 0   longitude           17000 non-null  float64
 1   latitude            17000 non-null  float64
 2   housing_median_age  17000 non-null  float64
 3   total_rooms         17000 non-null  float64
 4   total_bedrooms      17000 non-null  float64
 5   population          17000 non-null  float64
 6   households          17000 non-null  float64
 7   median_income       17000 non-null  float64
 8   median_house_value  17000 non-null  float64
dtypes: float64(9)
```

```
memory usage: 1.2 MB
```

7.2.1.2 *Try Dependent as Median House Value, and two Independent Variables*

Prepare independent variable

```
X = np.array(df[['total_rooms', 'median_income']]).reshape(-1,2)
```

Prepare dependent variable

```
y = np.array(df['total_bedrooms']).reshape(-1, 1)
```

Split train and test data

```
from sklearn.model_selection import train_test_split

X_train, X_test, y_train, y_test = train_test_split(X, y, test_size = 0.20)
```

Train the model

```
from sklearn.linear_model import LinearRegression

reg = LinearRegression()
model = reg.fit(X_train, y_train)
```

```
model.coef_, model.intercept_
```

```
(array([[  0.18665909, -44.67553951]]), array([218.63519336]))
```

Evaluate the model

```
from sklearn.metrics
    import mean_absolute_error,mean_squared_error, r2_score

y_pred = model.predict(X_test)
mae = mean_absolute_error(y_true=y_test,y_pred=y_pred)
mse = mean_squared_error(y_true=y_test,y_pred=y_pred)
rmse = mean_squared_error(y_true=y_test,y_pred=y_pred,squared=False)
mse = mean_squared_error(y_test, y_pred)
r2 = r2_score(y_test, y_pred)

print('MAE: {} MSE: {} RMSE: {} R^2 {}'.format(mae, mse, rmse, r2))
```

```
MAE: 82.63220433916297
MSE: 18266.31046933536
RMSE: 135.1529151344334
R^2 0.8964203264448544
```

Visualize your result

```
plt.scatter(y_pred, y_test)
plt.xlabel('y-pred')
plt.ylabel('y-actual')
```

Text(0, 0.5, 'y-actual')

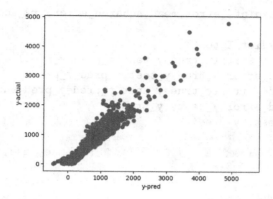

Figure 7.11   A Comparison with Predicted and True Values

7.2.1.3   Try with More Independent Variables

Prepare independent variable

```
X = np.array(df[['housing_median_age',
                 'total_rooms',
                 'population',
                 'households',
                 'median_income',
                 'median_house_value']]).reshape(-1,6)
```

Prepare dependent variable

```
y = np.array(df['total_bedrooms']).reshape(-1, 1)
```

Split train and test data

```
from sklearn.model_selection import train_test_split


X_train, X_test, y_train, y_test = train_test_split(X, y, test_size = 0.20)
```

Train the model

```
from sklearn.linear_model import LinearRegression

reg = LinearRegression()
model = reg.fit(X_train, y_train)
```

```
model.coef_, model.intercept_
```

```
(array([[-5.94684469e-01,  5.52456541e-02, -3.56695472e-02,
          8.76891707e-01, -2.09843990e+01,  8.70098041e-05]]),
 array([85.2479423]))
```

Evaluate the model

```
from sklearn.metrics
    import mean_absolute_error,mean_squared_error, r2_score

y_pred = model.predict(X_test)
mae = mean_absolute_error(y_true=y_test,y_pred=y_pred)
mse = mean_squared_error(y_true=y_test,y_pred=y_pred)
rmse = mean_squared_error(y_true=y_test,y_pred=y_pred,squared=False)
mse = mean_squared_error(y_test, y_pred)
r2 = r2_score(y_test, y_pred)

print('MAE: {} MSE: {} RMSE: {} R^2 {}'.format(mae, mse, rmse, r2))
```

```
MAE: 37.49868335804146
MSE: 4751.900928762269
RMSE: 68.9340331676761
R^2 0.9751011683609353
```

Visualize your result

```
plt.scatter(y_pred, y_test)
plt.xlabel('y-pred')
plt.ylabel('y-actual')
```

Text(0, 0.5, 'y-actual')

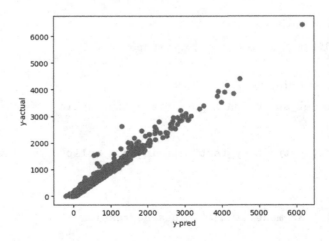

Figure 7.12 A Comparison with Predicted and True Values

7.3 REGULARIZATION

Regularization is a crucial technique in machine learning that helps prevent overfitting, a common problem where a model learns the training data too well but struggles to generalize to unseen data. Overfitting occurs when a model fits the training data noise instead of capturing the underlying patterns. Regularization is a set of techniques designed to mitigate overfitting by adding constraints to the model. Scikit-learn provides tools to implement regularization techniques effectively. You will explore practical implementation steps, including using regularization techniques such as Ridge (L2 regularization) and Lasso (L1 regularization) with the appropriate Ridge and Lasso classes in Scikit-learn, tuning hyperparameters to control the strength of regularization and balance bias and variance, and assessing model performance and comparing regularized models with non-regularized ones.

7.3.1 Tutorial – Regularization

Below is a step-by-step Python tutorial for regression analysis using a dataset, demonstrating Linear Regression, Polynomial Regression, and regularization techniques (Ridge, Lasso, Elastic Net) to handle overfitting.

7.3.1.1 Setup

You can either use a real dataset or generate a dummy dataset for this tutorial. For simplicity, let's create a dummy dataset using NumPy.

```python
import numpy as np
import pandas as pd
import matplotlib.pyplot as plt
from sklearn.model_selection import train_test_split
from sklearn.linear_model import LinearRegression, Ridge, Lasso, ElasticNet
from sklearn.preprocessing import PolynomialFeatures
from sklearn.metrics import r2_score, mean_squared_error
```

```python
# Generating a dummy dataset
X = np.linspace(0, 5, 100).reshape(-1, 1)
y = -5*X + X**2 + np.random.normal(0, 0.5, X.shape[0]).reshape(-1, 1)
```

```python
plt.scatter(X, y)
```

```
<matplotlib.collections.PathCollection at 0x79a048d0e680>
```

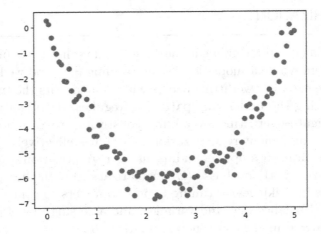

Figure 7.13 A Scatter Plot of X VS Y

7.3.1.2 Linear Regression

Let's start with Linear Regression to see how well it fits the data.

```
# Split the data into training and testing sets
X_train, X_test, y_train, y_test =
    train_test_split(X, y, test_size=0.2, random_state=0)

# Create and fit the linear regression model
linear_model = LinearRegression()
linear_model.fit(X_train, y_train)

# Make predictions on training and testing data
y_train_pred = linear_model.predict(X_train)
y_test_pred = linear_model.predict(X_test)

# Calculate R-squared and mean squared error for evaluation
linear_r2_train = r2_score(y_train, y_train_pred)
linear_r2_test = r2_score(y_test, y_test_pred)
linear_mse_train = mean_squared_error(y_train, y_train_pred)
linear_mse_test = mean_squared_error(y_test, y_test_pred)

print(f"Linear Regression:")
print(f"Training R-squared: {linear_r2_train:.4f}
    , Training MSE: {linear_mse_train:.4f}")
print(f"Testing R-squared: {linear_r2_test:.4f}
    , Testing MSE: {linear_mse_test:.4f}")
```

```
Linear Regression:
Training R-squared: 0.0008, Training MSE: 3.9027
Testing R-squared: -0.0453, Testing MSE: 3.5428
```

7.3.1.3 Polynomial Regression with Degree of 2

Now, let's perform Polynomial Regression with a degree of 2 to capture more complex relationships in the data.

```python
# Transform the features to include polynomial features of degree 2
poly = PolynomialFeatures(degree=2)
X_poly = poly.fit_transform(X)

# Split the polynomial features into training and testing sets
X_poly_train, X_poly_test, y_train, y_test
    = train_test_split(X_poly, y, test_size=0.2, random_state=0)

# Create and fit the polynomial regression model
poly_model = LinearRegression()
poly_model.fit(X_poly_train, y_train)

# Make predictions on training and testing data
y_train_pred_poly = poly_model.predict(X_poly_train)
y_test_pred_poly = poly_model.predict(X_poly_test)

# Calculate R-squared and mean squared error for evaluation
poly_r2_train = r2_score(y_train, y_train_pred_poly)
poly_r2_test = r2_score(y_test, y_test_pred_poly)
poly_mse_train = mean_squared_error(y_train, y_train_pred_poly)
poly_mse_test = mean_squared_error(y_test, y_test_pred_poly)

print(f"\nPolynomial Regression (Degree 2):")
print(f"Training R-squared: {poly_r2_train:.4f}
    , Training MSE: {poly_mse_train:.4f}")
print(f"Testing R-squared: {poly_r2_test:.4f}
    , Testing MSE: {poly_mse_test:.4f}")
```

```
Polynomial Regression (Degree 2):
Training R-squared: 0.9529, Training MSE: 0.1841
Testing R-squared: 0.9229, Testing MSE: 0.2612
```

7.3.1.4 Polynomial Regression with Higher Degree

Next, let's perform Polynomial Regression with a higher degree to observe overfitting. The training result is better than the testing result.

```python
# Transform the features to include polynomial features of higher
degree = 21
poly_high_degree = PolynomialFeatures(degree=degree)
X_poly_high_degree = poly_high_degree.fit_transform(X)

# Split the high-degree polynomial features into training and testing sets
X_poly_high_degree_train, X_poly_high_degree_test, y_train, y_test
    = train_test_split(X_poly_high_degree, y, test_size=0.2
```

```
            , random_state=0)

# Create and fit the high-degree polynomial regression model
poly_model_high_degree = LinearRegression()
poly_model_high_degree.fit(X_poly_high_degree_train, y_train)

# Make predictions on training and testing data
y_train_pred_high_degree
    = poly_model_high_degree.predict(X_poly_high_degree_train)
y_test_pred_high_degree
    = poly_model_high_degree.predict(X_poly_high_degree_test)

# Calculate R-squared and mean squared error for evaluation
poly_r2_train_high_degree
    = r2_score(y_train, y_train_pred_high_degree)
poly_r2_test_high_degree
    = r2_score(y_test, y_test_pred_high_degree)
poly_mse_train_high_degree
    = mean_squared_error(y_train, y_train_pred_high_degree)
poly_mse_test_high_degree
    = mean_squared_error(y_test, y_test_pred_high_degree)

print(f"\nPolynomial Regression (Degree {degree}):")
print(f"Training R-squared: {poly_r2_train_high_degree:.4f}
    , Training MSE: {poly_mse_train_high_degree:.4f}")
print(f"Testing R-squared: {poly_r2_test_high_degree:.4f}
    , Testing MSE: {poly_mse_test_high_degree:.4f}")
```

```
Polynomial Regression (Degree 21):
Training R-squared: 0.9616, Training MSE: 0.1501
Testing R-squared: 0.9100, Testing MSE: 0.3049
```

7.3.1.5 Regularization (Ridge, Lasso, Elastic Net)

Finally, let's introduce regularization techniques to mitigate overfitting in the high-degree Polynomial Regression.

```
# Regularization strengths
alpha_ridge = 0.001
alpha_lasso = 0.001
alpha_elasticnet = 0.001
l1_ratio_elasticnet = 0.5

# Create and fit the Ridge, Lasso, and ElasticNet regression models
ridge_model = Ridge(alpha=alpha_ridge)
ridge_model.fit(X_poly_high_degree_train, y_train)

lasso_model = Lasso(alpha=alpha_lasso)
lasso_model.fit(X_poly_high_degree_train, y_train)
```

```
elasticnet_model = ElasticNet(alpha=alpha_elasticnet
    , l1_ratio=l1_ratio_elasticnet)
elasticnet_model.fit(X_poly_high_degree_train, y_train)

# Make predictions on training and testing data for all regularized models
y_train_pred_ridge = ridge_model.predict(X_poly_high_degree_train)
y_test_pred_ridge = ridge_model.predict(X_poly_high_degree_test)

y_train_pred_lasso = lasso_model.predict(X_poly_high_degree_train)
y_test_pred_lasso = lasso_model.predict(X_poly_high_degree_test)

y_train_pred_elasticnet = elasticnet_model.predict(X_poly_high_degree_train)
y_test_pred_elasticnet = elasticnet_model.predict(X_poly_high_degree_test)

# Calculate R-squared and mean squared error for evaluation
ridge_r2_train = r2_score(y_train, y_train_pred_ridge)
ridge_r2_test = r2_score(y_test, y_test_pred_ridge)
ridge_mse_train = mean_squared_error(y_train, y_train_pred_ridge)
ridge_mse_test = mean_squared_error(y_test, y_test_pred_ridge)

lasso_r2_train = r2_score(y_train, y_train_pred_lasso)
lasso_r2_test = r2_score(y_test, y_test_pred_lasso)
lasso_mse_train = mean_squared_error(y_train, y_train_pred_lasso)
lasso_mse_test = mean_squared_error(y_test, y_test_pred_lasso)

elasticnet_r2_train = r2_score(y_train, y_train_pred_elasticnet)
elasticnet_r2_test = r2_score(y_test, y_test_pred_elasticnet)
elasticnet_mse_train = mean_squared_error(y_train, y_train_pred_elasticnet)
elasticnet_mse_test = mean_squared_error(y_test, y_test_pred_elasticnet)

print("\nRegularization:")
print(f"Ridge Regression - Training R-squared: {ridge_r2_train:.4f}
    , Testing R-squared: {ridge_r2_test:.4f}")
print(f"Lasso Regression - Training R-squared: {lasso_r2_train:.4f}
    , Testing R-squared: {lasso_r2_test:.4f}")
print(f"ElasticNet Regression - Training R-squared: {elasticnet_r2_
train:.4f}
    , Testing R-squared: {elasticnet_r2_test:.4f}")
```

```
Regularization:
Ridge Regression - Training R-squared: 0.9627, Testing R-squared: 0.9151
Lasso Regression - Training R-squared: 0.9554, Testing R-squared: 0.9225
ElasticNet Regression - Training R-squared: 0.9552, Testing R-squared: 0.9228
```

7.3.2   Case Study – California Housing Price

Let's use the California Housing Prices dataset to create a regularization tutorial for regression analysis. We will perform Ridge, Lasso, and Elastic Net regularization techniques to handle overfitting in a Linear Regression model.

This tutorial demonstrates the use of different regularization techniques (Ridge, Lasso, Elastic Net) for regression analysis on the California Housing Prices dataset. Users will be able to understand how regularization helps in controlling overfitting and improving the generalization of Linear Regression models. They can further explore other real-world datasets and apply different regularization strategies to improve the performance of regression models effectively.

7.3.2.1 Setup

We'll start by importing the necessary libraries for data manipulation, visualization, and regression analysis.

```python
import numpy as np
import pandas as pd
import matplotlib.pyplot as plt
from sklearn.datasets import fetch_california_housing
from sklearn.model_selection import train_test_split
from sklearn.linear_model import LinearRegression, Ridge, Lasso, ElasticNet
from sklearn.preprocessing import PolynomialFeatures, StandardScaler
from sklearn.metrics import r2_score, mean_squared_error
```

7.3.2.2 Load and Prepare the Dataset

Next, we'll load the California Housing Prices dataset and prepare it for regression analysis.

```python
# Load the California Housing Prices dataset
data = fetch_california_housing()
X = data.data
y = data.target

# Split the data into training and testing sets
X_train, X_test, y_train, y_test = train_test_split(X, y, test_size=0.2
    , random_state=42)

# Standardize the features
scaler = StandardScaler()
X_train_scaled = scaler.fit_transform(X_train)
X_test_scaled = scaler.transform(X_test)
```

7.3.2.3 Linear Regression (Baseline)

Let's start with a Simple Linear Regression model as a baseline.

```python
# Create and fit the linear regression model
linear_model = LinearRegression()
linear_model.fit(X_train_scaled, y_train)

# Make predictions on training and testing data
y_train_pred = linear_model.predict(X_train_scaled)
y_test_pred = linear_model.predict(X_test_scaled)
```

```
# Calculate R-squared and mean squared error for evaluation
linear_r2_train = r2_score(y_train, y_train_pred)
linear_r2_test = r2_score(y_test, y_test_pred)
linear_mse_train = mean_squared_error(y_train, y_train_pred)
linear_mse_test = mean_squared_error(y_test, y_test_pred)

print(f"Linear Regression (Baseline):")
print(f"Training R-squared: {linear_r2_train:.4f}
    , Training MSE: {linear_mse_train:.4f}")
print(f"Testing R-squared: {linear_r2_test:.4f}
    , Testing MSE: {linear_mse_test:.4f}")
```

```
Linear Regression (Baseline):
Training R-squared: 0.6126, Training MSE: 0.5179
Testing R-squared: 0.5758, Testing MSE: 0.5559
```

7.3.2.4 Polynomial Regression

Next, let's perform Polynomial Regression with different degrees.

```
# Polynomial degrees
degrees = [2, 3, 4]

# Create and fit the polynomial regression models with different degrees
polynomial_models = []
polynomial_r2_train_scores = []
polynomial_r2_test_scores = []

for degree in degrees:
    poly_features = PolynomialFeatures(degree=degree)
    X_train_poly = poly_features.fit_transform(X_train_scaled)
    X_test_poly = poly_features.transform(X_test_scaled)

    model = LinearRegression()
    model.fit(X_train_poly, y_train)
    polynomial_models.append(model)

    # Make predictions on training and testing data
    y_train_pred = model.predict(X_train_poly)
    y_test_pred = model.predict(X_test_poly)

    # Calculate R-squared for evaluation
    polynomial_r2_train = r2_score(y_train, y_train_pred)
    polynomial_r2_test = r2_score(y_test, y_test_pred)

    polynomial_r2_train_scores.append(polynomial_r2_train)
    polynomial_r2_test_scores.append(polynomial_r2_test)

# Find the best degree based on the testing R-squared score
best_degree = degrees[np.argmax(polynomial_r2_test_scores)]
```

```
print(f"\nPolynomial Regression:")
print(f"Best Degree: {best_degree}")
print(f"Training R-squared Scores: {polynomial_r2_train_scores}")
print(f"Testing R-squared Scores: {polynomial_r2_test_scores}")
```

```
Polynomial Regression:
Best Degree: 2
Training R-squared Scores:
    [0.685268198234495, 0.7441415681335484, 0.7893228446487628]
Testing R-squared Scores:
    [0.6456819729261878, -18.38870805843526, -11476.104183339065]
```

7.3.2.5 Ridge Regression

Now, let's perform Ridge Regression with different alpha values.

```
# Regularization strengths (alpha values)
alphas = [0.001, 0.01, 0.1, 1, 10, 30, 50]

poly_features = PolynomialFeatures(degree=2)
X_train_poly = poly_features.fit_transform(X_train_scaled)
X_test_poly = poly_features.transform(X_test_scaled)

# Create and fit the Ridge regression models with different alpha values
ridge_models = []
ridge_r2_train_scores = []
ridge_r2_test_scores = []

for alpha in alphas:
    ridge_model = Ridge(alpha=alpha)
    ridge_model.fit(X_train_poly, y_train)
    ridge_models.append(ridge_model)

    # Make predictions on training and testing data
    y_train_pred = ridge_model.predict(X_train_poly)
    y_test_pred = ridge_model.predict(X_test_poly)

    # Calculate R-squared for evaluation
    ridge_r2_train = r2_score(y_train, y_train_pred)
    ridge_r2_test = r2_score(y_test, y_test_pred)

    ridge_r2_train_scores.append(ridge_r2_train)
    ridge_r2_test_scores.append(ridge_r2_test)

# Find the best alpha based on the testing R-squared score
best_alpha_ridge = alphas[np.argmax(ridge_r2_test_scores)]

print(f"\nRidge Regression:")
print(f"Best Alpha: {best_alpha_ridge:.4f}")
```

```
print(f"Training R-squared Scores: {ridge_r2_train_scores}")
print(f"Testing R-squared Scores: {ridge_r2_test_scores}")
```

```
Ridge Regression:
Best Alpha: 50.0000
Training R-squared Scores:
    [0.6852681982309979, 0.6852681978848241, 0.6852681633541837,
    0.685264794671512, 0.6849940748677977, 0.6835523857209759,
    0.6816443257072609]
Testing R-squared Scores:
    [0.645683225805578, 0.6456944994375847, 0.6458070098962285,
    0.6469096540341595, 0.6558501677208112, 0.6655692803642396,
    0.6672535561034868]
```

7.3.2.6 Lasso Regression

Next, let's perform Lasso Regression with different alpha values.

```
# Create and fit the Lasso regression models with different alpha values
lasso_models = []
lasso_r2_train_scores = []
lasso_r2_test_scores = []

for alpha in alphas:
    lasso_model = Lasso(alpha=alpha)
    lasso_model.fit(X_train_poly, y_train)
    lasso_models.append(lasso_model)

    # Make predictions on training and testing data
    y_train_pred = lasso_model.predict(X_train_poly)
    y_test_pred = lasso_model.predict(X_test_poly)

    # Calculate R-squared for evaluation
    lasso_r2_train = r2_score(y_train, y_train_pred)
    lasso_r2_test = r2_score(y_test, y_test_pred)

    lasso_r2_train_scores.append(lasso_r2_train)
    lasso_r2_test_scores.append(lasso_r2_test)

# Find the best alpha based on the testing R-squared score
best_alpha_lasso = alphas[np.argmax(lasso_r2_test_scores)]

print(f"\nLasso Regression:")
print(f"Best Alpha: {best_alpha_lasso:.4f}")
print(f"Training R-squared Scores: {lasso_r2_train_scores}")
print(f"Testing R-squared Scores: {lasso_r2_test_scores}")
```

```
Lasso Regression:
Best Alpha: 0.0010
Training R-squared Scores:
```

```
    [0.6830030979089348, 0.6305732853769765, 0.500981674817156,
    0.033220008724097694, 0.0, 0.0,
    0.0]
Testing R-squared Scores:
    [0.6686741743527673, 0.533056472931786, 0.4823562161721351,
    0.032132551538488596, -0.00021908714592466794, -0.00021908714592466794,
    -0.00021908714592466794]
```

7.3.2.7 Elastic Net Regression

Finally, let's perform Elastic Net Regression with different alpha and l1_ratio values.

```python
# ElasticNet parameters (alpha and l1_ratio values)
alphas_elasticnet = [0.001, 0.01, 0.1, 1, 10, 50]
l1_ratios = [0.2, 0.5, 0.7, 0.9]

# Create and fit the models with different alpha and l1_ratio values
elasticnet_models = []
elasticnet_r2_train_scores = []
elasticnet_r2_test_scores = []

for alpha in alphas_elasticnet:
    for l1_ratio in l1_ratios:
        elasticnet_model = ElasticNet(alpha=alpha, l1_ratio=l1_ratio)
        elasticnet_model.fit(X_train_poly, y_train)
        elasticnet_models.append(elasticnet_model)

        # Make predictions on training and testing data
        y_train_pred = elasticnet_model.predict(X_train_poly)
        y_test_pred = elasticnet_model.predict(X_test_poly)

        # Calculate R-squared for evaluation
        elasticnet_r2_train = r2_score(y_train, y_train_pred)
        elasticnet_r2_test = r2_score(y_test, y_test_pred)

        elasticnet_r2_train_scores.append(elasticnet_r2_train)
        elasticnet_r2_test_scores.append(elasticnet_r2_test)

# Find the best alpha and l1_ratio based on the testing R-squared score
best_alpha_elasticnet, best_l1_ratio_elasticnet =
  alphas_elasticnet[np.argmax(elasticnet_r2_test_scores)//len(l1_ratios)],
  l1_ratios[np.argmax(elasticnet_r2_test_scores) % len(l1_ratios)]

print(f"\nElasticNet Regression:")
print(f"Best Alpha: {best_alpha_elasticnet:.4f}
    , Best l1_ratio: {best_l1_ratio_elasticnet:.1f}")
print(f"Training R-squared Scores: {elasticnet_r2_train_scores}")
print(f"Testing R-squared Scores: {elasticnet_r2_test_scores}")
```

```
ElasticNet Regression:
Best Alpha: 0.0010, Best l1_ratio: 0.9
```

```
Training R-squared Scores:
    [0.6840310978294589, 0.6837217689230024, 0.6834122448233106,
    0.6831585830280078, 0.6641895730066483, 0.654089814353995,
    0.6463124687609253, 0.6364839821265846, 0.5619051580675156,
    0.5325527976563843, 0.5104019630875991, 0.5043656964193155,
    0.3174625276332542, 0.21148526134241852, 0.08567216955936541,
    0.05311242187826348, 0.0, 0.0,
    0.0, 0.0, 0.0,
    0.0, 0.0, 0.0]
Testing R-squared Scores:
    [0.665131384671392, 0.6672768269417034, 0.6679746333269325,
    0.6687496873021064, 0.5953794418651244, 0.534895420337363,
    0.5324894830873397, 0.53544136023843, 0.5437773103890866,
    0.5153003945070083, 0.49307869728746057, 0.4864961977437864,
    0.30776990091131096, 0.2058625168336501, 0.0831325334530788,
    0.051496641763479345, -0.00021908714592466794, -0.00021908714592466794,
    -0.00021908714592466794, -0.00021908714592466794, -0.00021908714592466794,
    -0.00021908714592466794, -0.00021908714592466794, -0.00021908714592466794]
```

7.3.2.8   Visualization

You can visualize the R-squared scores for different regularization techniques.

```
# Plotting R-squared scores for different regularization techniques
plt.figure(figsize=(12, 6))

plt.subplot(1, 2, 1)
plt.plot(alphas, ridge_r2_test_scores, label="Ridge Regression")
plt.plot(alphas, lasso_r2_test_scores, label="Lasso Regression")
plt.plot(elasticnet_r2_test_scores, label="ElasticNet Regression")
plt.xlabel("Alpha (Regularization Strength)")
plt.ylabel("Testing R-squared")
plt.title("R-squared Scores for Different Regularization Techniques")
plt.legend()

plt.subplot(1, 2, 2)
plt.plot(degrees, polynomial_r2_test_scores, marker='o')
plt.xlabel("Polynomial Degree")
plt.ylabel("Testing R-squared")
plt.title("R-squared Scores for Different Polynomial Degrees")
plt.xticks(degrees)
plt.tight_layout()
plt.show()
```

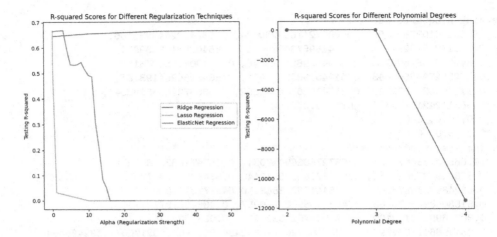

Figure 7.14 Performance Comparison between Polynomial Regression and Regularization

7.4 CROSS-VALIDATION

Cross-validation is a technique used to estimate how well a model will perform on unseen data by systematically splitting the dataset into multiple subsets. It helps in mitigating issues like overfitting and provides a more robust evaluation of model performance. Scikit-learn provides user-friendly tools to implement cross-validation effectively. You will explore practical implementation steps, including using the KFold or StratifiedKFold classes in Scikit-learn to create cross-validation folds, employing the cross_val_score function to evaluate model performance using cross-validation, and understanding the use of different scoring metrics (e.g., accuracy, mean squared error) for evaluation.

7.4.1 Tutorial – Cross-Validation

We will generate a dummy dataset for regression and demonstrate how to perform 3-fold, 5-fold, 10-fold, and leave-one-out cross-validation for regression models. Finally, we will compare the results to understand the performance of each approach.

7.4.1.1 Setup

```
import numpy as np
import pandas as pd
import matplotlib.pyplot as plt
from sklearn.model_selection import KFold, LeaveOneOut
from sklearn.linear_model import LinearRegression
from sklearn.metrics import mean_squared_error
```

7.4.1.2 Generate Dummy Dataset

Let's generate a dummy dataset for regression analysis using NumPy.

```
# Generating a dummy dataset
np.random.seed(0)
X = np.linspace(0, 10, 100).reshape(-1, 1)
y = X  + np.random.normal(0, 1, X.shape[0]).reshape(-1, 1)
plt.scatter(X, y)
```

```
<matplotlib.collections.PathCollection at 0x7c68f21d7e50>
```

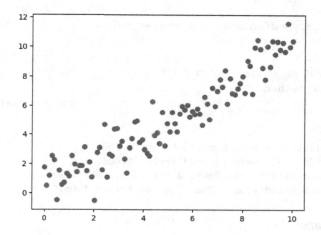

Figure 7.15 A Scatter Plot of X VS Y

7.4.1.3 Cross-Validation

Now, we'll perform cross-validation using different techniques and compare the results.

```
# Create a list to store the MSEs for different techniques
mse_scores = []

# List of cross-validation techniques to be used
cv_methods = ['3-fold', '5-fold', '10-fold', 'Leave-One-Out']

for cv_method in cv_methods:
    if cv_method == '3-fold':
        cv = KFold(n_splits=3, shuffle=True, random_state=0)
    elif cv_method == '5-fold':
        cv = KFold(n_splits=5, shuffle=True, random_state=0)
    elif cv_method == '10-fold':
        cv = KFold(n_splits=10, shuffle=True, random_state=0)
    else:
        cv = LeaveOneOut()
```

```
# Create and fit the linear regression model using cross-validation
model = LinearRegression()
mse_scores_cv = []

for train_idx, test_idx in cv.split(X):
    X_train, X_test = X[train_idx], X[test_idx]
    y_train, y_test = y[train_idx], y[test_idx]

    model.fit(X_train, y_train)
    y_pred = model.predict(X_test)

    mse = mean_squared_error(y_test, y_pred)
    mse_scores_cv.append(mse)

mse_scores.append(np.mean(mse_scores_cv))

# Display the mean squared errors for different cross-validation techniques
for i, cv_method in enumerate(cv_methods):
    print(f"{cv_method}
        Cross-Validation - Mean Squared Error: {mse_scores[i]:.4f}")
```

```
3-fold Cross-Validation - Mean Squared Error: 1.0650
5-fold Cross-Validation - Mean Squared Error: 1.0840
10-fold Cross-Validation - Mean Squared Error: 1.0566
Leave-One-Out Cross-Validation - Mean Squared Error: 1.0510
```

7.4.1.4 Visualization

We can also visualize the mean squared errors for different cross-validation techniques using a bar plot.

```
# Plotting mean squared errors for different cross-validation techniques
plt.figure(figsize=(8, 6))
plt.bar(cv_methods, mse_scores)
plt.xlabel("Cross-Validation Method")
plt.ylabel("Mean Squared Error")
plt.title("Mean Squared Error for Different Cross-Validation Techniques")
plt.show()
```

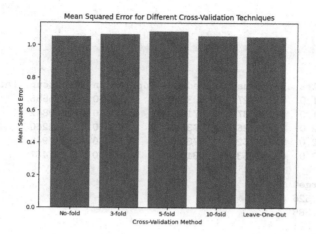

Figure 7.16 Mean Squared Error for Different Cross-Validation Techniques

7.4.2 Case Study – California Housing Price

Let's use the California Housing Prices dataset, which is available in Scikit-learn, for this tutorial. We'll perform cross-validation using 5-fold and leave-one-out techniques and compare the results.

7.4.2.1 Setup

We'll start by importing the necessary libraries for data manipulation, cross-validation, regression, and dataset loading.

```python
import numpy as np
import pandas as pd
import matplotlib.pyplot as plt
from sklearn.datasets import fetch_california_housing
from sklearn.model_selection import KFold, LeaveOneOut
from sklearn.linear_model import LinearRegression
from sklearn.metrics import mean_squared_error
```

7.4.2.2 Load and Explore the Dataset

Next, we'll load the California Housing Prices dataset and explore its features and target variable.

```python
# Load the California Housing Prices dataset
data = fetch_california_housing()
X = data.data
y = data.target

# Convert the dataset to a DataFrame for easier exploration
df = pd.DataFrame(data=np.c_[X, y]
    , columns=data.feature_names + ['target'])
```

```
# Print the first few rows of the dataset
print(df.head())
```

```
   MedInc  HouseAge  AveRooms  AveBedrms  Population  AveOccup  Latitude  \
0  8.3252      41.0  6.984127   1.023810       322.0  2.555556     37.88
1  8.3014      21.0  6.238137   0.971880      2401.0  2.109842     37.86
2  7.2574      52.0  8.288136   1.073446       496.0  2.802260     37.85
3  5.6431      52.0  5.817352   1.073059       558.0  2.547945     37.85
4  3.8462      52.0  6.281853   1.081081       565.0  2.181467     37.85

   Longitude  target
0    -122.23   4.526
1    -122.22   3.585
2    -122.24   3.521
3    -122.25   3.413
4    -122.25   3.422
```

7.4.2.3 Cross-Validation

Now, we'll perform cross-validation using different techniques and compare the results.

```
# Create a list to store the MSEs for different techniques
mse_scores = []

# List of cross-validation techniques to be used
cv_methods = ['3-fold', '5-fold', '10-fold', 'Leave-One-Out']

for cv_method in cv_methods:
    if cv_method == '3-fold':
        cv = KFold(n_splits=3, shuffle=True, random_state=0)
    elif cv_method == '5-fold':
        cv = KFold(n_splits=5, shuffle=True, random_state=0)
    elif cv_method == '10-fold':
        cv = KFold(n_splits=10, shuffle=True, random_state=0)
    else:
        cv = LeaveOneOut()

    # Create and fit the linear regression model using cross-validation
    model = LinearRegression()
    mse_scores_cv = []

    for train_idx, test_idx in cv.split(X):
        X_train, X_test = X[train_idx], X[test_idx]
        y_train, y_test = y[train_idx], y[test_idx]

        model.fit(X_train, y_train)
        y_pred = model.predict(X_test)

        mse = mean_squared_error(y_test, y_pred)
        mse_scores_cv.append(mse)
```

```
    mse_scores.append(np.mean(mse_scores_cv))

# Display the mean squared errors for different cross-validation techniques
for i, cv_method in enumerate(cv_methods):
    print(f"{cv_method}
        Cross-Validation - Mean Squared Error: {mse_scores[i]:.4f}")
```

```
3-fold Cross-Validation - Mean Squared Error: 0.5264
5-fold Cross-Validation - Mean Squared Error: 0.5277
10-fold Cross-Validation - Mean Squared Error: 0.5279
Leave-One-Out Cross-Validation - Mean Squared Error: 0.5282
```

7.4.2.4 Visualization

We can visualize the mean squared errors for different cross-validation techniques using a bar plot.

```
# Plotting mean squared errors for different cross-validation techniques
plt.figure(figsize=(8, 6))
plt.bar(cv_methods, mse_scores)
plt.xlabel("Cross-Validation Method")
plt.ylabel("Mean Squared Error")
plt.title("Mean Squared Error for Different Cross-Validation Techniques")
plt.show()
```

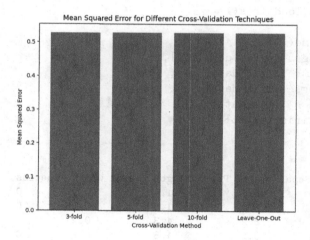

Figure 7.17 Mean Squared Error for Different Cross-Validation Techniques

7.5 ENSEMBLE METHODS

Ensemble methods are powerful techniques in machine learning that combine the predictions of multiple models to improve overall predictive performance. Ensemble methods leverage the wisdom of crowds by combining multiple models to make predictions that are often more accurate and robust than those of individual models.

They are particularly effective in reducing overfitting and improving generalization. In this section, you will gain a foundational understanding of ensemble methods. Bagging is an ensemble technique that builds multiple base models in parallel, each trained on a different subset of the training data. Boosting is an ensemble technique that builds base models sequentially, with each model focusing on the mistakes made by the previous ones. Stacking is an advanced ensemble technique that combines the predictions of multiple base models using a meta-learner. In this section, you will learn a comprehensive understanding of ensemble methods, including Bagging, Boosting, and Stacking, using the Scikit-learn package.

7.5.1   Tutorial – Iris Binary Classification Using Random Forests

https://scikit-learn.org/stable/modules/generated/sklearn.ensemble.Ra ndomForestClassifier.html

7.5.1.1   Setup

```
import numpy as np
import pandas as pd
import matplotlib.pyplot as plt
import seaborn as sns
from sklearn import datasets
```

Load the dataset iris

```
iris = datasets.load_iris()
```

```
df = pd.DataFrame(
    {'Sepal length': iris.data[:,0],
     'Sepal width': iris.data[:,1],
     'Petal length':iris.data[:,2],
     'Petal width':iris.data[:,3],
     'Species':iris.target})
df.head()
```

	Sepal length	Sepal width	Petal length	Petal width	Species
0	5.1	3.5	1.4	0.2	0
1	4.9	3.0	1.4	0.2	0
2	4.7	3.2	1.3	0.2	0
3	4.6	3.1	1.5	0.2	0
4	5.0	3.6	1.4	0.2	0

```
df = df[df['Species'] !=0]
```

```
df.info()
```

```
<class 'pandas.core.frame.DataFrame'>
Int64Index: 100 entries, 50 to 149
Data columns (total 5 columns):
 #   Column         Non-Null Count  Dtype
```

```
---  ------      --------------   -----
 0   Sepal length  100 non-null    float64
 1   Sepal width   100 non-null    float64
 2   Petal length  100 non-null    float64
 3   Petal width   100 non-null    float64
 4   Species       100 non-null    int64
dtypes: float64(4), int64(1)
memory usage: 4.7 KB
```

```
sns.relplot(data = df, x = 'Sepal length', y = 'Sepal width'
    , hue = 'Species')
```

```
<seaborn.axisgrid.FacetGrid at 0x7fe5f92a1d30>
```

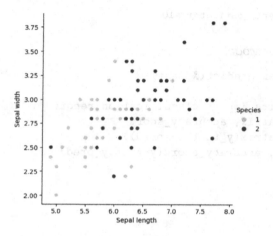

Figure 7.18   A Scatter Plot of Sepal Length VS Sepal Width with Species Differentiation

Train-test split   training and testing datasets are split with test_size as ratio. Here we use 80% for training and 20% for testing

```
from sklearn.model_selection import train_test_split

X = df[df.columns[:4]]
y = df[df.columns[-1]]
X_train, X_test, y_train, y_test = train_test_split(X, y, test_size = 0.20)
```

```
X_train
```

	Sepal length	Sepal width	Petal length	Petal width
147	6.5	3.0	5.2	2.0
109	7.2	3.6	6.1	2.5
69	5.6	2.5	3.9	1.1
92	5.8	2.6	4.0	1.2
145	6.7	3.0	5.2	2.3
..	...	...	...	...
136	6.3	3.4	5.6	2.4

138	6.0	3.0	4.8	1.8
76	6.8	2.8	4.8	1.4
114	5.8	2.8	5.1	2.4
55	5.7	2.8	4.5	1.3

```
[80 rows x 4 columns]
```

7.5.1.2 Train Your Model

```python
from sklearn.ensemble import RandomForestClassifier
classifier = RandomForestClassifier(n_estimators=10)
classifier.fit(X_train, y_train)
```

```
RandomForestClassifier(n_estimators=10)
```

7.5.1.3 Evaluate Your Model

```python
y_pred = classifier.predict(X_test)
```

```python
from sklearn.metrics import classification_report
    , confusion_matrix, accuracy_score
print(confusion_matrix(y_test, y_pred))
print('Accuracy:', accuracy_score(y_test,y_pred))
```

```
[[10  0]
 [ 1  9]]
Accuracy: 0.95
```

7.5.2 Tutorial – Iris Multi Classification Using Random Forests

https://scikit-learn.org/stable/modules/generated/sklearn.ensemble.Ra ndomForestClassifier.html

7.5.2.1 Setup

```python
import numpy as np
import pandas as pd
import matplotlib.pyplot as plt
import seaborn as sns
from sklearn import datasets
```

Load the dataset iris

```python
iris = datasets.load_iris()
```

```python
df = pd.DataFrame(
    {'Sepal length': iris.data[:,0],
     'Sepal width': iris.data[:,1],
     'Petal length':iris.data[:,2],
```

```
        'Petal width':iris.data[:,3],
        'Species':iris.target})
df.head()
```

	Sepal length	Sepal width	Petal length	Petal width	Species
0	5.1	3.5	1.4	0.2	0
1	4.9	3.0	1.4	0.2	0
2	4.7	3.2	1.3	0.2	0
3	4.6	3.1	1.5	0.2	0
4	5.0	3.6	1.4	0.2	0

```
df.info()
```

```
<class 'pandas.core.frame.DataFrame'>
RangeIndex: 150 entries, 0 to 149
Data columns (total 5 columns):
 #   Column        Non-Null Count   Dtype
---  ------        --------------   -----
 0   Sepal length  150 non-null     float64
 1   Sepal width   150 non-null     float64
 2   Petal length  150 non-null     float64
 3   Petal width   150 non-null     float64
 4   Species       150 non-null     int64
dtypes: float64(4), int64(1)
memory usage: 6.0 KB
```

```
sns.relplot(data = df, x = 'Sepal length', y = 'Sepal width'
    , hue = 'Species')
```

```
<seaborn.axisgrid.FacetGrid at 0x7fe8817e8cd0>
```

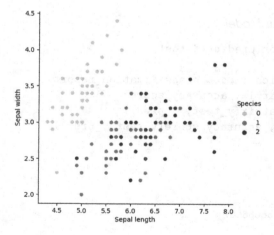

Figure 7.19   A Scatter Plot of Sepal Length VS Sepal Width with Species Differentiation

Train-test split   training and testing datasets are split with test_size as ratio. Here we use 80% for training and 20% for testing

```
from sklearn.model_selection import train_test_split

X = df[df.columns[:4]]
y = df[df.columns[-1]]
X_train, X_test, y_train, y_test = train_test_split(X, y, test_size = 0.20)
```

```
X_train
```

	Sepal length	Sepal width	Petal length	Petal width
118	7.7	2.6	6.9	2.3
45	4.8	3.0	1.4	0.3
28	5.2	3.4	1.4	0.2
57	4.9	2.4	3.3	1.0
98	5.1	2.5	3.0	1.1
..	...	...	...	...
126	6.2	2.8	4.8	1.8
91	6.1	3.0	4.6	1.4
43	5.0	3.5	1.6	0.6
90	5.5	2.6	4.4	1.2
110	6.5	3.2	5.1	2.0

```
[120 rows x 4 columns]
```

7.5.2.2   Train Your Model

```
from sklearn.ensemble import RandomForestClassifier
classifier = RandomForestClassifier(n_estimators=10)
classifier.fit(X_train, y_train)
```

```
RandomForestClassifier(n_estimators=10)
```

7.5.2.3   Evaluate Your Model

```
y_pred = classifier.predict(X_test)
```

```
from sklearn.metrics import classification_report
    , confusion_matrix, accuracy_score
print(confusion_matrix(y_test, y_pred))
print('Accuracy:', accuracy_score(y_test,y_pred))
```

```
[[11  0  0]
 [ 0  6  0]
 [ 0  1 12]]
Accuracy: 0.9666666666666667
```

7.5.3   Case Study – California Housing Price

Let's create a comprehensive tutorial that includes Linear Regression, Polynomial Regression, Polynomial Regression with regularization, Multivariable Regression (using multiple features), and ensemble methods using the California Housing Prices dataset.

We will explore three popular ensemble techniques: Bagging, Boosting, and Stacking. For this tutorial, we'll use the Gradient Boosting Regressor, Random Forest Regressor, and a Simple Linear Regression as base models.

This comprehensive tutorial covers various regression techniques, including Linear Regression, Polynomial Regression, Polynomial Regression with regularization (Ridge, Lasso, Elastic Net), Multivariable Regression, and Random Forest Regression using ensemble methods. Users will be able to understand the strengths and weaknesses of each method and how to select appropriate models for different regression tasks. They can further explore other real-world datasets and apply these regression models to make accurate predictions.

7.5.3.1 Import Libraries

We'll start by importing the necessary libraries for data manipulation, visualization, and regression analysis.

```
import numpy as np
import pandas as pd
import matplotlib.pyplot as plt
from sklearn.datasets import fetch_california_housing
from sklearn.model_selection import train_test_split
from sklearn.linear_model import LinearRegression, Ridge, Lasso, ElasticNet
from sklearn.preprocessing import PolynomialFeatures, StandardScaler
from sklearn.metrics import r2_score, mean_squared_error
from sklearn.ensemble import RandomForestRegressor
```

7.5.3.2 Load and Prepare the Dataset

Next, we'll load the California Housing Prices dataset and prepare it for regression analysis.

```
# Load the California Housing Prices dataset
data = fetch_california_housing()
X = data.data
y = data.target

# Split the data into training and testing sets
X_train, X_test, y_train, y_test = train_test_split(X, y, test_size=0.2
    , random_state=42)

# Standardize the features
scaler = StandardScaler()
X_train_scaled = scaler.fit_transform(X_train)
X_test_scaled = scaler.transform(X_test)
```

7.5.3.3 Linear Regression (Baseline)

Let's start with a Simple Linear Regression model as a baseline.

```
# Create and fit the linear regression model
linear_model = LinearRegression()
linear_model.fit(X_train_scaled, y_train)

# Make predictions on training and testing data
y_train_pred_linear = linear_model.predict(X_train_scaled)
y_test_pred_linear = linear_model.predict(X_test_scaled)

# Calculate R-squared and mean squared error for evaluation
linear_r2_train = r2_score(y_train, y_train_pred_linear)
linear_r2_test = r2_score(y_test, y_test_pred_linear)
linear_mse_train = mean_squared_error(y_train, y_train_pred_linear)
linear_mse_test = mean_squared_error(y_test, y_test_pred_linear)

print(f"Linear Regression (Baseline):")
print(f"Training R-squared: {linear_r2_train:.4f}
    , Training MSE: {linear_mse_train:.4f}")
print(f"Testing R-squared: {linear_r2_test:.4f}
    , Testing MSE: {linear_mse_test:.4f}")
```

```
Linear Regression (Baseline):
Training R-squared: 0.6126, Training MSE: 0.5179
Testing R-squared: 0.5758, Testing MSE: 0.5559
```

7.5.3.4 Polynomial Regression

Next, let's perform Polynomial Regression with different degrees.

```
# Polynomial degrees
degrees = [2, 3, 4]

# Create and fit the polynomial regression models with different degrees
polynomial_models = []
polynomial_r2_train_scores = []
polynomial_r2_test_scores = []

for degree in degrees:
    poly_features = PolynomialFeatures(degree=degree)
    X_train_poly = poly_features.fit_transform(X_train_scaled)
    X_test_poly = poly_features.transform(X_test_scaled)

    model = LinearRegression()
    model.fit(X_train_poly, y_train)
    polynomial_models.append(model)

    # Make predictions on training and testing data
    y_train_pred = model.predict(X_train_poly)
    y_test_pred = model.predict(X_test_poly)

    # Calculate R-squared for evaluation
```

```
        polynomial_r2_train = r2_score(y_train, y_train_pred)
        polynomial_r2_test = r2_score(y_test, y_test_pred)

        polynomial_r2_train_scores.append(polynomial_r2_train)
        polynomial_r2_test_scores.append(polynomial_r2_test)

# Find the best degree based on the testing R-squared score
best_degree = degrees[np.argmax(polynomial_r2_test_scores)]

print(f"\nPolynomial Regression:")
print(f"Best Degree: {best_degree}")
print(f"Training R-squared Scores: {polynomial_r2_train_scores}")
print(f"Testing R-squared Scores: {polynomial_r2_test_scores}")
```

```
Polynomial Regression:
Best Degree: 2
Training R-squared Scores:
    [0.6852681982344955, 0.7441415681335484, 0.7893228446487628]
Testing R-squared Scores:
    [0.6456819729261878, -18.38870805843526, -11476.104183339065]
```

7.5.3.5 Polynomial Regression with Regularization

Now, let's perform Polynomial Regression with regularization using Ridge, Lasso, and Elastic Net.

```
# Continue with degree of 2
poly_features = PolynomialFeatures(degree=2)
X_train_poly = poly_features.fit_transform(X_train_scaled)
X_test_poly = poly_features.transform(X_test_scaled)

# Regularization strengths (alpha values)
alphas = [0.001, 0.01, 0.1, 1, 10, 50]

# Create and fit the regression models with different alpha values
ridge_models = []
ridge_r2_train_scores = []
ridge_r2_test_scores = []

lasso_models = []
lasso_r2_train_scores = []
lasso_r2_test_scores = []

elasticnet_models = []
elasticnet_r2_train_scores = []
elasticnet_r2_test_scores = []

for alpha in alphas:
    ridge_model = Ridge(alpha=alpha)
    ridge_model.fit(X_train_poly, y_train)
```

```
        ridge_models.append(ridge_model)

        # Make predictions on training and testing data
        y_train_pred = ridge_model.predict(X_train_poly)
        y_test_pred = ridge_model.predict(X_test_poly)

        # Calculate R-squared for evaluation
        ridge_r2_train = r2_score(y_train, y_train_pred)
        ridge_r2_test = r2_score(y_test, y_test_pred)

        ridge_r2_train_scores.append(ridge_r2_train)
        ridge_r2_test_scores.append(ridge_r2_test)

        lasso_model = Lasso(alpha=alpha)
        lasso_model.fit(X_train_poly, y_train)
        lasso_models.append(lasso_model)

        # Make predictions on training and testing data
        y_train_pred = lasso_model.predict(X_train_poly)
        y_test_pred = lasso_model.predict(X_test_poly)

        # Calculate R-squared for evaluation
        lasso_r2_train = r2_score(y_train, y_train_pred)
        lasso_r2_test = r2_score(y_test, y_test_pred)

        lasso_r2_train_scores.append(lasso_r2_train)
        lasso_r2_test_scores.append(lasso_r2_test)

        for l1_ratio in [0.2, 0.5, 0.7, 0.9]:
            elasticnet_model = ElasticNet(alpha=alpha, l1_ratio=l1_ratio)
            elasticnet_model.fit(X_train_poly, y_train)
            elasticnet_models.append(elasticnet_model)

            # Make predictions on training and testing data
            y_train_pred = elasticnet_model.predict(X_train_poly)
            y_test_pred = elasticnet_model.predict(X_test_poly)

            # Calculate R-squared for evaluation
            elasticnet_r2_train = r2_score(y_train, y_train_pred)
            elasticnet_r2_test = r2_score(y_test, y_test_pred)

            elasticnet_r2_train_scores.append(elasticnet_r2_train)
            elasticnet_r2_test_scores.append(elasticnet_r2_test)

# Find the best alpha and l1_ratio based on the testing R-squared score
best_alpha_ridge = alphas[np.argmax(ridge_r2_test_scores)]
best_alpha_lasso = alphas[np.argmax(lasso_r2_test_scores)]
best_alpha_elasticnet = alphas[np.argmax(elasticnet_r2_test_scores)]
best_l1_ratio_elasticnet = [0.2, 0.5, 0.7, 0.9]
    [np.argmax(elasticnet_r2_test_scores) % 4]
```

```
print(f"\nPolynomial Regression with Regularization:")
print(f"Best Alpha (Ridge): {best_alpha_ridge:.4f}")
print(f"Best Alpha (Lasso): {best_alpha_lasso:.4f}")
print(f"Best Alpha (ElasticNet): {best_alpha_elasticnet:.4f}")
print(f"Best l1_ratio (ElasticNet): {best_l1_ratio_elasticnet:.1f}")
print(f"Ridge Training R-squared Scores: {ridge_r2_train_scores}")
print(f"Ridge Testing R-squared Scores: {ridge_r2_test_scores}")
print(f"Lasso Training R-squared Scores: {lasso_r2_train_scores}")
print(f"Lasso Testing R-squared Scores: {lasso_r2_test_scores}")
print(f"ElasticNet Training R-squared Scores: {elasticnet_r2_train_
scores}")
print(f"ElasticNet Testing R-squared Scores: {elasticnet_r2_test_scores}")
```

```
Polynomial Regression with Regularization:
Best Alpha (Ridge): 50.0000
Best Alpha (Lasso): 0.0010
Best Alpha (ElasticNet): 1.0000
Best l1_ratio (ElasticNet): 0.9
Ridge Training R-squared Scores:
    [0.6852681982309979, 0.6852681978848241, 0.6852681633541837,
    0.685264794671512, 0.6849940748677977, 0.6816443257072609]
Ridge Testing R-squared Scores:
    [0.645683225805578, 0.6456944994375847, 0.6458070098962285,
    0.6469096540341595, 0.6558501677208112, 0.6672535561034868]
Lasso Training R-squared Scores:
    [0.6830030979089348, 0.6305732853769765, 0.500981674817156,
    0.033220008724097694, 0.0, 0.0]
Lasso Testing R-squared Scores:
    [0.6686741743527673, 0.533056472931786, 0.4823562161721351,
    0.032132551538488596, -0.00021908714592466794, -0.00021908714592466794]
ElasticNet Training R-squared Scores:
    [0.6840310978294589, 0.6837217689230024, 0.6834122448233106,
    0.6831585830280078, 0.6641895730066483, 0.654089814353995,
    0.6463124687609253, 0.6364839821265846, 0.5619051580675156,
    0.5325527976563843, 0.5104019630875991, 0.5043656964193155,
    0.3174625276332542, 0.21148526134241852, 0.08567216955936541,
    0.05311242187826348, 0.0, 0.0, 0.0, 0.0, 0.0, 0.0, 0.0, 0.0]
ElasticNet Testing R-squared Scores:
    [0.665131384671392, 0.6672768269417034, 0.6679746333269325,
    0.6687496873021064, 0.5953794418651244, 0.534895420337363,
    0.5324894830873397, 0.53544136023843, 0.5437773103890866,
    0.5153003945070083, 0.49307869728746057, 0.486496197437864,
    0.30776990091131096, 0.2058625168336501, 0.0831325334530788,
    0.051496641763479345, -0.00021908714592466794, -0.00021908714592466794,
    -0.00021908714592466794, -0.00021908714592466794, -0.00021908714592466794,
    -0.00021908714592466794, -0.00021908714592466794, -0.00021908714592466794]
```

7.5.3.6 Multivariable Regression

Now, let's perform Multivariable Regression using all available features.

```
# Create and fit the multivariable regression model
multi_model = LinearRegression()
```

```
multi_model.fit(X_train_scaled, y_train)

# Make predictions on training and testing data
y_train_pred_multi = multi_model.predict(X_train_scaled)
y_test_pred_multi = multi_model.predict(X_test_scaled)

# Calculate R-squared and mean squared error for evaluation
multi_r2_train = r2_score(y_train, y_train_pred_multi)
multi_r2_test = r2_score(y_test, y_test_pred_multi)
multi_mse_train = mean_squared_error(y_train, y_train_pred_multi)
multi_mse_test = mean_squared_error(y_test, y_test_pred_multi)

print(f"\nMultivariable Regression:")
print(f"Training R-squared: {multi_r2_train:.4f}
    , Training MSE: {multi_mse_train:.4f}")
print(f"Testing R-squared: {multi_r2_test:.4f}
    , Testing MSE: {multi_mse_test:.4f}")
```

```
Multivariable Regression:
Training R-squared: 0.6126, Training MSE: 0.5179
Testing R-squared: 0.5758, Testing MSE: 0.5559
```

7.5.3.7 Ensemble Methods – Random Forest Regression

Finally, let's apply ensemble methods, specifically Random Forest Regression, to the dataset.

```
# Create and fit the Random Forest regression model
rf_model = RandomForestRegressor(n_estimators=100, random_state=42)
rf_model.fit(X_train_scaled, y_train)

# Make predictions on training and testing data
y_train_pred_rf = rf_model.predict(X_train_scaled)
y_test_pred_rf = rf_model.predict(X_test_scaled)

# Calculate R-squared and mean squared error for evaluation
rf_r2_train = r2_score(y_train, y_train_pred_rf)
rf_r2_test = r2_score(y_test, y_test_pred_rf)
rf_mse_train = mean_squared_error(y_train, y_train_pred_rf)
rf_mse_test = mean_squared_error(y_test, y_test_pred_rf)

print(f"\nRandom Forest Regression:")
print(f"Training R-squared: {rf_r2_train:.4f}
    , Training MSE: {rf_mse_train:.4f}")
print(f"Testing R-squared: {rf_r2_test:.4f}
    , Testing MSE: {rf_mse_test:.4f}")
```

```
Random Forest Regression:
Training R-squared: 0.9736, Training MSE: 0.0353
Testing R-squared: 0.8053, Testing MSE: 0.2552
```

7.5.3.8 Visualization

You can visualize the R-squared scores for different models.

```
# Plotting R-squared scores for different models
plt.figure(figsize=(12, 6))

models = ['Linear Regression', f'Polynomial (Degree {best_degree})'
    , 'Polynomial (Regularized)', 'Multivariable Regression'
    , 'Random Forest']

train_scores = [linear_r2_train
    , polynomial_r2_train_scores[np.argmax(polynomial_r2_test_scores)],
    max(ridge_r2_train_scores), multi_r2_train, rf_r2_train]

test_scores = [linear_r2_test
    , polynomial_r2_test_scores[np.argmax(polynomial_r2_test_scores)],
    max(ridge_r2_test_scores), multi_r2_test, rf_r2_test]

x = np.arange(len(models))
width = 0.35

plt.bar(x - width/2, train_scores, width, label='Training R-squared')
plt.bar(x + width/2, test_scores, width, label='Testing R-squared')

plt.xticks(x, models, rotation=45)
plt.ylabel('R-squared')
plt.title('R-squared Scores for Different Models')
plt.legend()
plt.tight_layout()
plt.show()
```

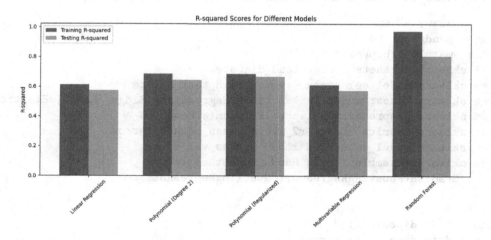

Figure 7.20 R-Squared Scores for Different Models

7.6 REGRESSION METHODS' COMPARISON

In this section, we will conduct a comprehensive case study to explore and compare the performance of various regression methods we have introduced using a single dataset. This hands-on approach will provide you with a practical understanding of how different regression techniques perform in real-world scenarios.

The case study aims to demonstrate the strengths and weaknesses of different regression methods, allowing you to make informed choices when selecting the most appropriate technique for a specific regression task. You will work with a dataset that is suitable for regression and apply the regression methods we have covered. Based on the case study results, you will gain insights into which regression method(s) perform best for the given dataset and regression task. You will also learn how to choose the most suitable regression technique based on specific requirements and characteristics of a problem.

7.6.1 Case Study – Diabetes

Let's play with the complete case study using the "Diabetes" dataset. We'll demonstrate all regression methods, including Simple Linear Regression, Polynomial Linear Regression, Polynomial Linear Regression with regularization (Ridge, Lasso, Elastic Net), Multivariable Regression, cross-validation with different folds (3, 5, 10), and ensemble methods (Bagging, Boosting, Stacking). At the end, we'll visualize the results of these models for comparison.

7.6.1.1 Setup the Dataset

Let's load the diabetes dataset from sklearn datasets. As the "Diabetes" dataset is already clean, there might not be significant data preprocessing steps required.

```python
import numpy as np
import pandas as pd
import matplotlib.pyplot as plt
from sklearn.datasets import load_diabetes
from sklearn.model_selection import train_test_split
from sklearn.linear_model import LinearRegression, Ridge, Lasso, ElasticNet
from sklearn.preprocessing import PolynomialFeatures
from sklearn.metrics import r2_score, mean_squared_error
from sklearn.model_selection import cross_val_score
from sklearn.ensemble import RandomForestRegressor
    , GradientBoostingRegressor, StackingRegressor

# Load the Diabetes dataset
data = load_diabetes()
X, y = data.data, data.target

# Convert to DataFrame for easier manipulation (optional)
df = pd.DataFrame(data=np.c_[X, y]
```

```
         , columns=data.feature_names + ['target'])

# Explore the dataset
print(df.head())
print(df.describe())
print(df.info())

# Split the data into training and testing sets
X_train, X_test, y_train, y_test = train_test_split(X, y, test_size=0.2
        , random_state=42)
```

```
        age       sex       bmi        bp        s1        s2        s3   \
0  0.038076  0.050680  0.061696  0.021872 -0.044223 -0.034821 -0.043401
1 -0.001882 -0.044642 -0.051474 -0.026328 -0.008449 -0.019163  0.074412
2  0.085299  0.050680  0.044451 -0.005670 -0.045599 -0.034194 -0.032356
3 -0.089063 -0.044642 -0.011595 -0.036656  0.012191  0.024991 -0.036038
4  0.005383 -0.044642 -0.036385  0.021872  0.003935  0.015596  0.008142

...
            target
count   442.000000
mean    152.133484
std      77.093005
min      25.000000
25%      87.000000
50%     140.500000
75%     211.500000
max     346.000000
<class 'pandas.core.frame.DataFrame'>
RangeIndex: 442 entries, 0 to 441
Data columns (total 11 columns):
 #   Column  Non-Null Count  Dtype
---  ------  --------------  -----
 0   age     442 non-null    float64
 1   sex     442 non-null    float64
 2   bmi     442 non-null    float64
 3   bp      442 non-null    float64
 4   s1      442 non-null    float64
 5   s2      442 non-null    float64
 6   s3      442 non-null    float64
 7   s4      442 non-null    float64
 8   s5      442 non-null    float64
 9   s6      442 non-null    float64
 10  target  442 non-null    float64
dtypes: float64(11)
memory usage: 38.1 KB
None
```

7.6.1.2 Simple Linear Regression

```python
# Create and fit the simple linear regression model
simple_linear_model = LinearRegression()
simple_linear_model.fit(X_train, y_train)

# Make predictions on training and testing data
y_train_pred_slr = simple_linear_model.predict(X_train)
y_test_pred_slr = simple_linear_model.predict(X_test)

# Calculate R-squared and mean squared error for evaluation
slr_r2_train = r2_score(y_train, y_train_pred_slr)
slr_r2_test = r2_score(y_test, y_test_pred_slr)
slr_mse_train = mean_squared_error(y_train, y_train_pred_slr)
slr_mse_test = mean_squared_error(y_test, y_test_pred_slr)

print(f"Simple Linear Regression:")
print(f"Training R-squared: {slr_r2_train:.4f}
    , Training MSE: {slr_mse_train:.4f}")
print(f"Testing R-squared: {slr_r2_test:.4f}
    , Testing MSE: {slr_mse_test:.4f}")
```

```
Simple Linear Regression:
Training R-squared: 0.5279, Training MSE: 2868.5497
Testing R-squared: 0.4526, Testing MSE: 2900.1936
```

7.6.1.3 Polynomial Linear Regression

```python
# Polynomial degrees
degrees = [2, 3, 4]

# Create and fit the polynomial regression models with different degrees
polynomial_models = []
polynomial_r2_train_scores = []
polynomial_r2_test_scores = []

for degree in degrees:
    poly_features = PolynomialFeatures(degree=degree)
    X_train_poly = poly_features.fit_transform(X_train)
    X_test_poly = poly_features.transform(X_test)

    model = LinearRegression()
    model.fit(X_train_poly, y_train)
    polynomial_models.append(model)

    # Make predictions on training and testing data
    y_train_pred = model.predict(X_train_poly)
    y_test_pred = model.predict(X_test_poly)

    # Calculate R-squared for evaluation
```

```
        polynomial_r2_train = r2_score(y_train, y_train_pred)
        polynomial_r2_test = r2_score(y_test, y_test_pred)

        polynomial_r2_train_scores.append(polynomial_r2_train)
        polynomial_r2_test_scores.append(polynomial_r2_test)

# Find the best degree based on the testing R-squared score
best_degree = degrees[np.argmax(polynomial_r2_test_scores)]

print(f"\nPolynomial Linear Regression:")
print(f"Best Degree: {best_degree}")
print(f"Training R-squared Scores: {polynomial_r2_train_scores}")
print(f"Testing R-squared Scores: {polynomial_r2_test_scores}")
```

```
Polynomial Linear Regression:
Best Degree: 2
Training R-squared Scores:
    [0.6061583502354679, 0.6311213891847405, 1.0]
Testing R-squared Scores:
    [0.41563993364080387, -15.50164602091279, -26.72808338196219]
```

7.6.1.4 Polynomial Linear Regression with Regularization

```
# Continue with degree of 2
poly_features = PolynomialFeatures(degree=degree)
X_train_poly = poly_features.fit_transform(X_train)
X_test_poly = poly_features.transform(X_test)

# Regularization strengths (alpha values)
alphas = [0.001, 0.01, 0.1, 1, 10]

# Create and fit the regression models with different alpha values
ridge_models = []
ridge_r2_train_scores = []
ridge_r2_test_scores = []

lasso_models = []
lasso_r2_train_scores = []
lasso_r2_test_scores = []

elasticnet_models = []
elasticnet_r2_train_scores = []
elasticnet_r2_test_scores = []

for alpha in alphas:
    ridge_model = Ridge(alpha=alpha)
    ridge_model.fit(X_train_poly, y_train)
    ridge_models.append(ridge_model)

    # Make predictions on training and testing data
```

```python
        y_train_pred = ridge_model.predict(X_train_poly)
        y_test_pred = ridge_model.predict(X_test_poly)

        # Calculate R-squared for evaluation
        ridge_r2_train = r2_score(y_train, y_train_pred)
        ridge_r2_test = r2_score(y_test, y_test_pred)

        ridge_r2_train_scores.append(ridge_r2_train)
        ridge_r2_test_scores.append(ridge_r2_test)

        lasso_model = Lasso(alpha=alpha)
        lasso_model.fit(X_train_poly, y_train)
        lasso_models.append(lasso_model)

        # Make predictions on training and testing data
        y_train_pred = lasso_model.predict(X_train_poly)
        y_test_pred = lasso_model.predict(X_test_poly)

        # Calculate R-squared for evaluation
        lasso_r2_train = r2_score(y_train, y_train_pred)
        lasso_r2_test = r2_score(y_test, y_test_pred)

        lasso_r2_train_scores.append(lasso_r2_train)
        lasso_r2_test_scores.append(lasso_r2_test)

        for l1_ratio in [0.2, 0.5, 0.8]:
            elasticnet_model = ElasticNet(alpha=alpha, l1_ratio=l1_ratio)
            elasticnet_model.fit(X_train_poly, y_train)
            elasticnet_models.append(elasticnet_model)

            # Make predictions on training and testing data
            y_train_pred = elasticnet_model.predict(X_train_poly)
            y_test_pred = elasticnet_model.predict(X_test_poly)

            # Calculate R-squared for evaluation
            elasticnet_r2_train = r2_score(y_train, y_train_pred)
            elasticnet_r2_test = r2_score(y_test, y_test_pred)

            elasticnet_r2_train_scores.append(elasticnet_r2_train)
            elasticnet_r2_test_scores.append(elasticnet_r2_test)

# Find the best alpha values based on the testing R-squared scores
best_alpha_ridge = alphas[np.argmax(ridge_r2_test_scores)]
best_alpha_lasso = alphas[np.argmax(lasso_r2_test_scores)]
best_alpha_elasticnet = alphas[np.argmax(elasticnet_r2_test_scores)]
best_l1_ratio_elasticnet = [0.2, 0.5, 0.8]
    [np.argmax(elasticnet_r2_test_scores) // len(alphas)]

print(f"\nPolynomial Linear Regression with Regularization:")
print(f"Best Alpha (Ridge): {best_alpha_ridge:.4f}")
```

```
print(f"Best Alpha (Lasso): {best_alpha_lasso:.4f}")
print(f"Best Alpha (ElasticNet): {best_alpha_elasticnet:.4f}")
print(f"Best l1_ratio (ElasticNet): {best_l1_ratio_elasticnet:.1f}")
print(f"Ridge Training R-squared Scores: {ridge_r2_train_scores}")
print(f"Ridge Testing R-squared Scores: {ridge_r2_test_scores}")
print(f"Lasso Training R-squared Scores: {lasso_r2_train_scores}")
print(f"Lasso Testing R-squared Scores: {lasso_r2_test_scores}")
print(f"ElasticNet Training R-squared Scores: {elasticnet_r2_train_
scores}")
print(f"ElasticNet Testing R-squared Scores: {elasticnet_r2_test_scores}")
```

Polynomial Linear Regression with Regularization:
Best Alpha (Ridge): 0.0010
Best Alpha (Lasso): 0.0010
Best Alpha (ElasticNet): 0.1000
Best l1_ratio (ElasticNet): 0.2
Ridge Training R-squared Scores:
    [0.5738225696816797, 0.5440556284976665, 0.523889352263707,
    0.44298458284557574, 0.16350659610783913]
Ridge Testing R-squared Scores:
    [0.510800687894738, 0.48429539225652785, 0.46593781159184344,
    0.41958874692366066, 0.161269221757383]
Lasso Training R-squared Scores:
    [0.5892701490358648, 0.5419119318329695, 0.5169410847799543,
    0.3646309911295581, 0.0]
Lasso Testing R-squared Scores:
    [0.5012980759269188, 0.49076078413751045, 0.4718547867276227,
    0.3575918767219115, -0.011962984778542296]
ElasticNet Training R-squared Scores:
    [0.5084098826948718, 0.5174639557698948, 0.5261690969450569,
    0.3283982611115136, 0.3856811985013552, 0.4671799800159241,
    0.0708338916850505, 0.1032878083423916, 0.19726642133866978,
    0.007112124669544362, 0.008901600088515704, 0.0162621249186663,
    2.5348994849738737e-05, 0.0, 0.0]
ElasticNet Testing R-squared Scores:
    [0.4610622729458884, 0.4643024301889397, 0.4665388951249436,
    0.3230312951444442, 0.37379052990319994, 0.43739385153422194,
    0.06419070712846853, 0.09865702265671039, 0.1960777104890853,
    -0.0042988350408805776, -0.0024652131111431164, 0.005259228957128381,
    -0.011937606996639039, -0.011962984778542296, -0.011962984778542296]

7.6.1.5 Multivariable Regression

```
# Create and fit the multivariable regression model
multi_linear_model = LinearRegression()
multi_linear_model.fit(X_train, y_train)

# Make predictions on training and testing data
y_train_pred_multi = multi_linear_model.predict(X_train)
y_test_pred_multi = multi_linear_model.predict(X_test)

# Calculate R-squared and mean squared error for evaluation
multi_r2_train = r2_score(y_train, y_train_pred_multi)
```

```
multi_r2_test = r2_score(y_test, y_test_pred_multi)
multi_mse_train = mean_squared_error(y_train, y_train_pred_multi)
multi_mse_test = mean_squared_error(y_test, y_test_pred_multi)

print(f"\nMultivariable Regression:")
print(f"Training R-squared: {multi_r2_train:.4f}
    , Training MSE: {multi_mse_train:.4f}")
print(f"Testing R-squared: {multi_r2_test:.4f}
    , Testing MSE: {multi_mse_test:.4f}")
```

```
Multivariable Regression:
Training R-squared: 0.5279, Training MSE: 2868.5497
Testing R-squared: 0.4526, Testing MSE: 2900.1936
```

7.6.1.6 Cross-Validation

We will perform cross-validation using 3-folds, 5-folds, and 10-folds to assess the performance of different regression models.

```
# Define a function to perform cross-validation
def perform_cross_validation(model, X, y, cv):
    cv_scores = cross_val_score(model, X, y, scoring='r2', cv=cv)
    mean_cv_score = np.mean(cv_scores)
    return mean_cv_score

# Cross-validation with 3-folds
cv_3folds_score = perform_cross_validation(multi_linear_model, X, y, cv=3)
print(f"Cross Validation (3-folds) R-squared: {cv_3folds_score:.4f}")

# Cross-validation with 5-folds
cv_5folds_score = perform_cross_validation(multi_linear_model, X, y, cv=5)
print(f"Cross Validation (5-folds) R-squared: {cv_5folds_score:.4f}")

# Cross-validation with 10-folds
cv_10folds_score = perform_cross_validation(multi_linear_model,X,y, cv=10)
print(f"Cross Validation (10-folds) R-squared: {cv_10folds_score:.4f}")
```

```
Cross Validation (3-folds) R-squared: 0.4887
Cross Validation (5-folds) R-squared: 0.4823
Cross Validation (10-folds) R-squared: 0.4620
```

7.6.1.7 Ensemble Methods

Now, let's apply ensemble methods using Bagging, Boosting, and Stacking techniques.

Bagging – Random Forest Regression

```
# Create and fit the Random Forest regression model
rf_model = RandomForestRegressor(n_estimators=100, max_features=3
    , random_state=42)
```

```
rf_model.fit(X_train, y_train)

# Make predictions on training and testing data
y_train_pred_rf = rf_model.predict(X_train)
y_test_pred_rf = rf_model.predict(X_test)

# Calculate R-squared and mean squared error for evaluation
rf_r2_train = r2_score(y_train, y_train_pred_rf)
rf_r2_test = r2_score(y_test, y_test_pred_rf)
rf_mse_train = mean_squared_error(y_train, y_train_pred_rf)
rf_mse_test = mean_squared_error(y_test, y_test_pred_rf)

print(f"\nRandom Forest Regression (Bagging):")
print(f"Training R-squared: {rf_r2_train:.4f}
    , Training MSE: {rf_mse_train:.4f}")
print(f"Testing R-squared: {rf_r2_test:.4f}
    , Testing MSE: {rf_mse_test:.4f}")
```

```
Random Forest Regression (Bagging):
Training R-squared: 0.9206, Training MSE: 482.5544
Testing R-squared: 0.4669, Testing MSE: 2824.4323
```

Boosting – Gradient Boosting Regression

```
# Create and fit the Gradient Boosting regression model
gb_model = GradientBoostingRegressor(n_estimators=100, learning_rate=0.1
    , random_state=42)
gb_model.fit(X_train, y_train)

# Make predictions on training and testing data
y_train_pred_gb = gb_model.predict(X_train)
y_test_pred_gb = gb_model.predict(X_test)

# Calculate R-squared and mean squared error for evaluation
gb_r2_train = r2_score(y_train, y_train_pred_gb)
gb_r2_test = r2_score(y_test, y_test_pred_gb)
gb_mse_train = mean_squared_error(y_train, y_train_pred_gb)
gb_mse_test = mean_squared_error(y_test, y_test_pred_gb)

print(f"\nGradient Boosting Regression (Boosting):")
print(f"Training R-squared: {gb_r2_train:.4f}
    , Training MSE: {gb_mse_train:.4f}")
print(f"Testing R-squared: {gb_r2_test:.4f}
    , Testing MSE: {gb_mse_test:.4f}")
```

```
Gradient Boosting Regression (Boosting):
Training R-squared: 0.8359, Training MSE: 997.1211
Testing R-squared: 0.4529, Testing MSE: 2898.4367
```

Stacking – Stacking Regressor

```python
# Create a list of base models for stacking
base_models = [
    ('ridge', Ridge(alpha=best_alpha_ridge)),
    ('lasso', Lasso(alpha=best_alpha_lasso)),
    ('elasticnet', ElasticNet(alpha=best_alpha_elasticnet
    , l1_ratio=best_l1_ratio_elasticnet))
]

# Create and fit the Stacking Regressor
stacking_model = StackingRegressor(estimators=base_models
    , final_estimator=multi_linear_model)
stacking_model.fit(X_train, y_train)

# Make predictions on training and testing data
y_train_pred_stack = stacking_model.predict(X_train)
y_test_pred_stack = stacking_model.predict(X_test)

# Calculate R-squared and mean squared error for evaluation
stack_r2_train = r2_score(y_train, y_train_pred_stack)
stack_r2_test = r2_score(y_test, y_test_pred_stack)
stack_mse_train = mean_squared_error(y_train, y_train_pred_stack)
stack_mse_test = mean_squared_error(y_test, y_test_pred_stack)

print(f"\nStacking Regressor (Stacking):")
print(f"Training R-squared: {stack_r2_train:.4f}
    , Training MSE: {stack_mse_train:.4f}")
print(f"Testing R-squared: {stack_r2_test:.4f}
    , Testing MSE: {stack_mse_test:.4f}")
```

```
Stacking Regressor (Stacking):
Training R-squared: 0.5264, Training MSE: 2877.9006
Testing R-squared: 0.4548, Testing MSE: 2888.4670
```

7.6.1.8 Visualize the Comparison

Let's visualize the R-squared scores of different regression methods. This bar chart will show the comparison of different regression methods, cross-validation, and ensemble methods based on their training and testing R-squared scores. The higher the R-squared score, the better the model fits the data. The chart will help you understand which regression method performs best for the 'Diabetes' dataset.

```python
# Create a DataFrame to store the R-squared scores
method_names = ['Simple Linear', f'Polynomial Degree {best_degree}'
    , 'Ridge', 'Lasso', 'ElasticNet','Multivariable Regression'
    , 'Bagging(Random Forest)', 'Boosting(Gradient Boosting)', 'Stacking']
train_r2_scores = [slr_r2_train
    , polynomial_r2_train_scores[np.argmax(polynomial_r2_test_scores)]
    , ridge_r2_train_scores[np.argmax(ridge_r2_test_scores)]
```

```
    , lasso_r2_train_scores[np.argmax(lasso_r2_test_scores)],
    , elasticnet_r2_train_scores[np.argmax(elasticnet_r2_test_scores)]
    , multi_r2_train, rf_r2_train, gb_r2_train, stack_r2_train]

test_r2_scores = [slr_r2_test
    , polynomial_r2_test_scores[np.argmax(polynomial_r2_test_scores)]
    , ridge_r2_test_scores[np.argmax(ridge_r2_test_scores)]
    , lasso_r2_test_scores[np.argmax(lasso_r2_test_scores)]
    , elasticnet_r2_test_scores[np.argmax(elasticnet_r2_test_scores)]
    , multi_r2_test, rf_r2_test, gb_r2_test, stack_r2_test]

r2_scores_df = pd.DataFrame({'Method': method_names
    , 'Training R-squared': train_r2_scores
    , 'Testing R-squared': test_r2_scores})

# Visualize the R-squared scores
plt.figure(figsize=(12, 6))
plt.bar(method_names,train_r2_scores,label='Training R-squared',alpha=0.7)
plt.bar(method_names,test_r2_scores,label='Testing R-squared',alpha=0.7)
plt.xlabel('Regression Method')
plt.ylabel('R-squared Score')
plt.title('Comparison of Regression Methods on Diabetes Dataset')
plt.legend()
plt.xticks(rotation=45, ha='right')
plt.ylim(0, 1)
plt.tight_layout()
plt.show()
```

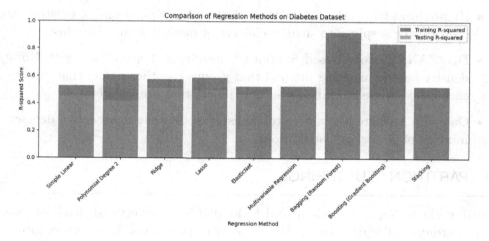

Figure 7.21   Comparison of Regression Methods on Diabetes Dataset

## CHAPTER 8

Clustering

C LUSTERING is an unsupervised learning task in which an algorithm groups a set of objects in such a way that objects in the same group (called a cluster) are more similar to each other than to those in other groups (clusters). The goal of clustering is to discover the inherent groupings or structure in the data.

There are many different clustering methods we use with Scikit-learn, but some of the most common include:

- K-Means: A method that partitions a dataset into k clusters, where each cluster is defined by the mean of the points assigned to that cluster.

- Hierarchical Clustering: A method that builds a hierarchy of clusters, where each cluster is split into smaller clusters or merged with other clusters.

- DBSCAN (Density-Based Spatial Clustering of Applications with Noise): A density-based clustering method that groups together points that are close to each other, while marking as outliers points that are isolated.

- Gaussian Mixture Model: A probabilistic model that represents a dataset as a mixture of Gaussian distributions.

8.1 PARTITION CLUSTERING

Partition clustering is a fundamental technique in unsupervised machine learning used to group similar data points into clusters or partitions. This section introduces partition clustering methods, including K-Means and K-Medoids, using the Scikit-learn package.

Partition clustering aims to discover natural groupings or clusters within a dataset, where data points within the same cluster are more similar to each other than to those in other clusters. It is widely used in various domains, including customer segmentation, image processing, and anomaly detection. Scikit-learn provides

DOI: 10.1201/9781003462781-8

user-friendly tools to implement partition clustering methods effectively. You will explore practical implementation steps, including using the K-Means and K-Medoids classes in Scikit-learn to perform clustering on a dataset, determining the optimal number of clusters using techniques like the elbow method or silhouette analysis, and visualizing cluster assignments and centroids/medoids for interpretation.

8.1.1 Tutorial

We learned both K-Means and K-Medoids as basic clustering methods. Let's play with them and observe the differences.

8.1.1.1 Prepare the Packages

- K-Means is included in sklearn package; we can import it directly.
- K-Medoids is included in sklearn extra package; we should install it first and then import it.
- We will need NumPy and Pandas to create some dummy dataset
- We will need Seaborn to visualize the result.

```
!pip install scikit-learn-extra
```

```
import numpy as np
import pandas as pd
from sklearn.cluster import KMeans
from sklearn_extra.cluster import KMedoids
import matplotlib.pyplot as plt
import seaborn as sns
```

8.1.1.2 Round 1: Let's Create Some Simple Dataset

For visualization purpose, we create datapoints with two dimensions.

Create three clusters of data points. Each cluster has 1,000 data points, and each data point has two dimensions. Data points have normal distribution with specified mean and std.

```
c1 = np.random.normal(5, 3, (100, 2))
c2 = np.random.normal(15, 5, (100, 2))
c3 = np.random.normal(-5, 2, (100, 2))
d = np.concatenate((c1, c2, c3), axis = 0)
d.shape
```

(300, 2)

Let's visualize the dataset using Seaborn

```
sns.scatterplot(data = d, x = d[:,0], y = d[:,1])
```

```
<matplotlib.axes._subplots.AxesSubplot at 0x7f547096a2d0>
```

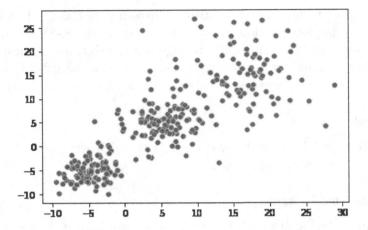

Figure 8.1 A Scatter Plot of X VS Y

Let's train a model using K-Means

```
kmeans = KMeans(n_clusters=3, random_state=0).fit(d)
```

```
sns.scatterplot(data = d, x = d[:,0], y = d[:,1],hue = kmeans.predict(d))
```

```
<matplotlib.axes._subplots.AxesSubplot at 0x7f546ef3fa10>
```

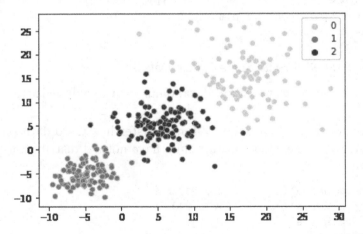

Figure 8.2 K-Means Result with Cluster Differentiation

Let's train a model using K-Medoids

```
kmedoids = KMedoids(n_clusters=3, random_state=0).fit(d)
```

Visualize the result

```
sns.scatterplot(data = d, x = d[:,0], y = d[:,1],hue = kmedoids.predict(d))
```

```
<matplotlib.axes._subplots.AxesSubplot at 0x7f54679ccc50>
```

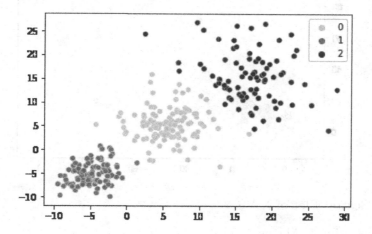

Figure 8.3 KMedoids Result with Cluster Differentiation

Conclusion: K-Means and K-Medoids did equally well for this dataset.

8.1.1.3 Round 2: Let Us Add One Outlier to the Dataset

Create the same random clusters

```
c1 = np.random.normal(5, 3, (100, 2))
c2 = np.random.normal(15, 5, (100, 2))
c3 = np.random.normal(-5, 2, (100, 2))
```

Create an outlier. The outlier is far away from all other data points.

```
outlier = np.array([[100, 100]])
```

```
d = np.concatenate((c1, c2, c3, outlier), axis = 0)
```

Visualize the dataset

```
sns.scatterplot(data = d, x = d[:,0], y = d[:,1])
```

```
<matplotlib.axes._subplots.AxesSubplot at 0x7f54678f9a90>
```

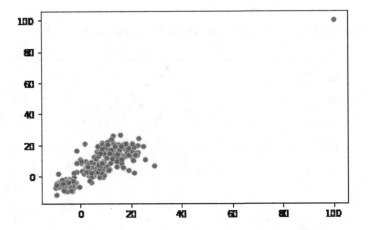

Figure 8.4   A Scatter Plot of X VS Y

Train a model using K-Means

```
kmeans = KMeans(n_clusters=3, random_state=0).fit(d)
```

Visualize the result

```
sns.scatterplot(data = d, x = d[:,0], y = d[:,1], hue = kmeans.predict(d))
```

```
<matplotlib.axes._subplots.AxesSubplot at 0x7f54678f6690>
```

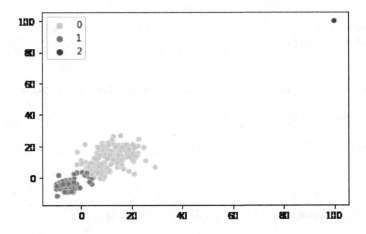

Figure 8.5   K-Means Result with Cluster Differentiation

Train a model using K-Medoids

```
kmedoids = KMedoids(n_clusters=3, random_state=0).fit(d)
```

Visualize the result

```
sns.scatterplot(data = d, x = d[:,0], y = d[:,1],hue = kmedoids.predict(d))
```

```
<matplotlib.axes._subplots.AxesSubplot at 0x7f5467861390>
```

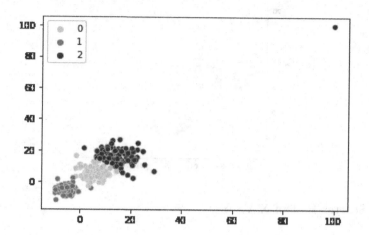

Figure 8.6   K-Medoids Result with Cluster Differentiation

Conclusion: K-Medoids did well even with an outlier. K-Means failed.

8.1.1.4   Round 3: Let's Create a More Realistic Dataset Using Pandas

Create a dataset

```
df = pd.DataFrame({'x': np.random.normal(5, 3, (100)),
    'y': np.random.normal(-2, 2, (100))})
df = df.append(pd.DataFrame({'x': np.random.normal(15, 2, (100)),
    'y': np.random.normal(22, 2, (100))}))
df = df.append(pd.DataFrame({'x': np.random.normal(-5, 3, (100)),
    'y': np.random.normal(8, 2, (100))}))
```

Visualize the dataset

```
sns.relplot(data = df, x = 'x', y = 'y')
```

```
<seaborn.axisgrid.FacetGrid at 0x7f5467792910>
```

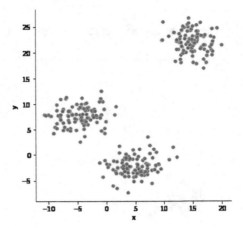

Figure 8.7 A Scatter Plot of X VS Y

Train a model using K-Means

```
kmeans = KMeans(n_clusters=3, random_state=0).fit(df)
```

Visualize the result

```
sns.scatterplot(data = df, x = 'x', y = 'y', hue = kmeans.predict(df))
```

```
<matplotlib.axes._subplots.AxesSubplot at 0x7f5467754890>
```

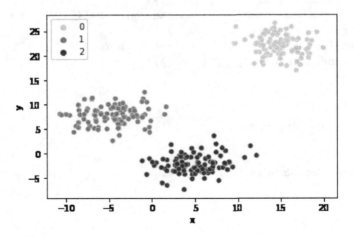

Figure 8.8 K-Means Result with Cluster Differentiation

Train a model using K-Medoids

```
kmedoids = KMedoids(n_clusters=3, random_state=0).fit(df)
```

Visualize the result

```
sns.scatterplot(data = df, x = 'x', y = 'y', hue = kmedoids.predict(df))
```

```
<matplotlib.axes._subplots.AxesSubplot at 0x7f5467685b90>
```

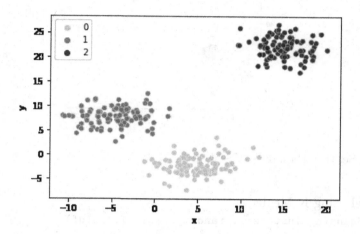

Figure 8.9 K-Medoids Result with Cluster Differentiation

Conclusion: K-Means and K-Medoids did equally well.

8.1.1.5 Round 4: Let's Add an Outlier

Create a dataset with an outlier

```
df = pd.DataFrame({'x': np.random.normal(5, 3, (100)),
    'y': np.random.normal(-2, 2, (100))})
df = df.append(pd.DataFrame({'x': np.random.normal(15, 2, (100)),
    'y': np.random.normal(22, 2, (100))}))
df = df.append(pd.DataFrame({'x': np.random.normal(-5, 3, (100)),
    'y': np.random.normal(8, 2, (100))}))
#outlier
df = df.append(pd.DataFrame({'x': [100], 'y': [100]}))
```

Visualize the dataset

```
sns.relplot(data = df, x = 'x', y = 'y')
```

```
<seaborn.axisgrid.FacetGrid at 0x7f54676c6250>
```

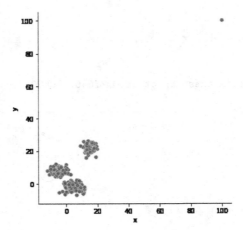

Figure 8.10 A Scatter Plot of X VS Y

Train a model using K-Means

```
kmeans = KMeans(n_clusters=3, random_state=0).fit(df)
```

Visualize the result

```
sns.scatterplot(data = df, x = 'x', y = 'y', hue = kmeans.predict(df))
```

```
<matplotlib.axes._subplots.AxesSubplot at 0x7f546786dbd0>
```

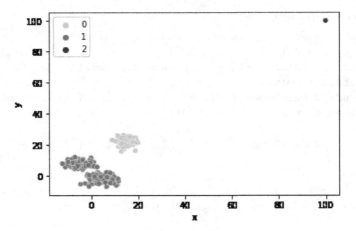

Figure 8.11 K-Means Result with Cluster Differentiation

Train a model using K-Medoids

```
kmedoids = KMedoids(n_clusters=3, random_state=0).fit(df)
```

Visualize the result

```
sns.scatterplot(data = df, x = 'x', y = 'y', hue = kmedoids.predict(df))
```

```
<matplotlib.axes._subplots.AxesSubplot at 0x7f5467634bd0>
```

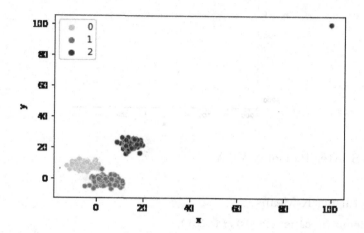

Figure 8.12   K-Medoids Result with Cluster Differentiation

Conclusion: K-Medoids did well even with an outlier. K-Means failed.

8.1.1.6   Round 5: Let's Add Two Outliers

Create a dataset with an outlier

```
df = pd.DataFrame({'x': np.random.normal(5, 3, (100)),
    'y': np.random.normal(-2, 2, (100))})
df = df.append(pd.DataFrame({'x': np.random.normal(15, 2, (100)),
    'y': np.random.normal(22, 2, (100))}))
df = df.append(pd.DataFrame({'x': np.random.normal(-5, 3, (100)),
    'y': np.random.normal(8, 2, (100))}))
#outlier
df = df.append(pd.DataFrame({'x': [200], 'y': [200]}))
df = df.append(pd.DataFrame({'x': [-200], 'y': [-200]}))
```

Visualize the dataset

```
sns.relplot(data = df, x = 'x', y = 'y')
```

```
<seaborn.axisgrid.FacetGrid at 0x7f54673ce1d0>
```

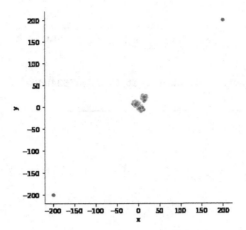

Figure 8.13 A Scatter Plot of X VS Y

Train a model using K-Means

```
kmeans = KMeans(n_clusters=3).fit(df)
```

Visualize the result

```
sns.scatterplot(data = df, x = 'x', y = 'y', hue = kmeans.predict(df))
```

```
<matplotlib.axes._subplots.AxesSubplot at 0x7f54673b0890>
```

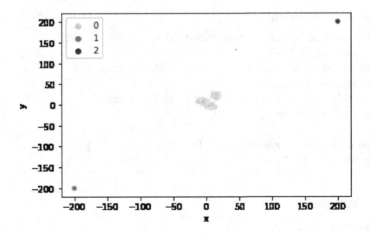

Figure 8.14 K-Means Result with Cluster Differentiation

Train a model using K-Medoids

```
kmedoids = KMedoids(n_clusters=3, random_state=0).fit(df)
```

Visualize the result

```
sns.scatterplot(data = df, x = 'x', y = 'y', hue = kmedoids.predict(df))
```

```
<matplotlib.axes._subplots.AxesSubplot at 0x7f54672d65d0>
```

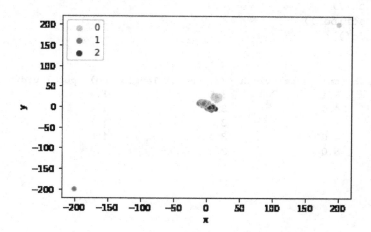

Figure 8.15   K-Medoids Result with Cluster Differentiation

Conclusion: K-Medoids did well even with more outliers. K-Means failed.

8.1.2   Case Study

Let's proceed with the tutorial on clustering analysis using the "Iris" dataset. We will demonstrate two popular clustering algorithms: K-Means and K-Medoids. We will compare these two methods based on their performance and clusters they form.

8.1.2.1   Setup

Dataset loading and exploration

```
!pip install scikit-learn-extra
```

```
import numpy as np
import pandas as pd
import matplotlib.pyplot as plt
from sklearn.datasets import load_iris
from sklearn.preprocessing import StandardScaler
from sklearn.cluster import KMeans
from sklearn_extra.cluster import KMedoids
from sklearn.metrics import silhouette_score, adjusted_rand_score

# Load the Iris dataset
data = load_iris()
X, y = data.data, data.target
```

```
# Convert to DataFrame for easier manipulation (optional)
df = pd.DataFrame(data=np.c_[X, y],
    columns=data.feature_names + ['target'])

# Explore the dataset
print(df.head())
print(df.describe())
print(df.info())
```

```
   sepal length (cm)  sepal width (cm)  petal length (cm)  petal width (cm)  \
0                5.1               3.5                1.4               0.2
1                4.9               3.0                1.4               0.2
2                4.7               3.2                1.3               0.2
3                4.6               3.1                1.5               0.2
4                5.0               3.6                1.4               0.2

   target
0     0.0
1     0.0
2     0.0
3     0.0
4     0.0
       sepal length (cm)  sepal width (cm)  petal length (cm)  \
count         150.000000        150.000000         150.000000
mean            5.843333          3.057333           3.758000
std             0.828066          0.435866           1.765298
min             4.300000          2.000000           1.000000
25%             5.100000          2.800000           1.600000
50%             5.800000          3.000000           4.350000
75%             6.400000          3.300000           5.100000
max             7.900000          4.400000           6.900000

       petal width (cm)      target
count        150.000000  150.000000
mean           1.199333    1.000000
std            0.762238    0.819232
min            0.100000    0.000000
25%            0.300000    0.000000
50%            1.300000    1.000000
75%            1.800000    2.000000
max            2.500000    2.000000
<class 'pandas.core.frame.DataFrame'>
RangeIndex: 150 entries, 0 to 149
Data columns (total 5 columns):
 #   Column             Non-Null Count  Dtype
---  ------             --------------  -----
 0   sepal length (cm)  150 non-null    float64
 1   sepal width (cm)   150 non-null    float64
 2   petal length (cm)  150 non-null    float64
 3   petal width (cm)   150 non-null    float64
 4   target             150 non-null    float64
dtypes: float64(5)
memory usage: 6.0 KB
```

None

8.1.2.2 Data Preprocessing

Before applying clustering algorithms, we need to preprocess the data to standardize the features.

```python
# Standardize the features
scaler = StandardScaler()
X_scaled = scaler.fit_transform(X)
```

8.1.2.3 K-Means Clustering

```python
# Initialize the K-means clustering algorithm with a specific k
kmeans = KMeans(n_clusters=3, random_state=42)

# Fit the model to the data
kmeans.fit(X_scaled)

# Get the cluster assignments for each sample
kmeans_labels = kmeans.labels_

# Calculate the silhouette score
kmeans_silhouette_score = silhouette_score(X_scaled, kmeans_labels)

# Calculate the adjusted Rand Index (ARI) score
kmeans_ari_score = adjusted_rand_score(y, kmeans_labels)

print(f"K-means Clustering:")
print(f"Silhouette Score: {kmeans_silhouette_score:.4f}")
print(f"Adjusted Rand Index Score: {kmeans_ari_score:.4f}")
```

```
K-means Clustering:
Silhouette Score: 0.4599
Adjusted Rand Index Score: 0.6201
```

8.1.2.4 K-Medoids Clustering

```python
# Initialize the K-medoids clustering algorithm with a specific k
kmedoids = KMedoids(n_clusters=3, random_state=42)

# Fit the model to the data
kmedoids.fit(X_scaled)

# Get the cluster assignments for each sample
kmedoids_labels = kmedoids.labels_

# Calculate the silhouette score
kmedoids_silhouette_score = silhouette_score(X_scaled, kmedoids_labels)
```

```
# Calculate the adjusted Rand Index (ARI) score
kmedoids_ari_score = adjusted_rand_score(y, kmedoids_labels)

print(f"\nK-medoids Clustering:")
print(f"Silhouette Score: {kmedoids_silhouette_score:.4f}")
print(f"Adjusted Rand Index Score: {kmedoids_ari_score:.4f}")
```

```
K-medoids Clustering:
Silhouette Score: 0.4590
Adjusted Rand Index Score: 0.6312
```

8.1.2.5 Compare K-Means and K-Medoids

```
# Visualization of K-means and K-medoids Clusters
plt.figure(figsize=(12, 6))
plt.subplot(1, 2, 1)
plt.scatter(X_scaled[:, 0], X_scaled[:, 1]
    , c=kmeans_labels, cmap='viridis')
plt.scatter(kmeans.cluster_centers_[:, 0]
    , kmeans.cluster_centers_[:, 1]
    , marker='X', s=200, c='red', label='Centroids')
plt.title('K-means Clustering')
plt.xlabel('Sepal Length (Scaled)')
plt.ylabel('Sepal Width (Scaled)')
plt.legend()

plt.subplot(1, 2, 2)
plt.scatter(X_scaled[:, 0]
    , X_scaled[:, 1], c=kmedoids_labels, cmap='viridis')
plt.scatter(kmedoids.cluster_centers_[:, 0]
    , kmedoids.cluster_centers_[:, 1]
    , marker='X', s=200, c='red', label='Medoids')
plt.title('K-medoids Clustering')
plt.xlabel('Sepal Length (Scaled)')
plt.ylabel('Sepal Width (Scaled)')
plt.legend()

plt.tight_layout()
plt.show()
```

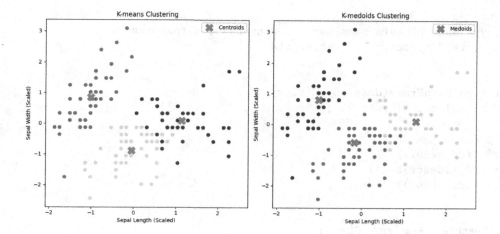

Figure 8.16 A Comparison with K-Means and K-Medoids Clustering

8.2 HIERARCHICAL CLUSTERING

Hierarchical clustering is a powerful technique in unsupervised machine learning used to discover hierarchical structures and natural groupings within a dataset. This section introduces hierarchical clustering using the Scikit-learn package.

Hierarchical clustering is a versatile method for exploring data with hierarchical relationships between clusters. It creates a tree-like structure (dendrogram) that visually represents the data's nested groupings. Scikit-learn provides tools to implement hierarchical clustering effectively. You will explore practical implementation steps, including using the AgglomerativeClustering class in Scikit-learn for agglomerative hierarchical clustering, customizing linkage methods (e.g., Ward, complete, average) to control the clustering strategy, and visualizing dendrograms and cluster assignments for interpretation.

8.2.1 Tutorial

Let's create a dummy dataset and demonstrate agglomerative hierarchical clustering using different numbers of clusters. We will observe how the number of clusters affects the clustering results and the dendrogram visualization.

8.2.1.1 Create a Dummy Dataset

```
import numpy as np
import pandas as pd
import matplotlib.pyplot as plt
from sklearn.datasets import make_blobs
from sklearn.preprocessing import StandardScaler
from sklearn.cluster import AgglomerativeClustering
from sklearn.metrics import silhouette_score
```

```
# Create a random dummy dataset with 100 samples and 2 features
X, y = make_blobs(n_samples=100, centers=4, n_features=2
    , random_state=42, cluster_std=1.5)

# Convert to DataFrame for easier manipulation (optional)
df = pd.DataFrame(data=np.c_[X, y]
    , columns=['Feature1', 'Feature2', 'Cluster'])

# Explore the dataset
print(df.head())
print(df.describe())
print(df.info())
```

```
    Feature1   Feature2  Cluster
0 -10.108518   5.051252      3.0
1  -5.659351  -8.726406      2.0
2  -3.213409   9.828126      0.0
3  -4.775436  -8.982886      2.0
4  -8.301647   8.164700      3.0
            Feature1     Feature2     Cluster
count  100.000000   100.000000  100.000000
mean    -3.582871     2.901643    1.500000
std      5.268073     6.293456    1.123666
min    -10.904832    -8.982886    0.000000
25%     -8.161044    -1.552449    0.750000
50%     -4.751208     4.685694    1.500000
75%      0.072281     8.205229    2.250000
max      6.856720    11.792703    3.000000
<class 'pandas.core.frame.DataFrame'>
RangeIndex: 100 entries, 0 to 99
Data columns (total 3 columns):
 #   Column    Non-Null Count  Dtype
---  ------    --------------  -----
 0   Feature1  100 non-null    float64
 1   Feature2  100 non-null    float64
 2   Cluster   100 non-null    float64
dtypes: float64(3)
memory usage: 2.5 KB
None
```

```
plt.scatter(df['Feature1'], df['Feature2'])
```

```
<matplotlib.collections.PathCollection at 0x7c20b88d3dc0>
```

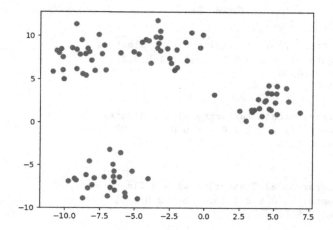

Figure 8.17 A Scatter Plot of Feature1 VS Feature2

8.2.1.2 Data Preprocessing

```
# Standardize the features
scaler = StandardScaler()
X_scaled = scaler.fit_transform(X)
```

8.2.1.3 Agglomerative Hierarchical Clustering

```
# Number of clusters to try
num_clusters_range = range(2, 8)

# Perform agglomerative hierarchical clustering with different numbers
for num_clusters in num_clusters_range:
    agglomerative = AgglomerativeClustering(n_clusters=num_clusters)
    agglomerative_labels = agglomerative.fit_predict(X_scaled)

    print(f"\nAgglomerative Hierarchical Clustering with
        {num_clusters} Clusters:")
    print(f"Cluster Assignments: {agglomerative_labels}")

    # Calculate the silhouette score
    silhouette_avg = silhouette_score(X_scaled, agglomerative_labels)
    print(f"Silhouette Score: {silhouette_avg:.4f}\n")
```

```
Agglomerative Hierarchical Clustering with 2 Clusters:
Cluster Assignments: [0 1 0 1 0 1 ... 0 0 0 0 0]
Silhouette Score: 0.5268
```

```
Agglomerative Hierarchical Clustering with 3 Clusters:
Cluster Assignments: [0 1 0 1 0 1 ... 0 0 2 0 2]
Silhouette Score: 0.6894
```

```
Agglomerative Hierarchical Clustering with 4 Clusters:
Cluster Assignments: [3 0 1 0 3 0 ... 1 1 1 2 3 2]
Silhouette Score: 0.6966


Agglomerative Hierarchical Clustering with 5 Clusters:
Cluster Assignments: [1 3 0 3 1 4 ... 0 0 0 2 1 2]
Silhouette Score: 0.5915


Agglomerative Hierarchical Clustering with 6 Clusters:
Cluster Assignments: [1 3 5 3 1 4 ... 5 5 2 0 1 0]
Silhouette Score: 0.5058


Agglomerative Hierarchical Clustering with 7 Clusters:
Cluster Assignments: [0 1 5 1 0 4 ... 5 5 2 6 0 3]
Silhouette Score: 0.4200
```

8.2.2 Case Study

Let's proceed with the tutorial on hierarchical clustering using the "Iris" dataset. We will demonstrate the agglomerative hierarchical clustering method, which is a popular hierarchical clustering approach.

8.2.2.1 Setup

Dataset loading and exploration

```python
import numpy as np
import pandas as pd
import matplotlib.pyplot as plt
from sklearn.datasets import load_iris
from sklearn.preprocessing import StandardScaler
from sklearn.cluster import AgglomerativeClustering
from scipy.cluster.hierarchy import dendrogram, linkage

# Load the Iris dataset
data = load_iris()
X, y = data.data, data.target

# Convert to DataFrame for easier manipulation (optional)
df = pd.DataFrame(data=np.c_[X, y]
    , columns=data.feature_names + ['target'])

# Explore the dataset
print(df.head())
print(df.describe())
print(df.info())
```

	sepal length (cm)	sepal width (cm)	petal length (cm)	petal width (cm) \
0	5.1	3.5	1.4	0.2
1	4.9	3.0	1.4	0.2
2	4.7	3.2	1.3	0.2
3	4.6	3.1	1.5	0.2
4	5.0	3.6	1.4	0.2

	target
0	0.0
1	0.0
2	0.0
3	0.0
4	0.0

	sepal length (cm)	sepal width (cm)	petal length (cm) \
count	150.000000	150.000000	150.000000
mean	5.843333	3.057333	3.758000
std	0.828066	0.435866	1.765298
min	4.300000	2.000000	1.000000
25%	5.100000	2.800000	1.600000
50%	5.800000	3.000000	4.350000
75%	6.400000	3.300000	5.100000
max	7.900000	4.400000	6.900000

	petal width (cm)	target
count	150.000000	150.000000
mean	1.199333	1.000000
std	0.762238	0.819232
min	0.100000	0.000000
25%	0.300000	0.000000
50%	1.300000	1.000000
75%	1.800000	2.000000
max	2.500000	2.000000

```
<class 'pandas.core.frame.DataFrame'>
RangeIndex: 150 entries, 0 to 149
Data columns (total 5 columns):
 #   Column             Non-Null Count  Dtype
---  ------             --------------  -----
 0   sepal length (cm)  150 non-null    float64
 1   sepal width (cm)   150 non-null    float64
 2   petal length (cm)  150 non-null    float64
 3   petal width (cm)   150 non-null    float64
 4   target             150 non-null    float64
dtypes: float64(5)
memory usage: 6.0 KB
None
```

8.2.2.2 Data Preprocessing

Before applying hierarchical clustering, we need to preprocess the data to standardize the features.

```
# Standardize the features
scaler = StandardScaler()
X_scaled = scaler.fit_transform(X)
```

8.2.2.3 Agglomerative Hierarchical Clustering

```
# Initialize the Agglomerative clustering algorithm
agglomerative = AgglomerativeClustering(n_clusters=3)

# Fit the model to the data
agglomerative.fit(X_scaled)

# Get the cluster assignments for each sample
agglomerative_labels = agglomerative.labels_

print(f"Agglomerative Hierarchical Clustering:")
print(f"Cluster Assignments: {agglomerative_labels}")
```

```
Agglomerative Hierarchical Clustering:
Cluster Assignments: [1 1 1 1 1 ... 0 0 0 0 0]
```

8.3 DENSITY-BASED CLUSTERING

Density-based clustering is a powerful technique in unsupervised machine learning used to discover clusters of varying shapes and sizes based on data density. This section introduces density-based clustering, specifically focusing on the DBSCAN algorithm using the Scikit-learn package.

Density-based clustering algorithms, such as DBSCAN (Density-Based Spatial Clustering of Applications with Noise), identify clusters based on the density of data points in the feature space. It is particularly useful for discovering clusters of irregular shapes and handling noise. Scikit-learn provides tools to implement DBSCAN effectively. You will explore practical implementation steps, including using the DBSCAN class in Scikit-learn to perform density-based clustering on a dataset, customizing DBSCAN parameters, such as epsilon (neighborhood distance) and minimum samples, and visualizing the resulting clusters and identifying noise points.

8.3.1 Tutorial

8.3.1.1 Setup

```
import numpy as np

from sklearn.cluster import DBSCAN
from sklearn import metrics
from sklearn.datasets import make_blobs
from sklearn.preprocessing import StandardScaler
```

```
# Generate sample data
centers = [[1, 1], [-1, -1], [1, -1]]
X, labels_true = make_blobs(
    n_samples=750, centers=centers, cluster_std=0.4, random_state=0
)

X = StandardScaler().fit_transform(X)
```

8.3.1.2 DBSCAN

```
# Compute DBSCAN
db = DBSCAN(eps=0.3, min_samples=10).fit(X)
core_samples_mask = np.zeros_like(db.labels_, dtype=bool)
core_samples_mask[db.core_sample_indices_] = True
labels = db.labels_
# Number of clusters in labels, ignoring noise if present.
n_clusters_ = len(set(labels)) - (1 if -1 in labels else 0)
n_noise_ = list(labels).count(-1)

print("Estimated number of clusters: %d" % n_clusters_)
print("Estimated number of noise points: %d" % n_noise_)
print("Homogeneity: %0.3f" %
    metrics.homogeneity_score(labels_true, labels))
print("Completeness: %0.3f" %
    metrics.completeness_score(labels_true, labels))
print("V-measure: %0.3f" %
    metrics.v_measure_score(labels_true, labels))
print("Adjusted Rand Index: %0.3f" %
    metrics.adjusted_rand_score(labels_true, labels))
print( "Adjusted Mutual Information: %0.3f"%
    metrics.adjusted_mutual_info_score(labels_true, labels))
print("Silhouette Coefficient: %0.3f" %
    metrics.silhouette_score(X, labels))

# Plot result
import matplotlib.pyplot as plt

# Black removed and is used for noise instead.
unique_labels = set(labels)
colors = [plt.cm.Spectral(each) for each in
    np.linspace(0, 1, len(unique_labels))]
for k, col in zip(unique_labels, colors):
    if k == -1:
        # Black used for noise.
        col = [0, 0, 0, 1]

    class_member_mask = labels == k

    xy = X[class_member_mask & core_samples_mask]
    plt.plot(
```

```
        xy[:, 0],
        xy[:, 1],
        "o",
        markerfacecolor=tuple(col),
        markeredgecolor="k",
        markersize=14,
    )

    xy = X[class_member_mask & ~core_samples_mask]
    plt.plot(
        xy[:, 0],
        xy[:, 1],
        "o",
        markerfacecolor=tuple(col),
        markeredgecolor="k",
        markersize=6,
    )

plt.title("Estimated number of clusters: %d" % n_clusters_)
plt.show()
```

```
Estimated number of clusters: 3
Estimated number of noise points: 18
Homogeneity: 0.953
Completeness: 0.883
V-measure: 0.917
Adjusted Rand Index: 0.952
Adjusted Mutual Information: 0.916
Silhouette Coefficient: 0.626
```

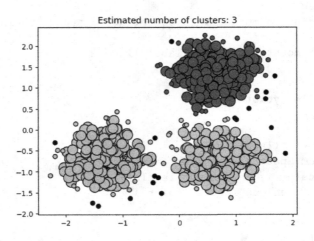

Figure 8.18 DBSCAN Result with Three Clusters

8.3.2 Case Study

Let's proceed with the tutorial on density-based clustering using the "Iris" dataset. We will demonstrate the DBSCAN (Density-Based Spatial Clustering of Applications with Noise) algorithm with multiple values of eps and min_samples for comparison.

8.3.2.1 Setup

Before applying DBSCAN, we need to preprocess the data to standardize the features.

```python
import numpy as np
import pandas as pd
import matplotlib.pyplot as plt
from sklearn.datasets import load_iris
from sklearn.preprocessing import StandardScaler
from sklearn.cluster import DBSCAN
from sklearn.metrics import silhouette_score, adjusted_rand_score

# Load the Iris dataset
data = load_iris()
X, y = data.data, data.target

# Convert to DataFrame for easier manipulation (optional)
df = pd.DataFrame(data=np.c_[X, y]
    , columns=data.feature_names + ['target'])

# Explore the dataset
print(df.head())
print(df.describe())
print(df.info())

# Standardize the features
scaler = StandardScaler()
X_scaled = scaler.fit_transform(X)
```

	sepal length (cm)	sepal width (cm)	petal length (cm)	petal width (cm)	\
0	5.1	3.5	1.4	0.2	
1	4.9	3.0	1.4	0.2	
2	4.7	3.2	1.3	0.2	
3	4.6	3.1	1.5	0.2	
4	5.0	3.6	1.4	0.2	

	target
0	0.0
1	0.0
2	0.0
3	0.0
4	0.0

	sepal length (cm)	sepal width (cm)	petal length (cm)	\
count	150.000000	150.000000	150.000000	
mean	5.843333	3.057333	3.758000	
std	0.828066	0.435866	1.765298	
min	4.300000	2.000000	1.000000	

25%	5.100000	2.800000	1.600000
50%	5.800000	3.000000	4.350000
75%	6.400000	3.300000	5.100000
max	7.900000	4.400000	6.900000

	petal width (cm)	target
count	150.000000	150.000000
mean	1.199333	1.000000
std	0.762238	0.819232
min	0.100000	0.000000
25%	0.300000	0.000000
50%	1.300000	1.000000
75%	1.800000	2.000000
max	2.500000	2.000000

```
<class 'pandas.core.frame.DataFrame'>
RangeIndex: 150 entries, 0 to 149
Data columns (total 5 columns):
 #   Column             Non-Null Count  Dtype
---  ------             --------------  -----
 0   sepal length (cm)  150 non-null    float64
 1   sepal width (cm)   150 non-null    float64
 2   petal length (cm)  150 non-null    float64
 3   petal width (cm)   150 non-null    float64
 4   target             150 non-null    float64
dtypes: float64(5)
memory usage: 6.0 KB
None
```

8.3.2.2 DBSCAN

DBSCAN clustering with different eps and min_samples

```
# Define a range of `eps` and `min_samples` values to try
eps_values = [0.2, 0.3, 0.4, 0.5]
min_samples_values = [2, 3, 4]

# Perform DBSCAN clustering
fig, axs = plt.subplots(len(eps_values), len(min_samples_values)
    , figsize=(15, 15))
fig.subplots_adjust(hspace=0.5)

for i, eps in enumerate(eps_values):
    for j, min_samples in enumerate(min_samples_values):
        dbscan = DBSCAN(eps=eps, min_samples=min_samples)
        dbscan_labels = dbscan.fit_predict(X_scaled)

        # Number of clusters in labels, ignoring noise if present
        n_clusters_ = len(set(dbscan_labels)) -
    (1 if -1 in dbscan_labels else 0)

        # Calculate the silhouette score and adjusted Rand Index score
        silhouette_avg = silhouette_score(X_scaled, dbscan_labels)
        ari_score = adjusted_rand_score(y, dbscan_labels)
```

```
        # Scatter plot for each combination of eps and min_samples
      axs[i, j].scatter(X_scaled[:, 0], X_scaled[:, 1]
, c=dbscan_labels, cmap='viridis', s=50)
      axs[i, j].set_title(f'DBSCAN Clustering (eps={eps},
                          min_samples={min_samples})\n'
                       f'Clusters: {n_clusters_},
                       Silhouette Score: {silhouette_avg:.2f},
                       ARI: {ari_score:.2f}')
      axs[i, j].set_xlabel('Feature 1 (Scaled)')
      axs[i, j].set_ylabel('Feature 2 (Scaled)')

plt.show()
```

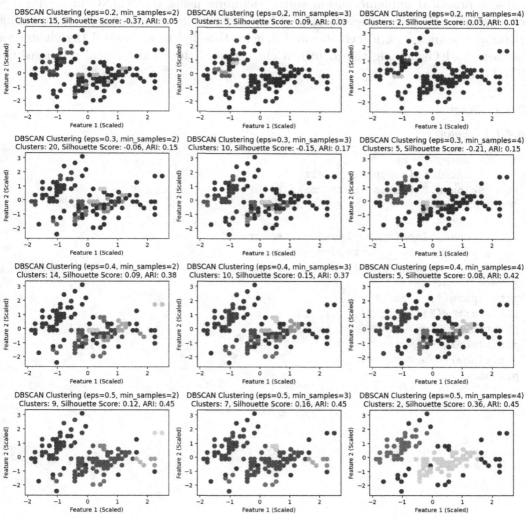

Figure 8.19 Comparison among DBSCAN Results

8.4 GRID-BASED CLUSTERING

Grid-based clustering is an innovative technique in unsupervised machine learning that partitions the feature space into a grid and then identifies clusters within these grid cells. This section introduces grid-based clustering methods, specifically focusing on STING (Statistical Information Grid) and OPTICS (Ordering Points To Identify Clustering Structure) using the Scikit-learn package.

Grid-based clustering methods offer a unique approach to cluster discovery by dividing the feature space into a grid of cells and identifying clusters within these cells. This technique is particularly useful for datasets with non-uniform density. Scikit-learn provides tools to implement grid-based clustering techniques effectively. You will explore practical implementation steps, including using the STING and OPTICS classes in Scikit-learn to perform grid-based clustering on a dataset, customizing parameters, such as grid cell size and density thresholds, to control the clustering process, and visualizing the identified clusters and their hierarchical relationships (OPTICS).

8.4.1 Tutorial

8.4.1.1 Setup

```python
import numpy as np
import matplotlib.pyplot as plt
from sklearn.datasets import make_blobs

# Generate a dummy dataset with grid-like structure
X, y = make_blobs(n_samples=500, centers=4
    , cluster_std=1.5, random_state=42)

# Plot the dataset
plt.figure(figsize=(8, 6))
plt.scatter(X[:, 0], X[:, 1], c='b', s=50)
plt.title("Dummy Grid-like Dataset")
plt.xlabel("Feature 1")
plt.ylabel("Feature 2")
plt.show()
```

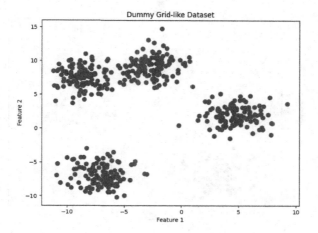

Figure 8.20 A Scatter Plot of Feature1 VS Feature2

```
!pip install scikit-learn-extra
```

8.4.1.2 STING

```
from sklearn_extra.cluster import KMedoids

# Perform STING clustering using KMedoids
grid_size = 10
# STING uses KMedoids as its clustering algorithm
sting = KMedoids(n_clusters=4, random_state=42)
sting_labels = sting.fit_predict(X)

print(f"STING Clustering:")
print(f"Cluster Assignments: {sting_labels}")
```

```
STING Clustering:
Cluster Assignments: [2 0 1 3 0 ... 2 3 0 0 1]
```

```
# Visualization of Clustering Results
plt.figure(figsize=(8, 6))
plt.scatter(X[:, 0], X[:, 1], c=sting_labels, cmap='viridis', s=50)
plt.title('STING Clustering')
plt.xlabel('Feature 1')
plt.ylabel('Feature 2')

plt.tight_layout()
plt.show()
```

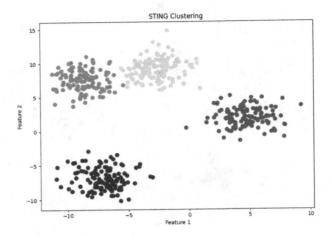

Figure 8.21   STING Clustering Result

8.4.1.3 *CLIQUE*

```
!pip install pyclustering
```

```python
from pyclustering.cluster.clique import clique, clique_visualizer

# Perform CLIQUE clustering
# create CLIQUE algorithm for processing

# defines amount of cells in grid in each dimension
intervals = 20
# lets consider each point as non-outlier
threshold = 3
clique_instance = clique(X.tolist(), intervals, threshold)


# start clustering process and obtain results
clique_instance.process()

# allocated clusters
clusters = clique_instance.get_clusters()
# points that are considered as outliers (in this example should be empty)
noise = clique_instance.get_noise()
# CLIQUE blocks that forms grid
cells = clique_instance.get_cells()

print("Amount of clusters:", len(clusters))

# visualize clustering results
# show grid that has been formed by the algorithm
clique_visualizer.show_grid(cells, X.tolist())
# show clustering results
clique_visualizer.show_clusters(X.tolist(), clusters, noise)
```

Amount of clusters: 4

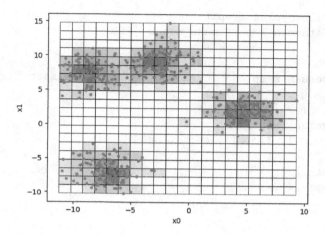

Figure 8.22   CLIQUE Clustering Result

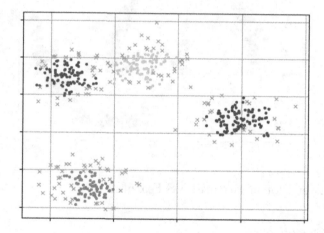

Figure 8.23   CLIQUE Clustering Result

8.4.2   Case Study

Grid clustering methods are particularly suitable for datasets with a spatial or grid-like structure, where data points are organized on a regular grid or lattice. One such dataset that is commonly used for grid clustering methods is the "Two Moons" dataset.

The "Two Moons" dataset consists of two crescent-shaped clusters that are not linearly separable, making it a good choice for demonstrating grid and density clustering algorithms.

Let's proceed with the "Two Moons" dataset and demonstrate STING, OPTICS, and DBSCAN.

8.4.2.1   *Setup*

```python
import numpy as np
import matplotlib.pyplot as plt
from sklearn.datasets import make_moons

# Generate the "Two Moons" dataset
X, y = make_moons(n_samples=500, noise=0.05, random_state=42)

# Plot the dataset
plt.figure(figsize=(8, 6))
plt.scatter(X[:, 0], X[:, 1], c='b', s=50)
plt.title("Two Moons Dataset")
plt.xlabel("Feature 1")
plt.ylabel("Feature 2")
plt.show()
```

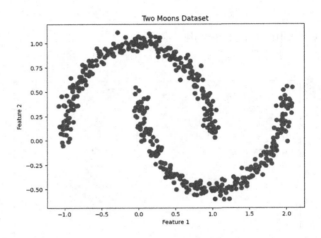

Figure 8.24   A Scatter Plot of Feature1 VS Feature2

8.4.2.2   *STING Clustering*

STING (STatistical INformation Grid) is a grid-based clustering method that partitions the dataset into a hierarchical grid and then groups cells based on statistical properties.

```python
!pip install scikit-learn-extra
```

```python
from sklearn_extra.cluster import KMedoids
from sklearn.cluster import DBSCAN
from sklearn.metrics import adjusted_rand_score

# Perform STING clustering
grid_size = 2
sting = KMedoids(n_clusters=2, random_state=42)
sting_labels = sting.fit_predict(X)
```

```
# Calculate the Adjusted Rand Index (ARI) score
ari_score_sting = adjusted_rand_score(y, sting_labels)

print(f"STING Clustering:")
print(f"Adjusted Rand Index Score: {ari_score_sting:.4f}")
```

```
STING Clustering:
Adjusted Rand Index Score: 0.2816
```

```
# Visualization of Clustering Results
plt.figure(figsize=(8, 6))
plt.scatter(X[:, 0], X[:, 1], c=sting_labels, cmap='viridis', s=50)
plt.title('STING Clustering')
plt.xlabel('Feature 1')
plt.ylabel('Feature 2')

plt.tight_layout()
plt.show()
```

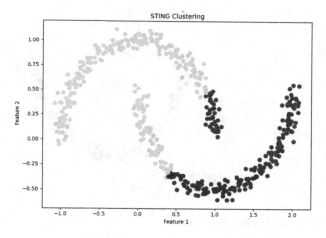

Figure 8.25 STING Clustering Result

Actually, density-based clustering methods are better for this dataset.

8.4.2.3 OPTICS Clustering

OPTICS is a density-based clustering method that builds a reachability plot to identify clusters with varying density.

```
from sklearn.cluster import OPTICS
from sklearn.metrics import adjusted_rand_score

# Perform OPTICS clustering
optics = OPTICS(min_samples=10, xi=0.15, min_cluster_size=0.15)
optics_labels = optics.fit_predict(X)
```

```
# Calculate the Adjusted Rand Index (ARI) score
ari_score_optics = adjusted_rand_score(y, optics_labels)

print(f"OPTICS Clustering:")
print(f"Adjusted Rand Index Score: {ari_score_optics:.4f}")
```

```
OPTICS Clustering:
Adjusted Rand Index Score: 1.0000
```

```
# Visualization of OPTICS Clustering Results
plt.figure(figsize=(8, 6))
plt.scatter(X[:, 0], X[:, 1], c=optics_labels, cmap='viridis', s=50)
plt.title('OPTICS Clustering')
plt.xlabel('Feature 1')
plt.ylabel('Feature 2')
plt.show()
```

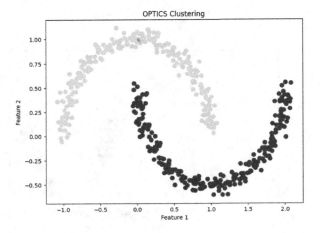

Figure 8.26 OPTICS Clustering Result

```
from sklearn.cluster import DBSCAN
from sklearn.metrics import adjusted_rand_score

# Perform DBSCAN clustering
dbscan = DBSCAN(eps=0.15, min_samples=10)
dbscan_labels = dbscan.fit_predict(X)

# Calculate the Adjusted Rand Index (ARI) score
ari_score_dbscan = adjusted_rand_score(y, dbscan_labels)

print(f"DBSCAN Clustering:")
print(f"Adjusted Rand Index Score: {ari_score_dbscan:.4f}")
```

```
DBSCAN Clustering:
Adjusted Rand Index Score: 1.0000
```

```
# Visualization of DBSCAN Clustering Results
plt.figure(figsize=(8, 6))
plt.scatter(X[:, 0], X[:, 1], c=dbscan_labels, cmap='viridis', s=50)
plt.title('DBSCAN Clustering')
plt.xlabel('Feature 1')
plt.ylabel('Feature 2')
plt.show()
```

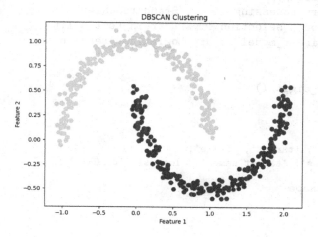

Figure 8.27 DBSCAN Clustering Result

8.5 PRINCIPAL COMPONENT ANALYSIS

Principal Component Analysis (PCA) is a fundamental dimensionality reduction technique widely used in machine learning and data analysis. This section introduces PCA, including both number-based and variance-based methods, using the Scikit-learn package.

PCA is a dimensionality reduction technique that aims to capture the most important information in a dataset by transforming the original features into a new set of orthogonal variables called principal components. It is used for data compression, visualization, and feature selection. Number-based PCA selection methods involve choosing a specific number of principal components based on the desired dimensionality reduction. Variance-based PCA selection methods aim to retain a sufficient amount of the total variance in the data. Scikit-learn provides user-friendly tools to implement PCA effectively. You will explore practical implementation steps, including using the PCA class in Scikit-learn to perform PCA on a dataset, determining the number of principal components to retain using methods like explained variance or cumulative variance, and transforming data into the PCA space for analysis or visualization.

8.5.1 Tutorial

8.5.1.1 Round 1: Using Digits Dataset

##Load dataset and preprocess it

```
from sklearn.datasets import load_digits
import pandas as pd
import matplotlib.pyplot as plt
from sklearn.preprocessing import StandardScaler
from sklearn.model_selection import train_test_split
from sklearn.linear_model import LogisticRegression


dataset = load_digits()
dataset.keys()
```

```
dict_keys(['data', 'target', 'frame',
    'feature_names', 'target_names', 'images', 'DESCR'])
```

```
dataset.data.shape
```

```
(1797, 64)
```

```
dataset.data[0]
```

```
array([ 0.,   0.,   5.,  13.,   9.,   1.,   0.,   0.,   0.,   0.,  13.,  15.,  10.,
       15.,   5.,   0.,   0.,   3.,  15.,   2.,   0.,  11.,   8.,   0.,   0.,   4.,
       12.,   0.,   0.,   8.,   8.,   0.,   0.,   5.,   8.,   0.,   0.,   9.,   8.,
        0.,   0.,   4.,  11.,   0.,   1.,  12.,   7.,   0.,   0.,   2.,  14.,   5.,
       10.,  12.,   0.,   0.,   0.,   0.,   6.,  13.,  10.,   0.,   0.,   0.])
```

```
dataset.data[0].reshape(8,8)
```

```
array([[ 0.,   0.,   5.,  13.,   9.,   1.,   0.,   0.],
       [ 0.,   0.,  13.,  15.,  10.,  15.,   5.,   0.],
       [ 0.,   3.,  15.,   2.,   0.,  11.,   8.,   0.],
       [ 0.,   4.,  12.,   0.,   0.,   8.,   8.,   0.],
       [ 0.,   5.,   8.,   0.,   0.,   9.,   8.,   0.],
       [ 0.,   4.,  11.,   0.,   1.,  12.,   7.,   0.],
       [ 0.,   2.,  14.,   5.,  10.,  12.,   0.,   0.],
       [ 0.,   0.,   6.,  13.,  10.,   0.,   0.,   0.]])
```

```
plt.gray()
plt.matshow(dataset.data[0].reshape(8,8))
```

```
<matplotlib.image.AxesImage at 0x7fa60ce2d2d0>
```

```
<Figure size 432x288 with 0 Axes>
```

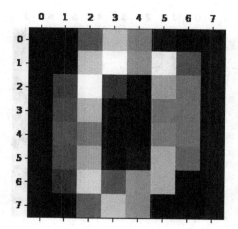

Figure 8.28 Digit 0

```
for i in range(10):
    plt.matshow(dataset.data[i].reshape(8,8))
```

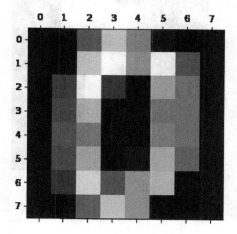

Figure 8.29 Digit 0

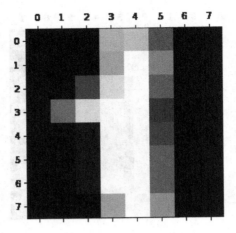

Figure 8.30   Digit 1

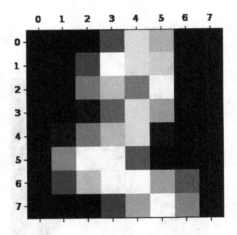

Figure 8.31   Digit 2

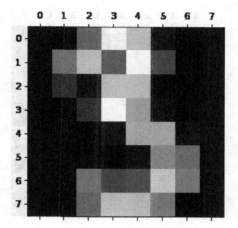

Figure 8.32 Digit 3

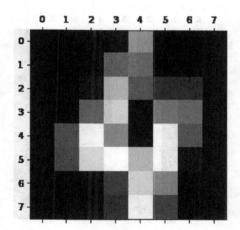

Figure 8.33 Digit 4

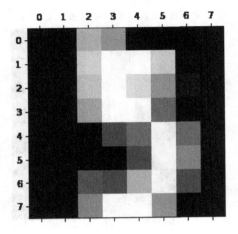

Figure 8.34   Digit 5

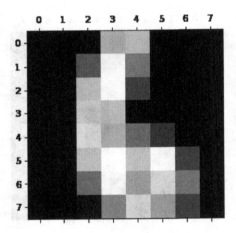

Figure 8.35   Digit 6

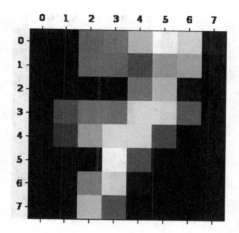

Figure 8.36   Digit 7

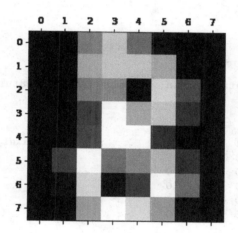

Figure 8.37   Digit 8

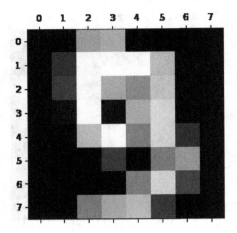

Figure 8.38 Digit 9

```
dataset.target
```

```
array([0, 1, 2, ..., 8, 9, 8])
```

```
df = pd.DataFrame(dataset.data, columns=dataset.feature_names)
df.head()
```

```
   pixel_0_0  pixel_0_1  pixel_0_2  ...  pixel_7_6  pixel_7_7
0       0.0        0.0        5.0  ...        0.0        0.0
1       0.0        0.0        0.0  ...        0.0        0.0
2       0.0        0.0        0.0  ...        0.0        0.0
3       0.0        0.0        7.0  ...        0.0        0.0
4       0.0        0.0        0.0  ...        0.0        0.0
[5 rows x 64 columns]
```

```
df.describe()
```

```
        pixel_0_0     pixel_0_1     pixel_0_2  ...     pixel_7_7
count     1797.0  1797.000000  1797.000000  ...  1797.000000
mean         0.0     0.303840     5.204786  ...     0.364496
std          0.0     0.907192     4.754826  ...     1.860122
min          0.0     0.000000     0.000000  ...     0.000000
25%          0.0     0.000000     1.000000  ...     0.000000
50%          0.0     0.000000     4.000000  ...     0.000000
75%          0.0     0.000000     9.000000  ...     0.000000
max          0.0     8.000000    16.000000  ...    16.000000
[8 rows x 64 columns]
```

```
X = df
y = dataset.target
```

```
scaler = StandardScaler()
X = scaler.fit_transform(X)
X
```

```
array([[ 0.        , -0.33501649, -0.04308102, ..., -1.14664746,
        -0.5056698 , -0.19600752],
       [ 0.        , -0.33501649, -1.09493684, ...,  0.54856067,
        -0.5056698 , -0.19600752],
       [ 0.        , -0.33501649, -1.09493684, ...,  1.56568555,
         1.6951369 , -0.19600752],
       ...,
       [ 0.        , -0.33501649, -0.88456568, ..., -0.12952258,
        -0.5056698 , -0.19600752],
       [ 0.        , -0.33501649, -0.67419451, ...,  0.8876023 ,
        -0.5056698 , -0.19600752],
       [ 0.        , -0.33501649,  1.00877481, ...,  0.8876023 ,
        -0.26113572, -0.19600752]])
```

Train a simple Logistic Regression classifier

```
X_train, X_test, y_train, y_test = train_test_split(X, y, test_size=0.2
    , random_state=30)
```

```
model = LogisticRegression(max_iter=1000)
model.fit(X_train, y_train)
model.score(X_test, y_test)
```

0.9722222222222222

Conclusion: With 100% information (64 features), we can achieve 97.2% accuracy.

8.5.1.2 Round 2: Use PCA with 0.95 for Analysis

Keep 95% information PCA for dimension deduction

```
X
```

```
array([[ 0.        , -0.33501649, -0.04308102, ..., -1.14664746,
        -0.5056698 , -0.19600752],
       [ 0.        , -0.33501649, -1.09493684, ...,  0.54856067,
        -0.5056698 , -0.19600752],
       [ 0.        , -0.33501649, -1.09493684, ...,  1.56568555,
         1.6951369 , -0.19600752],
       ...,
       [ 0.        , -0.33501649, -0.88456568, ..., -0.12952258,
        -0.5056698 , -0.19600752],
       [ 0.        , -0.33501649, -0.67419451, ...,  0.8876023 ,
        -0.5056698 , -0.19600752],
       [ 0.        , -0.33501649,  1.00877481, ...,  0.8876023 ,
        -0.26113572, -0.19600752]])
```

```
X.shape
```

(1797, 64)

```
from sklearn.decomposition import PCA

pca = PCA(0.95)
X_pca = pca.fit_transform(X)
X_pca.shape
```

(1797, 40)

```
pca.explained_variance_ratio_
```

```
array([0.12033916, 0.09561054, 0.08444415, 0.06498408, 0.04860155,
       0.0421412 , 0.03942083, 0.03389381, 0.02998221, 0.02932003,
       0.02781805, 0.02577055, 0.02275303, 0.0222718 , 0.02165229,
       0.01914167, 0.01775547, 0.01638069, 0.0159646 , 0.01489191,
       0.0134797 , 0.01271931, 0.01165837, 0.01057647, 0.00975316,
       0.00944559, 0.00863014, 0.00836643, 0.00797693, 0.00746471,
       0.00725582, 0.00691911, 0.00653909, 0.00640793, 0.00591384,
       0.00571162, 0.00523637, 0.00481808, 0.00453719, 0.00423163])
```

```
pca.n_components_
```

40

```
X_pca
```

```
array([[ 1.91421366, -0.95450157, -3.94603482, ...,  0.81405925,
         0.0249306 ,  0.32193146],
       [ 0.58898033,  0.9246358 ,  3.92475494, ...,  0.20026094,
         0.08710843, -0.48914299],
       [ 1.30203906, -0.31718883,  3.02333293, ..., -0.214596  ,
        -1.2788745 ,  0.54583387],
       ...,
       [ 1.02259599, -0.14791087,  2.46997365, ...,  0.60136463,
         0.41238798,  1.20886377],
       [ 1.07605522, -0.38090625, -2.45548693, ...,  0.43756556,
        -0.69863483, -0.44339963],
       [-1.25770233, -2.22759088,  0.28362789, ..., -0.38108638,
         0.12855104,  1.32137195]])
```

```
X_train_pca, X_test_pca, y_train, y_test
    = train_test_split(X_pca, y, test_size=0.2, random_state=30)
```

```
model = LogisticRegression(max_iter=1000)
model.fit(X_train_pca, y_train)
model.score(X_test_pca, y_test)
```

0.9638888888888889

Conclusion: With 95% information (40 features), we achieved 96.4% accuracy.

8.5.1.3 Round 3: Use PCA with 0.80 for Analysis

Keep 80% information PCA for dimension deduction

```
X
```

```
array([[ 0.        , -0.33501649, -0.04308102, ..., -1.14664746,
        -0.5056698 , -0.19600752],
       [ 0.        , -0.33501649, -1.09493684, ...,  0.54856067,
        -0.5056698 , -0.19600752],
       [ 0.        , -0.33501649, -1.09493684, ...,  1.56568555,
         1.6951369 , -0.19600752],
       ...,
       [ 0.        , -0.33501649, -0.88456568, ..., -0.12952258,
        -0.5056698 , -0.19600752],
       [ 0.        , -0.33501649, -0.67419451, ...,  0.8876023 ,
        -0.5056698 , -0.19600752],
       [ 0.        , -0.33501649,  1.00877481, ...,  0.8876023 ,
        -0.26113572, -0.19600752]])
```

```
X.shape
```

```
(1797, 64)
```

```
pca = PCA(0.80)
X_pca = pca.fit_transform(X)
X_pca.shape
```

```
(1797, 21)
```

```
pca.explained_variance_ratio_
```

```
array([0.12033916, 0.09561054, 0.08444415, 0.06498408, 0.04860155,
       0.0421412 , 0.03942083, 0.03389381, 0.02998221, 0.02932003,
       0.02781805, 0.02577055, 0.02275303, 0.0222718 , 0.02165229,
       0.01914167, 0.01775547, 0.01638069, 0.0159646 , 0.01489191,
       0.0134797 ])
```

```
pca.n_components_
```

```
21
```

```
X_pca
```

```
array([[ 1.91421366, -0.95450157, -3.94603482, ...,  0.41275404,
         0.43051695,  0.45099368],
       [ 0.58898033,  0.9246358 ,  3.92475494, ...,  0.55308473,
        -0.06967631,  0.90981832],
       [ 1.30203906, -0.31718883,  3.02333293, ..., -1.06555601,
```

```
      -1.13345406, -0.52591658],
      ...,
     [ 1.02259599, -0.14791087,  2.46997365, ..., -1.61210006,
       0.18230257,  0.16666651],
     [ 1.07605522, -0.38090625, -2.45548693, ..., -1.76918064,
       0.77471846, -0.13566828],
     [-1.25770233, -2.22759088,  0.28362789, ..., -2.43897852,
      -1.13276155, -1.11458695]])
```

```
X_train_pca, X_test_pca, y_train, y_test
    = train_test_split(X_pca, y, test_size=0.2, random_state=30)
```

```
model = LogisticRegression(max_iter=1000)
model.fit(X_train_pca, y_train)
model.score(X_test_pca, y_test)
```

0.9472222222222222

Conclusion: With 80% information (21 features), we achieved 94.7% accuracy.

8.5.1.4   Round 4: Use PCA with two features for analysis

Keep only two features PCA for dimension deduction

```
X
```

```
array([[ 0.        , -0.33501649, -0.04308102, ..., -1.14664746,
        -0.5056698 , -0.19600752],
       [ 0.        , -0.33501649, -1.09493684, ...,  0.54856067,
        -0.5056698 , -0.19600752],
       [ 0.        , -0.33501649, -1.09493684, ...,  1.56568555,
         1.6951369 , -0.19600752],
       ...,
       [ 0.        , -0.33501649, -0.88456568, ..., -0.12952258,
        -0.5056698 , -0.19600752],
       [ 0.        , -0.33501649, -0.67419451, ...,  0.8876023 ,
        -0.5056698 , -0.19600752],
       [ 0.        , -0.33501649,  1.00877481, ...,  0.8876023 ,
        -0.26113572, -0.19600752]])
```

```
X.shape
```

(1797, 64)

```
pca = PCA(n_components=2)
X_pca = pca.fit_transform(X)
X_pca.shape
```

(1797, 2)

```
pca.explained_variance_ratio_
```

```
array([0.12033916, 0.09561054])
```

```
pca.n_components_
```

2

```
X_pca
```

```
array([[ 1.91424073, -0.95439324],
       [ 0.58897815,  0.92467342],
       [ 1.30201409, -0.31731852],
       ...,
       [ 1.02261234, -0.14785558],
       [ 1.07607531, -0.38081854],
       [-1.25768733, -2.22764474]])
```

```
X_train_pca, X_test_pca, y_train, y_test
    = train_test_split(X_pca, y, test_size=0.2, random_state=30)
```

```
model = LogisticRegression(max_iter=1000)
model.fit(X_train_pca, y_train)
model.score(X_test_pca, y_test)
```

0.5666666666666667

Conclusion: With two features, we achieved 56.7% accuracy.

8.5.1.5 Round 5: Use PCA with ten Features for Analysis

Keep ten features PCA for dimension deduction

```
X
```

```
array([[ 0.         , -0.33501649, -0.04308102, ..., -1.14664746,
        -0.5056698 , -0.19600752],
       [ 0.         , -0.33501649, -1.09493684, ...,  0.54856067,
        -0.5056698 , -0.19600752],
       [ 0.         , -0.33501649, -1.09493684, ...,  1.56568555,
         1.6951369 , -0.19600752],
       ...,
       [ 0.         , -0.33501649, -0.88456568, ..., -0.12952258,
        -0.5056698 , -0.19600752],
       [ 0.         , -0.33501649, -0.67419451, ...,  0.8876023 ,
        -0.5056698 , -0.19600752],
       [ 0.         , -0.33501649,  1.00877481, ...,  0.8876023 ,
        -0.26113572, -0.19600752]])
```

```
X.shape
```

```
(1797, 64)
```

```
pca = PCA(n_components=10)
X_pca = pca.fit_transform(X)
X_pca.shape
```

```
(1797, 10)
```

```
pca.explained_variance_ratio_
```

```
array([0.12033916, 0.09561054, 0.08444414, 0.06498408, 0.04860031,
       0.04214069, 0.03941622, 0.03389025, 0.029981  , 0.0293009 ])
```

```
pca.n_components_
```

```
10
```

```
X_pca
```

```
array([[ 1.91419104, -0.95423662, -3.94596682, ...,  1.4875945 ,
         0.12958659, -0.80696961],
       [ 0.58907886,  0.92487031,  3.92502708, ...,  0.59412615,
         1.06303429,  0.01646066],
       [ 1.3020011 , -0.31734768,  3.02340561, ...,  1.15692023,
         0.78248132, -1.12782067],
       ...,
       [ 1.02278526, -0.14720481,  2.47042764, ...,  0.49576054,
         2.06471226, -1.94244605],
       [ 1.07606776, -0.38072138, -2.45549994, ...,  0.73116892,
         1.10143024, -0.22800896],
       [-1.25767195, -2.22777791,  0.2834488 , ..., -1.2334956 ,
         0.83499124, -1.77802894]])
```

```
X_train_pca, X_test_pca, y_train, y_test
    = train_test_split(X_pca, y, test_size=0.2, random_state=30)
```

```
model = LogisticRegression(max_iter=1000)
model.fit(X_train_pca, y_train)
model.score(X_test_pca, y_test)
```

```
0.8805555555555555
```

Conclusion: With ten features, we achieved 88.1% accuracy.

8.5.2 Case Study

8.5.2.1 Round 1: Using Wine Dataset

##Load dataset and preprocess it

```
from sklearn.datasets import load_wine
import pandas as pd
import matplotlib.pyplot as plt
from sklearn.preprocessing import StandardScaler
from sklearn.model_selection import train_test_split
from sklearn.linear_model import LogisticRegression


dataset = load_wine()
dataset.keys()
```

```
dict_keys(['data', 'target', 'frame',
    'target_names', 'DESCR', 'feature_names'])
```

```
dataset.data.shape
```

```
(178, 13)
```

```
dataset.data[0]
```

```
array([1.423e+01, 1.710e+00, 2.430e+00, 1.560e+01, 1.270e+02, 2.800e+00,
       3.060e+00, 2.800e-01, 2.290e+00, 5.640e+00, 1.040e+00, 3.920e+00,
       1.065e+03])
```

```
dataset.target
```

```
array([0, 0, 0, 0, 0, ... 2, 2, 2,
       2, 2])
```

```
df = pd.DataFrame(dataset.data, columns=dataset.feature_names)
df.head()
```

```
df.describe()
```

```
X = df
y = dataset.target
```

```
scaler = StandardScaler()
X = scaler.fit_transform(X)
X
```

```
array([[ 1.51861254, -0.5622498 ,  0.23205254, ...,  0.36217728,
         1.84791957,  1.01300893],
       [ 0.24628963, -0.49941338, -0.82799632, ...,  0.40605066,
         1.1134493 ,  0.96524152],
       [ 0.19687903,  0.02123125,  1.10933436, ...,  0.31830389,
         0.78858745,  1.39514818],
       ...,
       [ 0.33275817,  1.74474449, -0.38935541, ..., -1.61212515,
        -1.48544548,  0.28057537],
```

```
[ 0.20923168,  0.22769377,  0.01273209, ..., -1.56825176,
 -1.40069891,  0.29649784],
[ 1.39508604,  1.58316512,  1.36520822, ..., -1.52437837,
 -1.42894777, -0.59516041]])
```

Train a simple Logistic Regression classifier

```
X_train, X_test, y_train, y_test
    = train_test_split(X, y, test_size=0.2, random_state=30)
```

```
model = LogisticRegression(max_iter=1000)
model.fit(X_train, y_train)
model.score(X_test, y_test)
```

0.9722222222222222

Conclusion: With 100% information (13 features), we can achieve 97.2% accuracy.

8.5.2.2 Round 2: Use PCA with 0.95 for Analysis

Keep 95% information PCA for dimension deduction

```
X
```

```
array([[ 1.51861254, -0.5622498 ,  0.23205254, ...,  0.36217728,
         1.84791957,  1.01300893],
       [ 0.24628963, -0.49941338, -0.82799632, ...,  0.40605066,
         1.1134493 ,  0.96524152],
       [ 0.19687903,  0.02123125,  1.10933436, ...,  0.31830389,
         0.78858745,  1.39514818],
       ...,
       [ 0.33275817,  1.74474449, -0.38935541, ..., -1.61212515,
        -1.48544548,  0.28057537],
       [ 0.20923168,  0.22769377,  0.01273209, ..., -1.56825176,
        -1.40069891,  0.29649784],
       [ 1.39508604,  1.58316512,  1.36520822, ..., -1.52437837,
        -1.42894777, -0.59516041]])
```

```
X.shape
```

(178, 13)

```
from sklearn.decomposition import PCA

pca = PCA(0.95)
X_pca = pca.fit_transform(X)
X_pca.shape
```

(178, 10)

```
pca.explained_variance_ratio_
```

```
array([0.36198848, 0.1920749 , 0.11123631, 0.0706903 , 0.06563294,
       0.04935823, 0.04238679, 0.02680749, 0.02222153, 0.01930019])
```

```
pca.n_components_
```

10

```
X_pca
```

```
array([[ 3.31675081e+00, -1.44346263e+00, -1.65739045e-01, ...,
          6.51390947e-02,  6.41442706e-01,  1.02095585e+00],
        [ 2.20946492e+00,  3.33392887e-01, -2.02645737e+00, ...,
          1.02441595e+00, -3.08846753e-01,  1.59701372e-01],
        [ 2.51674015e+00, -1.03115130e+00,  9.82818670e-01, ...,
         -3.44216131e-01, -1.17783447e+00,  1.13360857e-01],
        ...,
        [-2.67783946e+00, -2.76089913e+00, -9.40941877e-01, ...,
          4.70238043e-02,  1.22214687e-03, -2.47997312e-01],
        [-2.38701709e+00, -2.29734668e+00, -5.50696197e-01, ...,
          3.90828774e-01,  5.74476725e-02,  4.91489502e-01],
        [-3.20875816e+00, -2.76891957e+00,  1.01391366e+00, ...,
         -2.92913734e-01,  7.41660423e-01, -1.17969019e-01]]])
```

```
X_train_pca, X_test_pca, y_train, y_test
    = train_test_split(X_pca, y, test_size=0.2, random_state=30)
```

```
model = LogisticRegression(max_iter=1000)
model.fit(X_train_pca, y_train)
model.score(X_test_pca, y_test)
```

0.9722222222222222

Conclusion: With 95% information (ten features), we achieved 97.2% accuracy (equally good as using 13 features).

8.5.2.3 Round 3: Use PCA with 0.80 for Analysis

Keep 80% information PCA for dimension deduction

```
X
```

```
array([[ 1.51861254, -0.5622498 ,  0.23205254, ...,  0.36217728,
          1.84791957,  1.01300893],
        [ 0.24628963, -0.49941338, -0.82799632, ...,  0.40605066,
          1.1134493 ,  0.96524152],
        [ 0.19687903,  0.02123125,  1.10933436, ...,  0.31830389,
          0.78858745,  1.39514818],
        ...,
        [ 0.33275817,  1.74474449, -0.38935541, ..., -1.61212515,
         -1.48544548,  0.28057537],
        [ 0.20923168,  0.22769377,  0.01273209, ..., -1.56825176,
```

```
        -1.40069891,  0.29649784],
      [ 1.39508604,  1.58316512,  1.36520822, ..., -1.52437837,
        -1.42894777, -0.59516041]])
```

```
X.shape
```

```
(178, 13)
```

```
pca = PCA(0.80)
X_pca = pca.fit_transform(X)
X_pca.shape
```

```
(178, 5)
```

```
pca.explained_variance_ratio_
```

```
array([0.36198848, 0.1920749 , 0.11123631, 0.0706903 , 0.06563294])
```

```
pca.n_components_
```

```
5
```

```
X_pca
```

```
array([[ 3.31675081e+00, -1.44346263e+00, -1.65739045e-01,
        -2.15631188e-01,  6.93042841e-01],
      [ 2.20946492e+00,  3.33392887e-01, -2.02645737e+00,
        -2.91358318e-01, -2.57654635e-01],
      [ 2.51674015e+00, -1.03115130e+00,  9.82818670e-01,
        7.24902309e-01, -2.51033118e-01],
      ...
      [-2.38701709e+00, -2.29734668e+00, -5.50696197e-01,
        -6.88284548e-01,  8.13955219e-01],
      [-3.20875816e+00, -2.76891957e+00,  1.01391366e+00,
        5.96903186e-01, -8.95192588e-01]])
```

```
X_train_pca, X_test_pca, y_train, y_test
    = train_test_split(X_pca, y, test_size=0.2, random_state=30)
```

```
model = LogisticRegression(max_iter=1000)
model.fit(X_train_pca, y_train)
model.score(X_test_pca, y_test)
```

```
0.9722222222222222
```

Conclusion: With 80% information (five features), we achieved 97.2% accuracy.

8.5.2.4 Round 4: Use PCA with two features for Analysis

Keep only two features PCA for dimension deduction

```
X
```

```
array([[ 1.51861254, -0.5622498 ,  0.23205254, ...,  0.36217728,
         1.84791957,  1.01300893],
       [ 0.24628963, -0.49941338, -0.82799632, ...,  0.40605066,
         1.1134493 ,  0.96524152],
       [ 0.19687903,  0.02123125,  1.10933436, ...,  0.31830389,
         0.78858745,  1.39514818],
       ...,
       [ 0.33275817,  1.74474449, -0.38935541, ..., -1.61212515,
        -1.48544548,  0.28057537],
       [ 0.20923168,  0.22769377,  0.01273209, ..., -1.56825176,
        -1.40069891,  0.29649784],
       [ 1.39508604,  1.58316512,  1.36520822, ..., -1.52437837,
        -1.42894777, -0.59516041]])
```

```
X.shape
```

```
(178, 13)
```

```
pca = PCA(n_components=2)
X_pca = pca.fit_transform(X)
X_pca.shape
```

```
(178, 2)
```

```
pca.explained_variance_ratio_
```

```
array([0.36198848, 0.1920749 ])
```

```
pca.n_components_
```

```
2
```

```
X_pca
```

```
array([[ 3.31675081, -1.44346263],
       [ 2.20946492,  0.33339289],
       [ 2.51674015, -1.0311513 ],
...
       [-2.67783946, -2.76089913],
       [-2.38701709, -2.29734668],
       [-3.20875816, -2.76891957]])
```

```
X_train_pca, X_test_pca, y_train, y_test
    = train_test_split(X_pca, y, test_size=0.2, random_state=30)
```

```
model = LogisticRegression(max_iter=1000)
model.fit(X_train_pca, y_train)
model.score(X_test_pca, y_test)
```

0.9722222222222222

Conclusion: With two features, we achieved 96.2% accuracy.

8.5.2.5 Round 5: Use PCA with one Feature for Analysis

Keep one feature PCA for dimension deduction

```
X
```

```
array([[ 1.51861254, -0.5622498 ,  0.23205254, ...,  0.36217728,
          1.84791957,  1.01300893],
       [ 0.24628963, -0.49941338, -0.82799632, ...,  0.40605066,
          1.1134493 ,  0.96524152],
       [ 0.19687903,  0.02123125,  1.10933436, ...,  0.31830389,
          0.78858745,  1.39514818],
       ...,
       [ 0.33275817,  1.74474449, -0.38935541, ..., -1.61212515,
         -1.48544548,  0.28057537],
       [ 0.20923168,  0.22769377,  0.01273209, ..., -1.56825176,
         -1.40069891,  0.29649784],
       [ 1.39508604,  1.58316512,  1.36520822, ..., -1.52437837,
         -1.42894777, -0.59516041]])
```

```
X.shape
```

(178, 13)

```
pca = PCA(n_components=1)
X_pca = pca.fit_transform(X)
X_pca.shape
```

(178, 1)

```
pca.explained_variance_ratio_
```

array([0.36198848])

```
pca.n_components_
```

1

```
X_pca
```

```
array([[ 3.31675081],
       [ 2.20946492],
```

```
[ 2.51674015],
...
       [-2.38701709],
       [-3.20875816]])
```

```
X_train_pca, X_test_pca, y_train, y_test
    = train_test_split(X_pca, y, test_size=0.2, random_state=30)
```

```
model = LogisticRegression(max_iter=1000)
model.fit(X_train_pca, y_train)
model.score(X_test_pca, y_test)
```

0.8888888888888888

Conclusion: With just one feature, we achieved 88.9% accuracy.

8.6 CLUSTERING METHODS' COMPARISON

In this section, we will conduct a comprehensive case study to explore and compare the performance of various clustering methods we have introduced using a single dataset. This hands-on approach will provide you with practical insights into how different clustering techniques perform in real-world scenarios.

The case study aims to evaluate and compare the performance of different clustering methods, allowing you to make informed choices when selecting the most appropriate technique for a specific clustering task. You will work with a dataset suitable for clustering and apply the clustering methods we have covered. Based on the case study results, you will gain insights into which clustering method(s) perform best for the given dataset and clustering task. You will also learn how to choose the most suitable clustering technique based on specific requirements and characteristics of a problem.

8.6.1 Case Study

Let's proceed with the clustering case study using the "penguins" dataset. We'll demonstrate four types of clustering methods: (1) partitioning methods, (2) hierarchical methods, and (3) density-based methods. We will visualize the clustering results and compare them using the Silhouette Score.

8.6.1.1 Setup

Load and explore the "penguins" dataset

```
import numpy as np
import pandas as pd
import matplotlib.pyplot as plt
import seaborn as sns

# Load the "penguins" dataset from Seaborn
```

```python
penguins = sns.load_dataset('penguins')

# Explore the basic information about the dataset
print(penguins.head())
print(penguins.info())
print(penguins.describe())

# Drop rows with missing values
penguins = penguins.dropna()

# Convert categorical variables to numerical using one-hot encoding
penguins = pd.get_dummies(penguins
    , columns=['species', 'island', 'sex'], drop_first=True)

# Extract the feature columns for clustering
X = penguins.drop('species_Chinstrap', axis=1)
```

```
   species     island  bill_length_mm  bill_depth_mm  flipper_length_mm  \
0  Adelie  Torgersen            39.1           18.7              181.0
1  Adelie  Torgersen            39.5           17.4              186.0
2  Adelie  Torgersen            40.3           18.0              195.0
3  Adelie  Torgersen             NaN            NaN                NaN
4  Adelie  Torgersen            36.7           19.3              193.0

   body_mass_g     sex
0       3750.0    Male
1       3800.0  Female
2       3250.0  Female
3          NaN     NaN
4       3450.0  Female
<class 'pandas.core.frame.DataFrame'>
RangeIndex: 344 entries, 0 to 343
Data columns (total 7 columns):
 #   Column             Non-Null Count  Dtype
---  ------             --------------  -----
 0   species            344 non-null    object
 1   island             344 non-null    object
 2   bill_length_mm     342 non-null    float64
 3   bill_depth_mm      342 non-null    float64
 4   flipper_length_mm  342 non-null    float64
 5   body_mass_g        342 non-null    float64
 6   sex                333 non-null    object
dtypes: float64(4), object(3)
memory usage: 18.9+ KB
None
       bill_length_mm  bill_depth_mm  flipper_length_mm   body_mass_g
count      342.000000     342.000000         342.000000    342.000000
mean        43.921930      17.151170         200.915205   4201.754386
std          5.459584       1.974793          14.061714    801.954536
min         32.100000      13.100000         172.000000   2700.000000
25%         39.225000      15.600000         190.000000   3550.000000
50%         44.450000      17.300000         197.000000   4050.000000
75%         48.500000      18.700000         213.000000   4750.000000
```

```
max            59.600000        21.500000        231.000000   6300.000000
```

8.6.1.2 Clustering with Partitioning Methods

```
from sklearn.cluster import KMeans
from sklearn.metrics import silhouette_score

# Perform K-means clustering
kmeans = KMeans(n_clusters=3, random_state=42)
kmeans_labels = kmeans.fit_predict(X)

# Visualize K-means clustering results
plt.scatter(X['bill_length_mm'], X['bill_depth_mm']
    , c=kmeans_labels, cmap='viridis', s=50)
plt.title('K-means Clustering')
plt.xlabel('Bill Length (mm)')
plt.ylabel('Bill Depth (mm)')
plt.show()

# Calculate the Silhouette Score for K-means clustering
silhouette_score_kmeans = silhouette_score(X, kmeans_labels)
print(f"Silhouette Score (K-means): {silhouette_score_kmeans:.4f}")
```

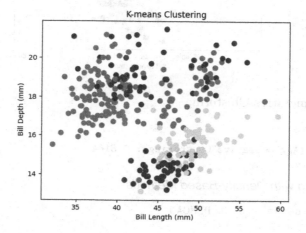

Figure 8.39   K-Means Clustering

```
Silhouette Score (K-means): 0.5752
```

8.6.1.3 Clustering with Hierarchical Methods

```
from sklearn.cluster import AgglomerativeClustering

# Perform Agglomerative Clustering
agglomerative = AgglomerativeClustering(n_clusters=3)
agglomerative_labels = agglomerative.fit_predict(X)
```

```python
# Visualize Agglomerative Clustering results
plt.scatter(X['bill_length_mm'], X['bill_depth_mm']
    , c=agglomerative_labels, cmap='viridis', s=50)
plt.title('Agglomerative Clustering')
plt.xlabel('Bill Length (mm)')
plt.ylabel('Bill Depth (mm)')
plt.show()

# Calculate the Silhouette Score for Agglomerative Clustering
silhouette_score_agglomerative = silhouette_score(X, agglomerative_labels)
print(f"Silhouette Score (Agglomerative Clustering):
    {silhouette_score_agglomerative:.4f}")
```

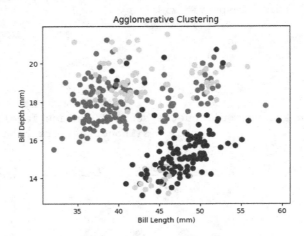

Figure 8.40 Agglomerative Clustering

Silhouette Score (Agglomerative Clustering): 0.5164

8.6.1.4 Clustering with Density-Based Methods

```python
from sklearn.cluster import DBSCAN

# Perform DBSCAN clustering
dbscan = DBSCAN(eps=20, min_samples=2)
dbscan_labels = dbscan.fit_predict(X)

# Visualize DBSCAN clustering results
plt.scatter(X['bill_length_mm'], X['bill_depth_mm']
    , c=dbscan_labels, cmap='viridis', s=50)
plt.title('DBSCAN Clustering')
plt.xlabel('Bill Length (mm)')
plt.ylabel('Bill Depth (mm)')
plt.show()
```

```
# Calculate the Silhouette Score for DBSCAN clustering
silhouette_score_dbscan = silhouette_score(X, dbscan_labels)
print(f"Silhouette Score (DBSCAN): {silhouette_score_dbscan:.4f}")
```

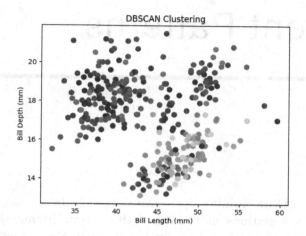

Figure 8.41   DBSCAN Clustering

```
Silhouette Score (DBSCAN): 0.6150
```

8.6.1.5   Compare the Results and Conclusion

```
# Compare the Silhouette Scores
silhouette_scores = [silhouette_score_kmeans
    , silhouette_score_agglomerative
    , silhouette_score_dbscan]
method_names = ['K-means', 'Agglomerative', 'DBSCAN']

for i, score in enumerate(silhouette_scores):
    print(f"Silhouette Score ({method_names[i]}): {score:.4f}")
```

```
Silhouette Score (K-means): 0.5752
Silhouette Score (Agglomerative): 0.5164
Silhouette Score (DBSCAN): 0.6150
```

## CHAPTER 9

Frequent Patterns

F REQUENT-PATTERN mining is a Data Mining task that aims to discover patterns or associations in a dataset that occur frequently. These patterns can be used to uncover relationships among items in the dataset and can be used for tasks such as market basket analysis, recommendation systems, and fraud detection.

There are many different frequent-pattern methods we use with Scikit-learn, but some of the most common include:

- Apriori: An algorithm that generates frequent itemsets by iteratively removing itemsets that do not meet a minimum support threshold.

- FP-Growth: An algorithm that generates frequent itemsets by building a compact data structure called a frequent-pattern tree, which allows for efficient generation of frequent itemsets.

9.1 FREQUENT ITEMSET AND ASSOCIATION RULES

Frequent itemset mining and association rule analysis are fundamental techniques in Data Mining used to discover associations and patterns within transactional datasets. This section introduces frequent itemsets and association rules using the mlxtend package, a versatile library for association analysis.

Frequent itemset mining identifies sets of items that frequently co-occur in transactions, while association rule analysis uncovers meaningful relationships and dependencies among items. These techniques provide valuable insights into customer behavior, product recommendations, and more. The mlxtend package offers a user-friendly environment to perform frequent itemset mining and association rule analysis efficiently. You will explore practical implementation steps, including using the apriori function in mlxtend to discover frequent itemsets based on specified support thresholds, extracting association rules from frequent itemsets using the association_rules function, and

DOI: 10.1201/9781003462781-9

visualizing itemset relationships, rule metrics, and support-confidence trade-offs for interpretation.

9.1.1 Tutorial – Finding Frequent Itemset

Below is a step-by-step tutorial on how to recognize frequent itemsets based on minimum support using the Apriori algorithm in Python.

9.1.1.1 Setup

Before proceeding, make sure you have the mlxtend library installed, which provides an efficient implementation of the Apriori algorithm.

```
!pip install mlxtend
```

9.1.1.2 Load and Preprocess the Dataset

For this tutorial, we'll use a sample dataset representing transactions (e.g., purchases in a store). Each transaction is represented as a list of items.

```python
import pandas as pd
from mlxtend.preprocessing import TransactionEncoder

# Sample dataset (list of transactions)
dataset = [
    ['Milk', 'Bread', 'Eggs'],
    ['Bread', 'Eggs', 'Butter'],
    ['Milk', 'Eggs'],
    ['Milk', 'Bread', 'Eggs', 'Butter'],
    ['Milk', 'Bread'],
    ['Bread', 'Eggs'],
    ['Milk', 'Bread', 'Butter'],
]

# Convert the dataset into a one-hot encoded format
te = TransactionEncoder()
te_ary = te.fit(dataset).transform(dataset)
df = pd.DataFrame(te_ary, columns=te.columns_)
print(df)
```

	Bread	Butter	Eggs	Milk
0	True	False	True	True
1	True	True	True	False
2	False	False	True	True
3	True	True	True	True
4	True	False	False	True
5	True	False	True	False
6	True	True	False	True

9.1.1.3 Perform Frequent Itemset Mining using Apriori

Now, we'll use the Apriori algorithm to mine frequent itemsets from the one-hot encoded dataset based on a minimum support threshold.

```python
from mlxtend.frequent_patterns import apriori

# Define the minimum support threshold
min_support = 0.4

# Perform frequent itemset mining using Apriori
frequent_itemsets = apriori(df, min_support=min_support, use_colnames=True)

print(frequent_itemsets)
```

```
   support         itemsets
0  0.857143          (Bread)
1  0.428571         (Butter)
2  0.714286           (Eggs)
3  0.714286           (Milk)
4  0.428571  (Butter, Bread)
5  0.571429    (Eggs, Bread)
6  0.571429    (Milk, Bread)
7  0.428571     (Eggs, Milk)
```

9.1.1.4 Analyze and Interpret the Results

The output will be a DataFrame containing frequent itemsets, their corresponding support values, and the length of each itemset. The support value represents the percentage of transactions in which the itemset appears.

You can analyze and interpret the results to identify the most frequent itemsets and their support. These frequent itemsets represent the combinations of items that appear frequently in the transactions and can provide valuable insights into item co-occurrences.

In this tutorial, we demonstrated how to recognize frequent itemsets based on a minimum support threshold using the Apriori algorithm in Python. You can adjust the min_support threshold to obtain more or fewer frequent itemsets based on your specific use case.

Frequent itemset mining is a powerful technique for identifying interesting associations between items in transactional data and can be applied to various domains, such as market basket analysis, customer behavior analysis, and recommendation systems.

9.1.2 Tutorial – Detecting Association Rules

In this tutorial, we'll create a dummy dataset, use the Apriori algorithm to find frequent itemsets, and display the support, confidence, lift, and other association rule metrics.

9.1.2.1 Setup

Install required packages: Make sure you have the mlxtend library installed, as it provides an efficient implementation of the Apriori algorithm.

```
!pip install mlxtend
```

9.1.2.2 Create and Preprocess the Dummy Dataset

For this tutorial, we'll create a simple dummy dataset representing transactions (e.g., purchases in a store). Each transaction is represented as a list of items.

```python
import pandas as pd
from mlxtend.preprocessing import TransactionEncoder

# Sample dataset (list of transactions)
dataset = [
    ['Milk', 'Bread', 'Eggs'],
    ['Bread', 'Eggs', 'Butter'],
    ['Milk', 'Eggs'],
    ['Milk', 'Bread', 'Eggs', 'Butter'],
    ['Milk', 'Bread'],
    ['Bread', 'Eggs'],
    ['Milk', 'Bread', 'Butter'],
]

# Convert the dataset into a one-hot encoded format
te = TransactionEncoder()
te_ary = te.fit(dataset).transform(dataset)
df = pd.DataFrame(te_ary, columns=te.columns_)
print(df)
```

	Bread	Butter	Eggs	Milk
0	True	False	True	True
1	True	True	True	False
2	False	False	True	True
3	True	True	True	True
4	True	False	False	True
5	True	False	True	False
6	True	True	False	True

9.1.2.3 Perform Frequent Itemset Mining using Apriori

Now, we'll use the Apriori algorithm to mine frequent itemsets from the one-hot encoded dataset.

```python
from mlxtend.frequent_patterns import apriori, association_rules

# Define the minimum support threshold
min_support = 0.4
```

```
# Perform frequent itemset mining using Apriori
frequent_itemsets = apriori(df, min_support=min_support, use_colnames=True)

print("Frequent Itemsets:")
print(frequent_itemsets)
```

```
Frequent Itemsets:
     support            itemsets
0   0.857143             (Bread)
1   0.428571            (Butter)
2   0.714286              (Eggs)
3   0.714286              (Milk)
4   0.428571     (Butter, Bread)
5   0.571429       (Eggs, Bread)
6   0.571429       (Milk, Bread)
7   0.428571        (Eggs, Milk)
```

9.1.2.4 Generate Association Rules

Next, we'll use the frequent itemsets to generate association rules and calculate various association metrics such as confidence and lift.

```
# Generate association rules with minimum confidence threshold (e.g., 0.6)
min_confidence = 0.6
association_rules_df = association_rules(frequent_itemsets
    , metric="confidence", min_threshold=min_confidence)

print("\nAssociation Rules:")
print(association_rules_df[['antecedents', 'consequents',
    'support', 'confidence','lift']])
```

```
Association Rules:
    antecedents consequents    support  confidence       lift
0      (Butter)     (Bread)   0.428571    1.000000   1.166667
1        (Eggs)     (Bread)   0.571429    0.800000   0.933333
2       (Bread)      (Eggs)   0.571429    0.666667   0.933333
3        (Milk)     (Bread)   0.571429    0.800000   0.933333
4       (Bread)      (Milk)   0.571429    0.666667   0.933333
5        (Eggs)      (Milk)   0.428571    0.600000   0.840000
6        (Milk)      (Eggs)   0.428571    0.600000   0.840000
```

9.1.2.5 Interpret the Results

The output will be DataFrames containing frequent itemsets and association rules along with the corresponding support, confidence, lift, and other metrics.

You can interpret the results to identify significant associations between items in transactions. The association rules represent interesting patterns of item co-occurrences with high confidence, indicating that if the antecedent of the rule is present in a transaction, the consequent is likely to be present as well.

In this tutorial, we demonstrated how to perform association rule mining using the Apriori algorithm in Python. The Apriori algorithm is a powerful technique for finding frequent itemsets and generating association rules, and it is widely used for market basket analysis and recommendation systems.

Feel free to experiment with different dataset examples and adjust the support and confidence thresholds to discover more or less frequent itemsets and association rules based on your specific use case.

9.2 APRIORI AND FP-GROWTH ALGORITHMS

Apriori and FP-Growth are classic algorithms used in frequent itemset mining and association rule analysis. This section introduces these two influential algorithms using the mlxtend package.

Apriori and FP-Growth are prominent algorithms for discovering frequent itemsets and generating association rules from transactional data. They play a crucial role in understanding customer behavior, product recommendations, and market basket analysis. The mlxtend package provides user-friendly tools to implement Apriori and FP-Growth efficiently. You will explore practical implementation steps, including using the apriori and fpgrowth functions in mlxtend to discover frequent itemsets based on specified support thresholds, extracting association rules from frequent itemsets using the association_rules function, and comparing the efficiency and performance of Apriori and FP-Growth.

9.2.1 Tutorial – Apriori Algorithm

Let's play with a tutorial for association rule mining using the Apriori algorithm with a dummy dataset representing transactions in a grocery store.

9.2.1.1 Setup

Make sure you have the mlxtend library installed, as it provides an efficient implementation of the Apriori algorithm.

You can install the mlxtend library using pip:

```
!pip install mlxtend
```

9.2.1.2 Create a Dummy Dataset

For this tutorial, we'll create a dummy dataset representing 1,000 transactions in a grocery store. Each transaction will contain a random selection of items from a list of ten unique items.

```
import pandas as pd
import numpy as np
from mlxtend.preprocessing import TransactionEncoder
```

```
# Set a random seed for reproducibility
np.random.seed(42)

# Number of records (transactions) in the dataset
num_records = 1000

# Number of unique items in the grocery store
num_items = 10

# Generate the dummy dataset
transactions = []
for _ in range(num_records):
    num_items_in_transaction = np.random.randint(1, num_items + 1)
    items = np.random.choice(range(1, num_items + 1)
        , num_items_in_transaction, replace=False)
    transactions.append([f"Item{item}" for item in items])

# Convert the dataset into a one-hot encoded format
te = TransactionEncoder()
te_ary = te.fit(transactions).transform(transactions)
df_encoded = pd.DataFrame(te_ary, columns=te.columns_)
print(df_encoded)
```

	Item1	Item10	Item2	Item3	Item4	Item5	Item6	Item7	Item8	Item9
0	True	True	True	True	False	False	True	True	False	True
1	True	True	True	True	False	False	True	True	True	True
2	False	False	False	True	False	False	False	True	False	False
3	True	True	True	True	True	True	True	True	True	True
4	True	True	True	True	True	True	True	False	True	True
..	...	...	...	...	...	...	...	...	...	...
995	True	False	True	True	False	False	False	False	False	True
996	False	False	False	False	False	False	False	True	False	False
997	True	False	False	True	True	True	False	True	False	True
998	False	True	False	True	False	False	False	True	False	False
999	False	False	False	False	True	False	False	True	True	True

[1000 rows x 10 columns]

9.2.1.3 Perform Frequent Itemset Mining using Apriori

Now, we'll use the Apriori algorithm to mine frequent itemsets from the one-hot encoded "Online Retail" dataset.

```
from mlxtend.frequent_patterns import apriori

# Define the minimum support threshold
min_support = 0.35

# Perform frequent itemset mining using Apriori
frequent_itemsets = apriori(df_encoded, min_support=min_support
```

```
        , use_colnames=True)

print("Frequent Itemsets:")
print(frequent_itemsets)
```

```
Frequent Itemsets:
      support              itemsets
0      0.530              (Item1)
1      0.546             (Item10)
2      0.543              (Item2)
3      0.545              (Item3)
4      0.527              (Item4)
5      0.540              (Item5)
6      0.533              (Item6)
7      0.532              (Item7)
8      0.533              (Item8)
9      0.545              (Item9)
10     0.358      (Item1, Item5)
11     0.358     (Item2, Item10)
12     0.359     (Item3, Item10)
13     0.351     (Item4, Item10)
14     0.353     (Item5, Item10)
15     0.364     (Item9, Item10)
16     0.351      (Item2, Item4)
17     0.357      (Item2, Item6)
18     0.352      (Item8, Item2)
19     0.362      (Item2, Item9)
20     0.354      (Item3, Item4)
21     0.362      (Item3, Item5)
22     0.357      (Item3, Item6)
23     0.360      (Item3, Item7)
24     0.362      (Item3, Item8)
25     0.356      (Item3, Item9)
26     0.358      (Item4, Item5)
27     0.350      (Item8, Item4)
28     0.352      (Item4, Item9)
29     0.352      (Item5, Item6)
30     0.352      (Item8, Item5)
31     0.356      (Item5, Item9)
32     0.354      (Item8, Item6)
33     0.355      (Item8, Item9)
```

9.2.1.4 Generate Association Rules

Next, we'll use the frequent itemsets to generate association rules and calculate various association metrics such as confidence, lift, and support.

```
from mlxtend.frequent_patterns import association_rules

# Generate association rules with minimum confidence threshold (e.g., 0.5)
min_confidence = 0.67
association_rules_df = association_rules(frequent_itemsets
    , metric="confidence", min_threshold=min_confidence)
```

```
print("\nAssociation Rules:")
print(association_rules_df)
```

```
Association Rules:
     antecedents consequents  antecedent support  consequent support  support  \
0      (Item1)     (Item5)              0.530               0.540        0.358
1      (Item4)     (Item3)              0.527               0.545        0.354
2      (Item5)     (Item3)              0.540               0.545        0.362
3      (Item7)     (Item3)              0.532               0.545        0.360
4      (Item8)     (Item3)              0.533               0.545        0.362
5      (Item4)     (Item5)              0.527               0.540        0.358

   confidence      lift  leverage  conviction  zhangs_metric
0    0.675472  1.250874  0.071800    1.417442       0.426721
1    0.671727  1.232526  0.066785    1.386040       0.398855
2    0.670370  1.230037  0.067700    1.380337       0.406558
3    0.676692  1.241636  0.070060    1.407326       0.415836
4    0.679174  1.246192  0.071515    1.418216       0.423031
5    0.679317  1.257994  0.073420    1.434438       0.433581
```

9.2.2 Tutorial – FP-Growth Algorithm

Let's go through the step-by-step tutorial for association rule mining using the FP-Growth algorithm with a dummy dataset. We'll generate the dataset, apply FP-Growth to find frequent itemsets, and mine association rules.

9.2.2.1 Setup

Import necessary libraries.

```
!pip install mlxtend
```

```
import pandas as pd
from mlxtend.preprocessing import TransactionEncoder
from mlxtend.frequent_patterns import fpgrowth, association_rules
```

9.2.2.2 Prepare the Dataset

Generate the dummy dataset and convert the dataset into a one-hot encoded format.

```
# Sample dataset (list of transactions)
dataset = [
    ['Milk', 'Bread', 'Eggs'],
    ['Bread', 'Eggs', 'Butter'],
    ['Milk', 'Eggs'],
    ['Milk', 'Bread', 'Eggs', 'Butter'],
    ['Milk', 'Bread'],
    ['Bread', 'Eggs'],
    ['Milk', 'Bread', 'Butter'],
]
```

```
# Convert the dataset into a one-hot encoded format
te = TransactionEncoder()
te_ary = te.fit(dataset).transform(dataset)
df = pd.DataFrame(te_ary, columns=te.columns_)
print(df)
```

	Bread	Butter	Eggs	Milk
0	True	False	True	True
1	True	True	True	False
2	False	False	True	True
3	True	True	True	True
4	True	False	False	True
5	True	False	True	False
6	True	True	False	True

9.2.2.3 Apply FP-Growth to Find Frequent Itemsets

```
# Apply FP-growth to find frequent itemsets
frequent_itemsets = fpgrowth(df, min_support=0.4, use_colnames=True)

print(frequent_itemsets)
```

	support	itemsets
0	0.857143	(Bread)
1	0.714286	(Milk)
2	0.714286	(Eggs)
3	0.428571	(Butter)
4	0.571429	(Milk, Bread)
5	0.571429	(Eggs, Bread)
6	0.428571	(Eggs, Milk)
7	0.428571	(Butter, Bread)

9.2.2.4 Mine Association Rules from Frequent Itemsets

```
# Generate association rules with minimum confidence threshold (e.g., 0.6)
min_confidence = 0.6
association_rules_df = association_rules(frequent_itemsets
    , metric="confidence", min_threshold=min_confidence)

print("\nAssociation Rules:")
print(association_rules_df[['antecedents', 'consequents',
    'support', 'confidence','lift']])
```

Association Rules:

	antecedents	consequents	support	confidence	lift
0	(Milk)	(Bread)	0.571429	0.800000	0.933333
1	(Bread)	(Milk)	0.571429	0.666667	0.933333
2	(Eggs)	(Bread)	0.571429	0.800000	0.933333
3	(Bread)	(Eggs)	0.571429	0.666667	0.933333
4	(Eggs)	(Milk)	0.428571	0.600000	0.840000
5	(Milk)	(Eggs)	0.428571	0.600000	0.840000

```
6    (Butter)    (Bread)   0.428571    1.000000  1.166667
```

9.2.3 Case Study – Online Retail

Let's play with a Market Basket Analysis Data for Apriori algorithm and association rule mining.

9.2.3.1 Setup

Make sure you have the mlxtend library installed, as it provides an efficient implementation of the Apriori algorithm.

You can install the mlxtend library using pip:

```
!pip install mlxtend
```

9.2.3.2 Load the Dataset

For this tutorial, we'll use a dataset "Market Basket Analysis Data". You should upload the .csvfile to your Google Colab. Also, don't forget to set index_col = 0 when you use pd.read_csv().

```python
import pandas as pd
from mlxtend.preprocessing import TransactionEncoder

# Upoad the dataset
df = pd.read_csv('/content/basket_analysis.csv', index_col=0)
print(df.info())
df[:10]
```

```
<class 'pandas.core.frame.DataFrame'>
Int64Index: 999 entries, 0 to 998
Data columns (total 16 columns):
 #   Column        Non-Null Count  Dtype
---  ------        --------------  -----
 0   Apple         999 non-null    bool
 1   Bread         999 non-null    bool
 2   Butter        999 non-null    bool
 3   Cheese        999 non-null    bool
 4   Corn          999 non-null    bool
 5   Dill          999 non-null    bool
 6   Eggs          999 non-null    bool
 7   Ice cream     999 non-null    bool
 8   Kidney Beans  999 non-null    bool
 9   Milk          999 non-null    bool
 10  Nutmeg        999 non-null    bool
 11  Onion         999 non-null    bool
 12  Sugar         999 non-null    bool
 13  Unicorn       999 non-null    bool
 14  Yogurt        999 non-null    bool
 15  chocolate     999 non-null    bool
dtypes: bool(16)
```

```
memory usage: 23.4 KB
None
```

	Apple	Bread	Butter	Cheese	Corn	Dill	Eggs	Ice cream	Kidney Beans	\
0	False	True	False	False	True	True	False	True	False	
1	False	False	False	False	False	False	False	False	False	
2	True	False	True	False	False	True	False	True	False	
3	False	False	True	True	False	True	False	False	False	
4	True	True	False	False	False	False	False	False	False	
5	True	True	True	True	False	True	False	True	False	
6	False	False	True	False	False	False	True	True	True	
7	True	False	False	True	False	False	True	False	False	
8	True	False	False	False	True	True	True	True	False	
9	True	False	False	False	False	True	True	True	False	

	Milk	Nutmeg	Onion	Sugar	Unicorn	Yogurt	chocolate
0	False	False	False	True	False	True	True
1	True	False	False	False	False	False	False
2	True	False	False	False	False	True	True
3	True	True	True	False	False	False	False
4	False	False	False	False	False	False	False
5	False	True	False	False	True	True	True
6	True	True	True	False	False	True	False
7	False	True	False	True	False	True	False
8	True	True	True	True	True	True	True
9	True	False	True	True	True	False	True

9.2.3.3 Perform Frequent Itemset Mining using Apriori

Now, we'll use the Apriori algorithm to mine frequent itemsets from the one-hot encoded "Online Retail" dataset.

```python
from mlxtend.frequent_patterns import apriori

# Define the minimum support threshold
min_support = 0.2

# Perform frequent itemset mining using Apriori
frequent_itemsets = apriori(df, min_support=min_support, use_colnames=True)

print("Frequent Itemsets:")
print(frequent_itemsets)
```

```
Frequent Itemsets:
    support        itemsets
0  0.383383        (Apple)
1  0.384384        (Bread)
2  0.420420       (Butter)
3  0.404404       (Cheese)
4  0.407407         (Corn)
5  0.398398         (Dill)
6  0.384384         (Eggs)
```

```
7    0.410410                  (Ice cream)
8    0.408408                (Kidney Beans)
9    0.405405                       (Milk)
10   0.401401                     (Nutmeg)
11   0.403403                      (Onion)
12   0.409409                      (Sugar)
13   0.389389                    (Unicorn)
14   0.420420                     (Yogurt)
15   0.421421                  (chocolate)
16   0.207207       (Butter, Ice cream)
17   0.202202     (Butter, Kidney Beans)
18   0.202202       (Butter, chocolate)
19   0.200200     (Cheese, Kidney Beans)
20   0.202202    (chocolate, Ice cream)
21   0.211211         (Milk, chocolate)
```

9.2.3.4 Generate Association Rules

Next, we'll use the frequent itemsets to generate association rules and calculate various association metrics such as confidence, lift, and support.

```python
from mlxtend.frequent_patterns import association_rules

# Generate association rules with minimum confidence threshold (e.g., 0.5)
min_confidence = 0.5
association_rules_df = association_rules(frequent_itemsets
    , metric="confidence", min_threshold=min_confidence)

print("\nAssociation Rules:")
print(association_rules_df)
```

```
Association Rules:
     antecedents   consequents   antecedent support   consequent support   support  \
0   (Ice cream)      (Butter)             0.410410             0.420420  0.207207
1        (Milk)   (chocolate)             0.405405             0.421421  0.211211
2   (chocolate)        (Milk)             0.421421             0.405405  0.211211

    confidence       lift  leverage   conviction   zhangs_metric
0     0.504878   1.200889  0.034662     1.170579        0.283728
1     0.520988   1.236263  0.040365     1.207857        0.321413
2     0.501188   1.236263  0.040365     1.192021        0.330310
```

9.2.3.5 Interpret the Results

The output will be DataFrames containing frequent itemsets and association rules along with the corresponding support, confidence, lift, and other metrics.

You can interpret the results to identify significant associations between items in transactions. The association rules represent interesting patterns of item co-occurrences with high confidence, indicating that if the antecedent of the rule is present in a transaction, the consequent is likely to be present as well.

In this case study, we demonstrated how to perform association rule mining using the Apriori algorithm with the "Groceries" dataset. The Apriori algorithm is a powerful technique for finding frequent itemsets and generating association rules, and it is widely used for market basket analysis and recommendation systems.

Feel free to experiment with different datasets and adjust the support and confidence thresholds to discover more or less frequent itemsets and association rules based on your specific use case.

## CHAPTER 10

Outlier Detection

O UTLIER DETECTION, also known as anomaly detection, is a technique used to identify observations in a dataset that deviate significantly from the majority of the data. These observations are often referred to as "outliers" or "anomalies". Outlier detection is useful in a variety of fields such as finance, healthcare, and cybersecurity, for identifying unusual patterns, fraud, or errors in data.

There are many different outlier detection methods we use with Scikit-learn, but some of the most common include:

- Isolation Forest: A method that isolates observations by randomly selecting a feature and then randomly selecting a split value between the maximum and minimum values of the selected feature.

- Local Outlier Factor (LOF): A method that calculates the local density of a data point and compares it with the densities of its neighbors. Data points with a low local density are considered outliers.

- One-Class SVM: A method that learns a boundary that separates the majority of the data from the outlier data.

- DBSCAN: A density-based clustering algorithm that can be used for outlier detection. DBSCAN groups together data points that are close to each other based on a density threshold, called Eps, and a minimum number of points, called MinPts. Data points that are not part of any dense group are considered outliers.

- IQR: A statistical measure that can be used to detect outliers in a dataset. It is defined as the difference between the third quartile (Q3) and the first quartile (Q1) of a dataset. The IQR is a measure of the spread of the middle 50% of the data, and it is robust to outliers.

DOI: 10.1201/9781003462781-10

10.1 OUTLIER DETECTION

Outlier detection is a critical task in data analysis, aiming to identify data points that deviate significantly from the norm. This section introduces various outlier detection methods using the Scikit-learn package.

Outliers are data points that exhibit unusual behavior compared to the majority of data in a dataset. Detecting outliers is essential in various domains, including fraud detection, quality control, and anomaly detection. Scikit-learn offers a wide range of tools to implement outlier detection methods efficiently. You will explore practical implementation steps, including using Scikit-learn's modules to apply various outlier detection techniques, such as Z-score, IQR, One-Class SVM, Isolation Forest, DBSCAN, and LOF, customizing parameters and thresholds for each method to adapt to specific datasets, and visualizing outlier detection results to understand data anomalies.

10.1.1 Tutorial

10.1.1.1 Dataset Creation

In this code, we generate 500 normal data points following a normal distribution with mean [5, 10] and standard deviation [1, 2]. Then, we introduce 50 outliers by adding noise to the data with mean [20, 30] and standard deviation [5, 8]. The dataset is then combined, and a binary target variable (Outlier) is assigned to indicate whether a data point is an outlier (1) or not (0).

The scatter plot visualizes the dataset, where outliers are shown in a different color.

```python
import numpy as np
import pandas as pd
import matplotlib.pyplot as plt

# Set a random seed for reproducibility
np.random.seed(42)

# Number of data points (normal data points and outliers)
num_data_points = 500

# Mean and standard deviation for the normal distribution
mean_normal = [5, 10]
std_normal = [1, 2]

# Generate normal data points
normal_data_points = np.random.normal(loc=mean_normal
    , scale=std_normal, size=(num_data_points, 2))

# Introduce outliers by adding noise to the data
outliers = np.random.normal(loc=[20, 30], scale=[5, 8], size=(50, 2))

# Combine normal data points and outliers
data = np.vstack([normal_data_points, outliers])
```

```
target = np.hstack([np.zeros(num_data_points), np.ones(50)])

# Create a DataFrame for the dataset
df = pd.DataFrame(data, columns=['Feature1', 'Feature2'])
df['Outlier'] = target.astype(int)

# Visualize the dataset
plt.scatter(df['Feature1'], df['Feature2']
    , c=df['Outlier'], cmap='viridis')
plt.xlabel('Feature 1')
plt.ylabel('Feature 2')
plt.title('Dummy Dataset for Outlier Detection')
plt.colorbar(label='Outlier (1: Yes, 0: No)')
plt.show()
```

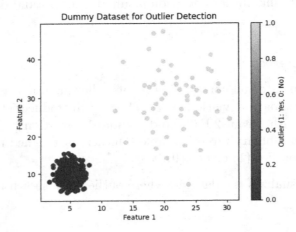

Figure 10.1 A Scatter Plot of Feature1 VS Feature2 with Colorbar

10.1.1.2 Z-score

In this code, we calculate the Z-scores for each data point with respect to both Feature1 and Feature2. We set a threshold value (in this case, 3) to determine outliers. Data points with a Z-score greater than the threshold in either feature are considered outliers.

The scatter plot visualizes the dataset, where normal data points are shown in blue, and the outliers detected by the Z-score method are shown in red.

```
from scipy import stats

# Apply Z-score method for outlier detection
z_scores = np.abs(stats.zscore(df[['Feature1', 'Feature2']]))
threshold = 3  # Adjust the threshold based on your preference

# Identify outliers based on the threshold
outliers_zscore = df[(z_scores['Feature1'] > threshold) |
    (z_scores['Feature2'] > threshold)]
```

```
# Visualize the dataset with outliers detected by Z-score method
plt.scatter(df['Feature1'], df['Feature2']
    , c='blue', label='Normal Data Points')
plt.scatter(outliers_zscore['Feature1']
    , outliers_zscore['Feature2'], c='red', label='Outliers (Z-score)')
plt.xlabel('Feature 1')
plt.ylabel('Feature 2')
plt.title('Outlier Detection using Z-score')
plt.legend()
plt.show()
```

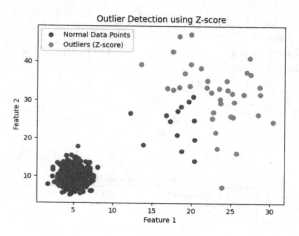

Figure 10.2   Outlier Detection by Z-Score

10.1.1.3   IQR

Let's use the same dummy dataset and apply the Interquartile Range (IQR) method for outlier detection. The IQR method is based on the range between the first quartile (Q1) and the third quartile (Q3) of the data. Data points outside a specified range (usually defined as Q1 - 1.5 * IQR and Q3 + 1.5 * IQR) are considered outliers.

In this code, we calculate the first quartile (Q1), third quartile (Q3), and IQR for each feature (Feature1 and Feature2). We then define the outlier range as Q1 - 1.5 * IQR and Q3 + 1.5 * IQR for each feature. Data points falling outside this range in either feature are considered outliers.

The scatter plot visualizes the dataset, where normal data points are shown in blue, and the outliers detected by the IQR method are shown in red.

```
# Calculate Q1, Q3, and IQR for each feature
Q1 = df[['Feature1', 'Feature2']].quantile(0.25)
Q3 = df[['Feature1', 'Feature2']].quantile(0.75)
IQR = Q3 - Q1

# Define the outlier range based on IQR
```

```
outlier_range_lower = Q1 - 1.5 * IQR
outlier_range_upper = Q3 + 1.5 * IQR

# Identify outliers based on the IQR range
outliers_iqr = df[
    (df['Feature1'] < outlier_range_lower['Feature1']) |
    (df['Feature1'] > outlier_range_upper['Feature1']) |
    (df['Feature2'] < outlier_range_lower['Feature2']) |
    (df['Feature2'] > outlier_range_upper['Feature2'])
]

# Visualize the dataset with outliers detected by IQR method
plt.scatter(df['Feature1'], df['Feature2']
    , c='blue', label='Normal Data Points')
plt.scatter(outliers_iqr['Feature1'], outliers_iqr['Feature2']
    , c='red', label='Outliers (IQR)')
plt.xlabel('Feature 1')
plt.ylabel('Feature 2')
plt.title('Outlier Detection using IQR')
plt.legend()
plt.show()
```

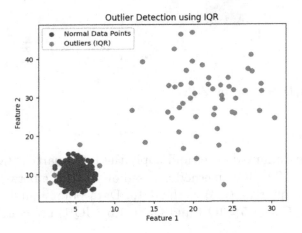

Figure 10.3 Outlier Detection by IQR

10.1.1.4 One-Class SVM

Let's continue with the same dummy dataset and apply the One-Class SVM method for outlier detection. One-Class SVM is a machine learning algorithm that is useful for novelty detection, where the goal is to identify data points that deviate significantly from the majority of the data.

In this code, we fit the One-Class SVM model to the combined feature array X, which contains both Feature1 and Feature2. The nu hyperparameter controls the fraction of data points considered as outliers by the model. You can adjust the nu value based on your preference and the nature of your data.

The ocsvm.predict(X) method returns an array of predictions, where -1 indicates an outlier and 1 indicates an inlier. We convert the predictions to Boolean values, where True represents an outlier and False represents an inlier.

The scatter plot visualizes the dataset, where normal data points are shown in blue, and the outliers detected by the One-Class SVM method are shown in red.

```
from sklearn.svm import OneClassSVM

# Combine the features into a single array
X = df[['Feature1', 'Feature2']].values

# Fit the One-Class SVM model
ocsvm = OneClassSVM(nu=0.15)
ocsvm.fit(X)

# Predict outliers using the One-Class SVM model
outliers_ocsvm = ocsvm.predict(X)
outliers_ocsvm = outliers_ocsvm == -1

# Visualize the dataset with outliers detected by One-Class SVM method
plt.scatter(X[:, 0], X[:, 1], c='blue', label='Normal Data Points')
plt.scatter(X[outliers_ocsvm, 0], X[outliers_ocsvm, 1]
    , c='red', label='Outliers (One-Class SVM)')
plt.xlabel('Feature 1')
plt.ylabel('Feature 2')
plt.title('Outlier Detection using One-Class SVM')
plt.legend()
plt.show()
```

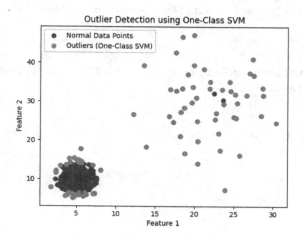

Figure 10.4 Outlier Detection by One-Class SVM

10.1.1.5 Isolation Forest

Let's continue with the same dummy dataset and apply the Isolation Forest method for outlier detection. The Isolation Forest algorithm is another popular unsupervised outlier detection technique based on the concept of isolating anomalies (outliers) in the data.

In this code, we fit the Isolation Forest model to the combined feature array X, which contains both Feature1 and Feature2. The contamination parameter controls the expected proportion of outliers in the data. You can adjust the contamination value based on your preference and the nature of your data.

The isolation_forest.predict(X) method returns an array of predictions, where -1 indicates an outlier and 1 indicates an inlier. We convert the predictions to Boolean values, where True represents an outlier and False represents an inlier.

The scatter plot visualizes the dataset, where normal data points are shown in blue, and the outliers detected by the Isolation Forest method are shown in red.

```python
from sklearn.ensemble import IsolationForest

# Combine the features into a single array
X = df[['Feature1', 'Feature2']].values

# Fit the Isolation Forest model
isolation_forest = IsolationForest(contamination=0.09)
isolation_forest.fit(X)

# Predict outliers using the Isolation Forest model
outliers_isolation_forest = isolation_forest.predict(X)
outliers_isolation_forest = outliers_isolation_forest == -1

# Visualize the dataset with outliers detected by Isolation Forest method
plt.scatter(X[:, 0], X[:, 1], c='blue', label='Normal Data Points')
plt.scatter(X[outliers_isolation_forest,0], X[outliers_isolation_forest,1]
    , c='red', label='Outliers (Isolation Forest)')
plt.xlabel('Feature 1')
plt.ylabel('Feature 2')
plt.title('Outlier Detection using Isolation Forest')
plt.legend()
plt.show()
```

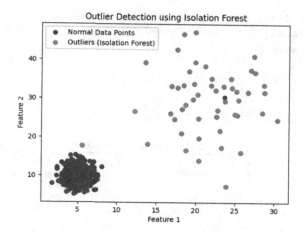

Figure 10.5 Outlier Detection by Isolation Forest

10.1.1.6 DBSCAN

Let's continue with the same dummy dataset and apply the Density-Based Spatial Clustering of Applications with Noise (DBSCAN) algorithm for outlier detection. DBSCAN is a density-based clustering algorithm that can be used for outlier detection by identifying points that are not part of any dense cluster.

In this code, we fit the DBSCAN model to the combined feature array X, which contains both Feature1 and Feature2. The eps parameter defines the maximum distance between two samples for them to be considered as part of the same cluster. The min_samples parameter specifies the minimum number of samples in a neighborhood for a point to be considered as a core point.

The dbscan.labels_ attribute contains the cluster labels assigned by DBSCAN. Points that are not part of any cluster are assigned the label -1, which indicates outliers.

The scatter plot visualizes the dataset, where normal data points are shown in blue, and the outliers detected by the DBSCAN algorithm are shown in red.

```python
from sklearn.cluster import DBSCAN

# Combine the features into a single array
X = df[['Feature1', 'Feature2']].values

# Fit the DBSCAN model
dbscan = DBSCAN(eps=2.5, min_samples=10)
dbscan.fit(X)

# Identify outliers based on the DBSCAN clustering results
outliers_dbscan = dbscan.labels_ == -1  # DBSCAN assigns -1 to outliers

# Visualize the dataset with outliers detected by DBSCAN
plt.scatter(X[:, 0], X[:, 1], c='blue', label='Normal Data Points')
```

```
plt.scatter(X[outliers_dbscan, 0], X[outliers_dbscan, 1]
    , c='red', label='Outliers (DBSCAN)')
plt.xlabel('Feature 1')
plt.ylabel('Feature 2')
plt.title('Outlier Detection using DBSCAN')
plt.legend()
plt.show()
```

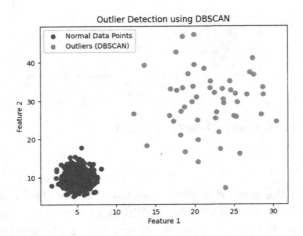

Figure 10.6 Outlier Detection by DBSCAN

10.1.1.7 LOF

Let's continue with the same dummy dataset and apply the Local Outlier Factor (LOF) method for outlier detection. LOF is a density-based outlier detection method that measures the local density deviation of a data point with respect to its neighbors. Outliers are identified as data points with significantly lower local density compared to their neighbors.

In this code, we fit the LOF model to the combined feature array X, which contains both Feature1 and Feature2. The n_neighbors parameter defines the number of neighbors considered for calculating the local density deviation of each data point. The contamination parameter controls the expected proportion of outliers in the data.

The lof.fit_predict(X) method returns an array of predictions, where -1 indicates an outlier and 1 indicates an inlier. We convert the predictions to Boolean values, where True represents an outlier and False represents an inlier.

The scatter plot visualizes the dataset, where normal data points are shown in blue, and the outliers detected by the LOF method are shown in red.

```
from sklearn.neighbors import LocalOutlierFactor

# Combine the features into a single array
X = df[['Feature1', 'Feature2']].values
```

```
# Fit the LOF model
lof = LocalOutlierFactor(n_neighbors=100, contamination=0.10)
outliers_lof = lof.fit_predict(X)

# Identify outliers based on the LOF scores
outliers_lof = outliers_lof == -1  # LOF assigns -1 to outliers

# Visualize the dataset with outliers detected by LOF
plt.scatter(X[:, 0], X[:, 1], c='blue', label='Normal Data Points')
plt.scatter(X[outliers_lof, 0], X[outliers_lof, 1]
    , c='red', label='Outliers (LOF)')
plt.xlabel('Feature 1')
plt.ylabel('Feature 2')
plt.title('Outlier Detection using Local Outlier Factor (LOF)')
plt.legend()
plt.show()
```

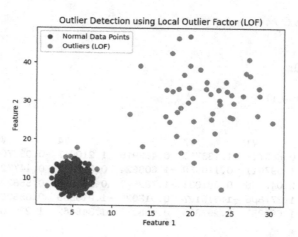

Figure 10.7 Outlier Detection by LOF

10.1.2 Case Study

Let's proceed with the tutorial for outlier detection using the "Credit Card Fraud Detection" dataset. We'll cover the following steps:

1. Load the dataset.
2. Apply Z-score method for outlier detection.
3. Apply IQR method for outlier detection.
4. Apply One-Class SVM method for outlier detection.
5. Apply Isolation Forest method for outlier detection.
6. Apply DBSCAN method for outlier detection.
7. Apply LOF method for outlier detection.
8. Let's start with Step 1: Load the dataset.

10.1.2.1 Load the Dataset

In this code, we load the dataset into a Pandas DataFrame named df using the pd.read_csv() function. We then print the first few rows of the dataset using df.head(), display the data types and non-null counts of each column using df.info(), and provide basic statistical summaries using df.describe().

```python
import pandas as pd
import numpy as np
import matplotlib.pyplot as plt
from sklearn.preprocessing import StandardScaler
from sklearn.decomposition import PCA
from sklearn.svm import OneClassSVM
from sklearn.ensemble import IsolationForest
from sklearn.neighbors import LocalOutlierFactor
from sklearn.cluster import DBSCAN

# Step 1: Load the dataset
df = pd.read_csv('/content/creditcard.csv')
df= df.sample(10000)
# Explore the dataset
print(df.head())
print(df.info())
print(df.describe())
```

```
           Time       V1        V2        V3        V4        V5        V6   \
128634  78785.0 -0.659717  1.183753  0.483915  1.210817 -0.035700  0.188756
224924 144024.0  1.997011  0.110559 -1.608624  0.337948  0.447722 -0.561137
266887 162525.0  2.047366  0.081031 -1.782673  0.251559  0.558326 -0.433816
72073   54554.0  1.377808 -1.975197  0.013025 -1.915389  0.035267  4.520147
145549  87041.0 -1.690957  2.297320  0.088259 -1.348462  1.239065 -1.195810

             V7        V8        V9  ...       V21       V22       V23   \
128634  0.587158  0.505609 -0.997043  ...  0.248231  0.827323  0.105537
224924  0.109484 -0.100417  0.157042  ... -0.286172 -0.745629  0.344806
266887  0.059302 -0.059358  0.291644  ... -0.330798 -0.896494  0.302621
72073  -2.459011  1.203601 -0.376902  ... -0.340203 -0.349072 -0.073197
145549  2.715813 -2.112286  3.660540  ... -0.446350  1.275375 -0.325042

             V24       V25       V26       V27       V28  Amount  Class
128634  0.051588 -0.439095 -0.252372  0.335354  0.191205   74.00      0
224924  0.621968 -0.315746  0.146097 -0.061768 -0.037233    8.99      0
266887  0.248781 -0.267571  0.169080 -0.068661 -0.043473    1.98      0
72073   1.032692  0.533805 -0.069993  0.106404  0.032108   52.95      0
145549  0.023081 -0.428979 -0.423186  0.290195 -0.963410    1.38      0

[5 rows x 31 columns]
<class 'pandas.core.frame.DataFrame'>
Int64Index: 10000 entries, 128634 to 133610
Data columns (total 31 columns):
 #   Column  Non-Null Count  Dtype
---  ------  --------------  -----
```

```
0    Time     10000 non-null  float64
1    V1       10000 non-null  float64
2    V2       10000 non-null  float64
3    V3       10000 non-null  float64
4    V4       10000 non-null  float64
5    V5       10000 non-null  float64
6    V6       10000 non-null  float64
7    V7       10000 non-null  float64
8    V8       10000 non-null  float64
9    V9       10000 non-null  float64
10   V10      10000 non-null  float64
11   V11      10000 non-null  float64
12   V12      10000 non-null  float64
13   V13      10000 non-null  float64
14   V14      10000 non-null  float64
15   V15      10000 non-null  float64
16   V16      10000 non-null  float64
17   V17      10000 non-null  float64
18   V18      10000 non-null  float64
19   V19      10000 non-null  float64
20   V20      10000 non-null  float64
21   V21      10000 non-null  float64
22   V22      10000 non-null  float64
23   V23      10000 non-null  float64
24   V24      10000 non-null  float64
25   V25      10000 non-null  float64
26   V26      10000 non-null  float64
27   V27      10000 non-null  float64
28   V28      10000 non-null  float64
29   Amount   10000 non-null  float64
30   Class    10000 non-null  int64
dtypes: float64(30), int64(1)
memory usage: 2.4 MB
None
               Time             V1             V2             V3             V4  \
count  10000.000000   10000.000000   10000.000000   10000.000000   10000.000000
mean   94887.874900       0.002672      -0.020461       0.006153      -0.007649
std    47357.353834       1.927744       1.588162       1.511947       1.409433
min        9.000000     -34.148234     -25.041752     -33.680984      -4.678263
25%    54267.250000      -0.940641      -0.617593      -0.879722      -0.869958
50%    85197.500000       0.019107       0.038539       0.174602      -0.019430
75%   139291.000000       1.332319       0.774920       1.042169       0.768741
max   172764.000000       2.412720      18.902453       3.877099       9.074932

                 V5             V6             V7             V8             V9  \
count  10000.000000   10000.000000   10000.000000   10000.000000   10000.000000
mean       0.000447      -0.006421       0.002671       0.008939       0.010266
std        1.368033       1.322849       1.208984       1.112960       1.103543
min      -23.669726     -13.591286     -24.419483     -37.353443      -4.679402
25%       -0.694127      -0.762416      -0.549120      -0.208433      -0.643822
50%       -0.062717      -0.259929       0.043512       0.016011      -0.039315
75%        0.604511       0.399681       0.558851       0.321598       0.621245
max       19.180525      15.568823      28.069822      16.635979       6.965981

       ...            V21            V22            V23            V24  \
```

```
count    ...    10000.000000    10000.000000    10000.000000    10000.000000
mean     ...        0.011401        0.005769        0.003773        0.001991
std      ...        0.685554        0.707334        0.553777        0.599677
min      ...       -9.332602       -8.887017      -16.136984       -2.659700
25%      ...       -0.223521       -0.525469       -0.162007       -0.353868
50%      ...       -0.025647        0.019093       -0.014429        0.041452
75%      ...        0.191557        0.521004        0.148461        0.440166
max      ...       27.202839        4.858497       17.768462        3.664552

                    V25             V26             V27             V28          Amount    \
count    10000.000000    10000.000000    10000.000000    10000.000000    10000.000000
mean         0.002423       -0.003846       -0.002565        0.004327       89.248071
std          0.516714        0.486862        0.418014        0.392181      235.961113
min         -3.919077       -1.732008       -9.895244       -8.310167        0.000000
25%         -0.318246       -0.333213       -0.068061       -0.053335        5.980000
50%          0.027028       -0.064101        0.002981        0.011874       23.000000
75%          0.356523        0.249469        0.093867        0.078157       79.917500
max          3.655826        2.733698        5.352193       15.866721     7766.600000

                 Class
count    10000.00000
mean         0.00160
std          0.03997
min          0.00000
25%          0.00000
50%          0.00000
75%          0.00000
max          1.00000

[8 rows x 31 columns]
```

```
df['Class'].value_counts()
```

```
0    9984
1      16
Name: Class, dtype: int64
```

10.1.2.2 Apply Z-score Method

```python
# Step 2: Apply Z-score method for outlier detection
z_scores = np.abs(StandardScaler().fit_transform(df.drop('Class', axis=1)))
threshold = 3

# Identify outliers based on the threshold
outliers_zscore = (z_scores > threshold).any(axis=1)

# Visualize the number of outliers detected by Z-score method
plt.bar(['Normal', 'Outlier']
    , [len(df) - outliers_zscore.sum(), outliers_zscore.sum()])
plt.xlabel(f'Data Points {len(df) -
    outliers_zscore.sum()}:{outliers_zscore.sum()}')
plt.ylabel('Count')
```

```
plt.title('Outliers Detected by Z-score Method')
plt.show()
df[outliers_zscore]['Class'].value_counts()
```

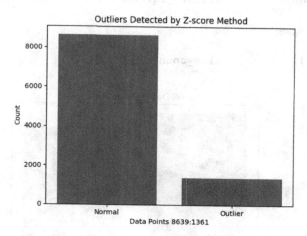

Figure 10.8   Outlier Detection by Z-Score

```
0      1348
1        13
Name: Class, dtype: int64
```

10.1.2.3   Apply IQR Method

In this code, we apply the IQR method to the features (excluding the "Class" column) to identify outliers. We calculate the first quartile (Q1), third quartile (Q3), and IQR for each feature. Data points falling outside the range (Q1 - 1.5 * IQR, Q3 + 1.5 * IQR) in at least one feature are considered outliers.

We then visualize the number of outliers detected by the IQR method using a bar chart.

```
# Step 3: Apply IQR method for outlier detection
Q1 = df.drop('Class', axis=1).quantile(0.25)
Q3 = df.drop('Class', axis=1).quantile(0.75)
IQR = Q3 - Q1

# Define the outlier range based on IQR
outlier_range_lower = Q1 - 1.5 * IQR
outlier_range_upper = Q3 + 1.5 * IQR

# Identify outliers based on the IQR range
outliers_iqr = ((df.drop('Class', axis=1) < outlier_range_lower) |
    (df.drop('Class', axis=1) > outlier_range_upper)).any(axis=1)

# Visualize the number of outliers detected by IQR method
```

```
plt.bar(['Normal', 'Outlier']
        , [len(df) - outliers_iqr.sum(), outliers_iqr.sum()])
plt.xlabel(f'Data Points {len(df) -
    outliers_iqr.sum()}:{outliers_iqr.sum()}')
plt.ylabel('Count')
plt.title('Outliers Detected by IQR Method')
plt.show()
df[outliers_iqr]['Class'].value_counts()
```

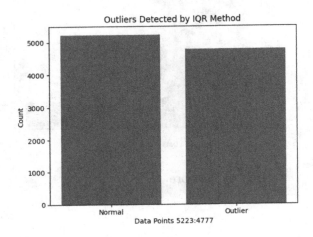

Figure 10.9 Outlier Detection by IQR

```
0    4761
1      16
Name: Class, dtype: int64
```

10.1.2.4 Apply One-Class SVM Method

In this code, we apply the One-Class SVM method for outlier detection. The nu parameter controls the fraction of data points considered as outliers by the model. You can adjust the nu value based on your preference.

We then visualize the number of outliers detected by the One-Class SVM method using a bar chart.

```
# Step 4: Apply One-Class SVM method for outlier detection
df_svm = df.dropna()
ocsvm = OneClassSVM(nu=0.1)
outliers_ocsvm = ocsvm.fit_predict(df_svm.drop('Class', axis=1))

# Identify outliers based on the One-Class SVM predictions
outliers_ocsvm = outliers_ocsvm == -1

# Visualize the number of outliers detected by One-Class SVM method
plt.bar(['Normal', 'Outlier']
```

```
    , [len(df_svm) - outliers_ocsvm.sum(), outliers_ocsvm.sum()])
plt.xlabel(f'Data Points {len(df_svm) -
    outliers_ocsvm.sum()}:{outliers_ocsvm.sum()}')
plt.ylabel('Count')
plt.title('Outliers Detected by One-Class SVM Method')
plt.show()
df[outliers_ocsvm]['Class'].value_counts()
```

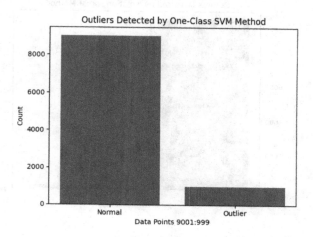

Figure 10.10 Outlier Detection by One-Class SVM

```
0       998
1         1
Name: Class, dtype: int64
```

10.1.2.5 Apply Isolation Forest Method

In this code, we apply the Isolation Forest method for outlier detection. The contamination parameter controls the expected proportion of outliers in the data. You can adjust the contamination value based on your preference.

We then visualize the number of outliers detected by the Isolation Forest method using a bar chart.

```
# Step 5: Apply Isolation Forest method for outlier detection
isolation_forest = IsolationForest(contamination=0.02)
outliers_isolation_forest =
    isolation_forest.fit_predict(df.drop('Class', axis=1))

# Identify outliers based on the Isolation Forest predictions
outliers_isolation_forest = outliers_isolation_forest == -1

# Visualize the number of outliers detected by Isolation Forest method
plt.bar(['Normal', 'Outlier'], [len(df) -
    outliers_isolation_forest.sum(), outliers_isolation_forest.sum()])
```

```
plt.xlabel(f'Data Points {len(df) -
    outliers_isolation_forest.sum()}:{outliers_isolation_forest.sum()}')
plt.ylabel('Count')
plt.title('Outliers Detected by Isolation Forest Method')
plt.show()
df[outliers_isolation_forest]['Class'].value_counts()
```

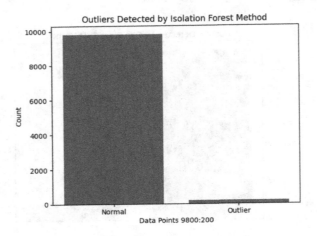

Figure 10.11 Outlier Detection by Isolation Forest

```
0    190
1     10
Name: Class, dtype: int64
```

10.1.2.6 Apply DBSCAN Method

In this code, we apply the DBSCAN method for outlier detection. The eps parameter defines the maximum distance between two samples for them to be considered as part of the same cluster. The min_samples parameter specifies the minimum number of samples in a neighborhood for a point to be considered as a core point.

We then visualize the number of outliers detected by the DBSCAN method using a bar chart.

```
# Step 6: Apply DBSCAN method for outlier detection
dbscan = DBSCAN(eps=100, min_samples=5)
outliers_dbscan = dbscan.fit_predict(df.drop('Class', axis=1))

# Identify outliers based on the DBSCAN clustering results
outliers_dbscan = outliers_dbscan == -1

# Visualize the number of outliers detected by DBSCAN method
plt.bar(['Normal', 'Outlier'], [len(df) -
    outliers_dbscan.sum(), outliers_dbscan.sum()])
plt.xlabel(f'Data Points {len(df) -
```

```
        outliers_dbscan.sum()}:{outliers_dbscan.sum()}')
plt.ylabel('Count')
plt.title('Outliers Detected by DBSCAN Method')
plt.show()
df[outliers_dbscan]['Class'].value_counts()
```

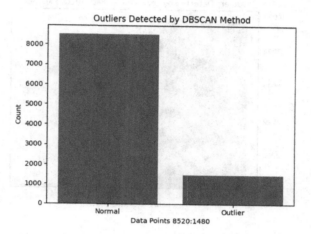

Figure 10.12 Outlier Detection by DBSCAN

```
0      1472
1         8
Name: Class, dtype: int64
```

10.1.2.7 Apply LOF Method

In this code, we apply the Local Outlier Factor (LOF) method for outlier detection. The n_neighbors parameter defines the number of neighbors considered for calculating the local density deviation of each data point. The contamination parameter controls the expected proportion of outliers in the data.

We then visualize the number of outliers detected by the LOF method using a bar chart.

```
# Step 7: Apply LOF method for outlier detection
lof = LocalOutlierFactor(n_neighbors=50, contamination=0.02)
outliers_lof = lof.fit_predict(df.drop('Class', axis=1))

# Identify outliers based on the LOF scores
outliers_lof = outliers_lof == -1

# Visualize the number of outliers detected by LOF method
plt.bar(['Normal', 'Outlier'], [len(df) -
    outliers_lof.sum(), outliers_lof.sum()])
plt.xlabel(f'Data Points {len(df) -
    outliers_lof.sum()}:{outliers_lof.sum()}')
```

```
plt.ylabel('Count')
plt.title('Outliers Detected by Local Outlier Factor (LOF) Method')
plt.show()
df[outliers_lof]['Class'].value_counts()
```

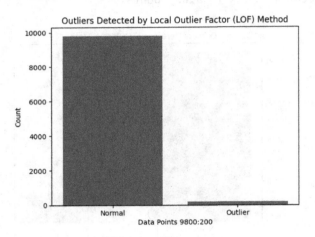

Figure 10.13 Outlier Detection by LOF

```
0     198
1       2
Name: Class, dtype: int64
```

10.1.2.8 Conclusion

In this specific context, not every model works well!

That completes the tutorial for outlier detection using different methods on the "Credit Card Fraud Detection" dataset. You can compare the performances of each method and adjust the hyperparameters to fine-tune the outlier detection for your specific use case.

Index

Printed in the United States
by Baker & Taylor Publisher Services